THE
RED
LINE

THE GRIPPING STORY OF THE RAF'S
BLOODIEST RAID ON HITLER'S GERMANY

JOHN NICHOL

Collins

First published in 2013 by Collins

HarperCollins*Publishers*
77–85 Fulham Palace Road
London W6 8JB

www.harpercollins.co.uk

1 3 5 7 9 10 8 6 4 2

A catalogue record for this book is
available from the British Library.

HB ISBN: 978-0-00-748683-0
TPB ISBN: 978-0-00-748684-7
EB ISBN: 978-0-00-748686-1

Printed and bound in Great Britain by
Clays Ltd, St Ives plc.

MIX
Paper from
responsible sources
FSC C007454

FSC™ is a non-profit international organisation established to promote
the responsible management of the world's forests. Products carrying the
FSC label are independently certified to assure consumers that they come
from forests that are managed to meet the social, economic and
ecological needs of present and future generations,
and other controlled sources.

Find out more about HarperCollins and the environment at
www.harpercollins.co.uk/green

For Sophie

This book is dedicated to all members of Bomber Command, on the ground and in the air, who served during the Second World War with such incredible courage, dedication and fortitude.

Contents

Acknowledgements

There are many people who gave me their valuable time and considerable expertise whilst I researched and wrote this book. It is simply impossible to mention every person individually, but I am truly grateful to them all. My sincere thanks also go to:

Doug Radcliffe and Vivien Hammer from the Bomber Command Association for their advice and support during this project, which ensured unrivalled access to so many veterans. And to Sergeant Ollie Smith who dispatched my thousands of letters and carried out valuable research.

Dan Waddell for his expertise and dedication, and Christian Kuhrt for his diligent research and translation of the German interviewees.

Sarah Standeven of OfficeOffice for her continuing skill and speed in transcribing my many interviews.

Peter Elliot from the RAF Museum Hendon, Anne Wickes from The Second World War Experience in Leeds and Simon Williams, editor of *RAF News*.

Fred, Harold and Andrew Panton from The Lincolnshire Aviation Heritage Centre for allowing me to spend so much time in their Lancaster bomber, *Just Jane*.

My editor Iain MacGregor and the excellent team at Collins for their patience and expertise.

My agent and friend Mark Lucas, who has been a constant source of advice, skill and encouragement.

I am indebted to the countless Bomber Command historians, researchers and enthusiasts whose work I have referenced or who assisted me in locating veterans. It is impossible to name them all, but the following provided important leads, accounts and background information: Ken Ballantyne, Theo Boiten, Corporal Dee Boneham, Hugh Cawdron, Sean Feast, Martin Ford-Jones, Pete Jacobs, Christine Kininmonth, Bill Lowther, Kevin Malandain, Martin Middlebrook, Alan Mitcheson, Alan Parr, Rita Prince, Howard Sandall, Peter Scoley, David Swallow, David Williams.

To my wife Suzannah and daughter Sophie for their ever-present love and continuing support.

Finally, to the countless veterans and their relatives who sent me many hundreds of letters and personal accounts, I am truly grateful – I could only use a fraction of the stories I received, but I hope I have done you all justice.

'In Bomber Command we had to lay on and, more often than not, carry through, at least one and occasionally more than one major battle every twenty-four hours. That was a situation which no naval or military command has ever had to compete with. Navies fight two or three major battles per war. Armies, maybe a dozen. We had to lay on, during my three and a half years, well over a thousand.'

SIR ARTHUR HARRIS

Foreword

They had waited 67 years and journeyed from every far-flung corner of the world for this day. A lifetime ago, young and idealistic, they had come together to battle against the Nazi scourge which threatened to engulf their homelands. Once sprightly, upright figures were now stooped by age or confined to wheelchairs, but medals were polished to perfection and trousers pressed to a razor-sharp crease, and nothing would prevent them from gathering to witness the closing chapter in their extraordinary and controversial story.

The sun shone down on London's Green Park on 28 June 2012 as more than 800 Royal Air Force veterans paraded to witness the unveiling of the Bomber Command Memorial – their memorial. Some came from as far away as New Zealand, Canada and Australia, some just a few minutes' bus-ride from nearby suburbs of the British capital. They were joined by widows, families, celebrities, political leaders and royalty. I was incredibly proud to be part of their day.

My association with the men of Bomber Command began in 1991. As a young Tornado navigator, I had been shot down over Iraq during the first Gulf War, captured, tortured and paraded on television screens around the world. My short but deeply unpleasant experience of captivity entitled me to join the RAF Ex-Prisoner of War Association.

Until that point, I had known little about my forebears who had flown the early bombers into the heart of German-occupied

Europe during the darkest days of the Second World War. I'd watched the classic films like *The Dambusters* and *The Great Escape,* of course. I'd met veterans at various military functions, chatted politely and listened to the occasional war story. But I'm ashamed to admit I hadn't got to know these men; I understood little of their personal stories, their astonishing sacrifice and their incredible bravery.

Now I was able to join their illustrious gatherings – some raucous, laughter- and beer-filled, some poignant and sombre, when awe-inspiring stories of survival brought the occasional tear at the memory of lost friends, or moments of stillness at the recollection of life-threatening danger. Men like Lancaster navigator Harry Evans invited me into their homes to 'share a brew' and talk about wartime memories. Harry was just 18 when he joined up. 'I'd seen the fighter pilots in the skies over London and wanted to be part of it all; it looked so exciting. I wanted to be one of those Brylcreem Boys who were fighting back against the Germans.' He got his wish – and went on to be part of one of the most deadly chapters in aviation history.

Over the years, their reunions have become fewer and the numbers attending have diminished to the point where many Second World War old-comrade associations have now disbanded. At last year's Remembrance Ceremony, only four surviving WWII prisoners-of-war managed to join us on parade at London's Cenotaph. The eldest, Alfie Fripp, shot down in 1939, died on 3 January this year, aged 98. And so it was with a mixture of pride, pleasure and sorrow that I took my seat amidst the crowd of nearly 7,000, gathered around the memorial to honour and remember a truly extraordinary group of people.

I chatted with Lancaster pilot Rusty Waughman, who had come down from Coventry, the scene of a massive German blitz. Alongside his navigator, Alec Cowan, and bomb aimer, Norman Westby, who had travelled from Andorra in the Pyrenees, they relived experiences few could comprehend.

Rusty spoke for so many when he told me, 'We have waited a long time for this … The memorial is not a celebration of our work, it is recognition of the sacrifice so many of our friends made. We are proud to have been part of it all, to have made just a small contribution towards winning the war. I wasn't an educated lad with a brilliant mind. You just did your job to the best of your ability. Luck played the major part in it really. We knew so many who were lost.'

Rusty and his crew truly understood the 'luck factor'; they had witnessed those terrible losses at close quarters.

★   ★   ★

Every one of the 125,000 men who served with Bomber Command was a volunteer and their average age was 22. If the names and ages of each of the 55,573 who gave their lives had been read out at the unveiling ceremony, the roll of honour would have taken two full days – 48 hours – to complete. Yet the furore surrounding the RAF's bombing of German cities and the lack of moral fibre of successive generations of politicians meant that they were denied the recognition their brethren in Fighter Command had been swiftly granted for their outstanding achievements in the Battle of Britain – and many of the survivors of the bomber war suffered downright hostility instead.

Some trace the roots of this invidious state of affairs back to that icon amongst British heroes, Winston Churchill. In the final year of the war he pressed Bomber Command to crush German resistance with 'carpet bombing' raids on cities in eastern Germany; his wish was to deliver a 'basting [to] the Germans in their retreat'. When the Air Ministry demurred, he told them in no uncertain terms to get on with the job. 'I asked whether Berlin, and no doubt other large cities in East Germany, should not now be considered especially attractive targets,' he wrote. 'I am glad this is "under examination". Pray report to me tomorrow what is going to be done.'

Bomber Command was issued with a clear and unambiguous instruction to execute 'one big attack on Berlin and attacks on Dresden, Leipzig, Chemnitz, or other cities where a severe blitz will not only cause confusion in the evacuation from the east but will also hamper the movement of troops from the west'.

The horrific loss of life in Dresden in particular came to epitomise the strategy, and perhaps prompted his astonishing U-turn six weeks later. 'The destruction of Dresden remains a serious query against the conduct of Allied bombing,' he told the Chiefs of Staff in a briefing paper, laying the blame for the death and destruction of which he was the architect squarely at the open bomb doors of Sir Arthur Harris and his ceaselessly loyal aircrews.

It remained there for many years.

No memorial was granted them; no campaign medal. But the survivors would not let their fallen comrades be exiled to the margins of history. A small but stubborn group finally determined to right this wrong. It took them five years and cost some £7 million – money raised by the men themselves, through newspaper appeals and personal donations that ranged from a few pence of a child's pocket money to many thousands of pounds, and in one case an incredible £2 million. Alongside such luminaries as Bee Gee Robin Gibb (who sadly did not live to see the culmination of his incredible work), I joined their campaign. It was now my privilege to witness its outcome.

★   ★   ★

Just after midday, Her Majesty the Queen pulled aside the drapes to reveal Philip Jackson's stunning sculpture, the centre-piece of architect Liam O'Connor's beautiful Portland stone memorial. There were gasps of pleasure and admiration from the front of the crowd, and cheers from those of us further back who, for the time being, could only imagine the sight.

The bronze statues depict seven members of a bomber crew,

recently returned from yet another sortie through enemy skies. Exhaustion and relief are etched on their faces. Five of the figures gaze skywards, praying for a glimpse of friends destined never to return; two stare downwards, perhaps reflecting on the ordeal they have just endured – and knowing they must do it all again before the sun rises tomorrow.

The sacrifice of thousands of young lives is woven into every fibre of the monument. A stainless steel lattice in its ceiling depicts the geometric fuselage construction of the early Wellington bombers. Aluminium from a crashed Halifax lines the roof; eight young men were killed when she was shot down over Belgium in May 1944, and three were still at their stations when she was discovered in 1997. Even the rivets connecting the pieces are scale replicas of those used in the aircraft. And as a symbol of generous reconciliation, a yew tree donated by the people of Germany grows alongside the memorial.

The verdict amongst those who shared the day was unanimous. Andy Wiseman, a Halifax bomb aimer, echoed the thoughts of many as he gazed at the bronze faces of the crew. 'I understand just how they feel,' he said softly. 'This was us, every single night. My only sadness is that it took so long to get the memorial. It would have meant so much to the mothers and fathers who lost so many sons.'

★   ★   ★

The service of dedication was dignified yet simple. The Chief of the Air Staff, Air Chief Marshal Sir Stephen Dalton, promised the relatives of the dead that 'they will now know that their service and raw courage has been recognised'. He spoke of the collective heroism of the men, highlighting the story of Canadian pilot Charles Mynarski, who refused to bale out of his burning aircraft until he had saved his rear gunner. Mynarksi died in the crash while the tail gunner was thrown clear. He was awarded a posthumous Victoria Cross.

As the Venerable Ray Pentland, RAF Chaplain-in-Chief, began the dedication, four Tornado bombers roared overhead, to a chorus of cheers from the crowd and a wail of protest from a handful of car alarms. And then came the moment we had all been waiting for: 'May this memorial commemorate the lives of all who have served and died in Bomber Command, as we acknowledge their sacrifice and service to others.'

As we reflected upon his words, the familiar drone of four Merlin engines filled the crowded park. And here she was, overhead: the last surviving airworthy Lancaster bomber. Many of those in wheelchairs struggled to their feet as our tear-filled eyes turned skywards and her massive bomb doors opened – to scatter thousands of blood-red poppies in a timeless Act of Remembrance.

We cheered and clapped in both celebration and sorrow, and in an instant she was gone.

'You've waited a long time for it,' the Queen had told Marshal of the Royal Air Force Sir Michael Beetham, himself a distinguished wartime pilot and one of the leaders of the campaign. 'Well done.'

★　　★　　★

As the service ended, thousands queued to file through the memorial, to offer a quiet prayer or remember a fallen friend or loved one. The Royal Family wandered amongst the crowd, chatting to old and young alike; children played amidst the drifts of fallen poppies, and the bar began a roaring trade.

On stage in the entertainment area, TV presenter Carol Vorderman interviewed Rusty Waughman and his Lancaster crew about their experiences. Although more than a little uncomfortable about being singled out, Rusty was delighted with the day and its highlight: 'Shaking hands with Prince Charles and being kissed by Carol Vorderman … twice!'

Although it was now late afternoon, bomb aimer Norman Westby had arranged a special feast at a local hotel. They were to be served bacon and eggs, the meal they had all enjoyed on the successful completion of each operation over enemy territory nearly 70 years before.

As Rusty and his crew departed for their own private Act of Remembrance, I have no doubt they reflected on the morning of 31 March 1944, when so many of their friends and fellow crew members had been absent from Bomber Command's traditional 'survivors' breakfast.

JOHN NICHOL
Hertfordshire
13 January 2013

CHAPTER I

The Home Front

Cyril Barton

There is nothing out of the ordinary about Joyce Voysey's semi-detached house in New Malden or the quiet suburban street on which she lives. The garden is well kept, the house immaculate and neatly furnished. Joyce and her sister, Cynthia Maidment, are two white-haired ladies with kindly faces and easy smiles, eager to welcome their visitors, especially those who have come to talk about their beloved brother, Cyril Barton.

His portrait, an oil-painted copy of his official RAF photograph, gazes from the wall of the sitting room. His broad, boyish grin is equal parts innocence and mischief and his eyes shine with pride. While Cyril looks down, his sisters serve tea in china cups and saucers on a polished mahogany table. At one end is a large scrapbook, filled with papers and cuttings, and a stack of files, all of them focused on Cyril's service in Bomber Command. The scrapbook is well thumbed, its pages now faded and yellowing. At first glance there is nothing to suggest that they contain one of the most extraordinary stories of the Second World War.

Cynthia, Joyce and their three brothers and sisters idolised Cyril. They always looked forward to the week when he made the long journey home from his RAF base in Burn, North Yorkshire. Cyril was the oldest, wisest and most confident of the six Barton children, and life at their semi-detached Edwardian house seemed more fun whenever he was there. He was mischievous and playful but also like 'a little father to us',[1] Cynthia remembers, who often put them to bed at night when their dad, an electrical engineer, worked late shifts. He and their brother Ken, who was two years younger, had also taught the girls to sew, knit, draw and read.

Cyril flew with 578 Squadron. He and his crew had been operational since August 1943. Becoming a pilot had been a lifetime's ambition. As a five-year-old he had once stuffed feathers from a recently plucked chicken into the sleeves of his pullover and jumped off a wall, flapping furiously, determined to defy gravity. The family had little money, but whenever funds allowed he was bought model aeroplanes, which he would build assiduously. Sometimes he would even allow his little sisters to help finish off the wings with yellow tissue paper. He was always willing to give them a ride on the back of Ichabod, his trusty bicycle, named after the son of Phineas in the Book of Samuel, and loosely translated from the Hebrew as 'The Glory has departed'.

When they were teenagers, Cyril and Ken had heard the distinctive rumble of a Vickers Wellesley in the night sky. They went out into their quiet suburban street for a closer look. The light bomber had lurched into an uncontrollable spin, and the pilot had parachuted out. Seconds later, there was a world-

Cyril Barton

shaking bang. Cyril and Ken shoved Cynthia into their younger sister Pamela's pushchair so they could get to the crash site quicker than Cynthia could run. A few streets away the tail section of the plane jutted from a tiled roof. No one had been injured, but the house's pregnant inhabitant gave birth earlier than expected. Cyril's only regret was the absence of debris which he could claim as a souvenir.

His dream of flying seemed to have been dashed when his late childhood was blighted by serious illness. Severe bouts of meningitis and peritonitis hospitalised him for months, interrupted his schooling and at times threatened his life. His parents were twice summoned to the hospital to see him for the last time.

3

Each time he recovered, he managed to catch up at school, and throughout his ordeal he remained typically selfless; a diary entry from his sickbed recorded his principal concern: 'I don't know what to get Dad for his birthday.'

His love of aviation never wavered. At the age of 14 he went to work at Parnall's, a manufacturer of military and civil aircraft. They had recently taken over Nash & Thompson in Kingston, who designed gun turrets for RAF bombers, and it was here that Cyril started as an apprentice draughtsman, taking one day a week off to study at college for his National Certificate in Aeronautical Engineering. His early apprenticeship was as blighted by illness as his schooldays had been, but he managed to complete it, and when war broke out, though he might have claimed the protection of a reserved occupation, he knew his chance to fly had finally arrived.

The minute he reached enlistment age in 1941 he asked his father if he could volunteer for the RAF. The family had moved to the safety of the countryside, leaving Cyril lodging in Surrey with his Sunday school teacher, so parental permission had to be sought by letter.

Mr Barton couldn't hide his reluctance to agree to Cyril's request; he had survived the horror of the trenches in the Great War and was in no hurry to see his much-loved son follow in his footsteps. 'Dear Cyril,' he wrote,

After all these … forms, the phone calls and so on, I weighed up your position and feel that the matter should rest entirely with you. Naturally your mother and I are not too keen on your "joining up", more especially as I know by experience what such a step entails, but in view of what you have said regarding your present state at Parnells [sic], I rather grudgingly give my consent …

I am writing as requested to both the Air Ministry and Parnells and in doing so I wish you every success and a happy ending to your enthusiasm. Stick to your principles and faith (this will be very hard in the

*RAF) and I am confident that you will win. We at home will be wait-
ing and watching in all that the future may hold for you.*

*I'll close now and may God bless you and help you in the days that
lie ahead. That is my greatest wish and hope …*

Goodbye and 'happy landings'.

Dad

Unsurprisingly, Cynthia and Joyce's parents worried constantly
about Cyril's frequent and serious ill health, and their concern
made his homecoming even more precious. Most of those
serving an operational tour with Bomber Command were
given one week off in every six. Cynthia, Joyce and Pamela,
then aged seven, would wait eagerly for him to return to New
Malden – the family had grown bored with country life and
moved back to Surrey by then – wondering what new skills
he would pass on, what practical jokes he might pull and what
words of wisdom he would impart.

Their house always reverberated with laughter during these
visits, and even when he was away in the United States, completing his pilot training in Albany, Georgia, he wrote streams
of letters, including one to his sisters in May 1942, enclosing
photos of the young daughters of the family he was staying
with, but promising, 'I'm not going to stay and be their big
brother … I'll try and come home for Christmas!'

That February visit of 1944, the ground was still blanketed
with snow. Without even changing out of his uniform, Cyril
headed straight to the garden shed. He pulled out an old tea
chest and attached some metal runners to it. His three sisters
screeched with delight as he dragged them up and down the
street on their makeshift sleigh.

But once the excitement had died down, Cynthia noticed a
change in her brother's usually gregarious nature. He still found
time to teach Joyce how to conjure up a watercolour sunset by
wetting the paper and then blending in the paints, but much of

the time he was withdrawn and silent. Their mother told the girls that Cyril had 'grown up', but it concerned them to see him so distant and preoccupied. He had always possessed a serious side and a strong religious conviction, but the Cyril they knew best was a playful extrovert.

One morning, as he sat quietly on the sofa, staring into space, Cynthia was unable to contain herself for a minute longer. There had been talk of a girl he had met, and she felt a surge of jealousy that there was someone else on the scene who might share his leave. Was that bothering him?

'What's wrong?' she asked.

Cyril remained silent for a few seconds. Then he nodded. 'As you're a young lady now, I'll tell you.' He patted the empty space on the sofa beside him. When she sat down, he turned to face her. 'You know I'm having to bomb people in Germany?'

Cynthia did know, even if she didn't fully understand. Cyril and his crew had completed more than a dozen ops. Their parents rarely mentioned the dangers he faced, especially in front of the younger children, but as they heard the drone of engines overhead and stood in the garden counting the bombers in their droves, his mother couldn't help saying plaintively: 'Oh, I hope Cyril's not in one of them.'

It was the same story in thousands of other homes across the country; the worry was never voiced, but it hung in the air like mist. Most evenings the Barton family gathered in the kitchen and switched on their Consul Marconi wireless. Sitting around the table, warmed by a Triplex oven, they listened to their favourite programmes, whilst their mother and father waited anxiously for the latest news bulletins from the front.

'Well, I don't like doing it,' Cyril said, 'because it means I have to bomb other people's children.'

Cynthia had never known him speak so seriously to her.

'I'm a Christian and I find it difficult to cope with bombing innocent people,' he continued. 'But I do it because of you three young girls. I don't want Hitler to ruin your lives. He has some terrible plans for the human race. He has to be stopped. So that's why I'm having to do it. For you, Joyce and Pamela.'

Cyril remained subdued for the remainder of his stay, but at least Cynthia now understood why. She was grateful that he had spoken to her so openly; she was only 13, but he was treating her like an adult. And the next time they went for a stroll, he took her arm. 'Right,' he said, 'you don't hold my hand any more. You're a young lady now.'

Cynthia still remembers her feeling of pride as he escorted her down the shopping parade.

Then the day came that the whole family dreaded: the day of Cyril's return to active service. Joyce always walked him to the station hand in hand. As they stood awkwardly outside the entrance, Cyril noticed the state of her nails. 'I think you ought to use that manicure set more often, don't you?' He smiled. When he had arrived back from the USA two years before, he had brought Cynthia a gold watch and Joyce a gold-plated manicure set in a green leather case. It was one of her most treasured possessions.

★   ★   ★

The Pantons' small stone gamekeeper's cottage in Old Boling-broke, Lincolnshire, was less than a mile away from RAF East Kirby, the home of two Bomber Command squadrons, so the deafening roar of 3,000 rpm Merlin engines provided the soundtrack for 13-year-old Fred Panton and his younger brother Harold's everyday life. The boys ran down the hill with rising excitement whenever they heard them, and stood with the other onlookers on the main road adjoining the runway as the lumbering machines, fully bombed up, strained to get airborne.

The pilots and flight engineers at their side always stared straight ahead, eyes fixed on the task of getting the aircraft safely off the ground, but the mid-upper and tail-end gunners often wiggled their guns to acknowledge the crowd.

Fred and 10-year-old Harold watched and waited until the bombers had gathered above them, and would not go home until they were just grey dots in the distance. Much later, the shadows of the returning planes would flit across their bedroom wall. Sometimes they were so close that Fred could make out the eerie glow cast by the instruments in the cockpit.

When the sky was silent once more, they wondered whether their big brother would be joining that night's raid. Nineteen-year-old Chris was a flight engineer with 433 Squadron at Skipton-on-Swale, part of a maverick crew that included a Danish-born volunteer from the USA called Chris Nielsen and several Canadians. Despite his youth, Chris was already well on his way to becoming an officer and nearing the 30 ops that signalled the end of a tour. He still had dreams of being a pilot. There had been some close calls. On one trip the hydraulics on their bomb- and fuel-laden Halifax had failed on take-off, so the undercarriage and flaps would not retract. They were struggling to gain enough height to clear an oncoming hill, so Chris pumped furiously on the manual controls. They regained enough hydraulic pressure just in time to ensure the bomber cleared the hill. All on board were stunned into silence. Except for Nielsen. 'It's OK,' he said in a bored American drawl. 'I've got it.'

The two boys lived for the times he came back on leave. With eight children in their cramped cottage, Fred and Chris had to share a bed. Fred was always bursting with questions as they lay there, listening to the bombers return, but Chris would only talk about his experiences to their father, a veteran of the First World War. Fred sometimes heard the rumble of their conversation, but could never make out what they were saying.

Fred and Harold joined their older brother on rabbit-hunting expeditions (Chris had trained as a gamekeeper, aiming to follow in his father's footsteps), but what he had seen and done in the skies above Germany was never discussed then either. For a few precious moments the war seemed a lifetime away, and they didn't want to bring it rushing back. Watching the planes come and go, wave after wave, night after night, Fred knew the dangers they faced. He and Harold often visited crash sites once the bodies of the crewmen had been removed, and just stared, transfixed, at the twisted, smoking metal carcasses.

But finally, that winter's evening, he could contain his curiosity no more. 'Don't you worry about crashing?'

There was a pause. 'Not really,' Chris replied casually. 'It'd just be further experience.'[2]

His brother's insouciance astounded Fred. He longed to know more, but didn't dare ask. He didn't dare ask his father either. Their late-night chats were man's talk, to be shared only by those who had experienced the realities of war.

Once, when Chris had been home on leave, Fred had slipped on his big brother's RAF jacket, trying to imagine what it was like to be him. His father caught him red-handed. 'Don't you be going out that door with that on,' he'd said sternly. In his dad's eyes, Fred hadn't earned the right.

The questions would have to wait for another time, hopefully not too far off, when Chris's tour – and the war – were over.

★   ★   ★

Alan Payne, a bomb aimer with 630 Squadron, was part of one of the crews Fred and Harold had seen straining to take off at East Kirby. On the early evening of 29 March, Alan was preparing to leave his parents' home in Wendover. He gave his mother a final cheery wave before putting on his helmet and climbing on to his motorbike.

For the entire week they had not spoken once about his experiences with Bomber Command. They never asked and he never told them, and that suited him just fine. He knew the truth would only upset them and cause them to worry even more than they already did.

The rain started to pour as he saddled up. It was going to be a long ride back to East Kirby in this weather. While he felt the usual sadness of leaving his loved ones, at least he was returning to his surrogate family. Alan and his crew, like so many others in Bomber Command, were tight. They spent all their time together, more often than not at The Red Lion in nearby Revesby. And while they sank their pints, their conversations, like those with his real family, rarely turned to war. They knew all too well that young men like them were being lost every night, in ever-increasing numbers, during the winter of 1943–44. But they kept those thoughts at bay as they laughed and joked around the bar. The prospect of death never weighed heavily on Alan. He always felt there was a gap in the sky where he and his crew would find safety

The rain hammered down and the wind howled around his ears as Alan tore up the A1. He headed straight for the Peacock Hotel in Boston, where, sopping wet, he found time for a couple of pints before catching a bus to the camp, where Pat was waiting for him. She was a young Geordie girl who served the crews' meals in the mess, and they had been courting for a few weeks; she had joined him and his crew at the pub so often she had almost become their eighth member. They had a quick chat and then it was time to get out of his wet clothes, unpack his bag and get some sleep.[3]

Tomorrow was 30 March. Yet another day at the cutting edge of Bomber Command.

CHAPTER 2

Sowing the Wind

Rusty Waughman

On a Sunday evening in December 1940, in the middle of the Blitzkrieg, Sir Arthur Harris, then the Air Ministry's Deputy Chief of Air Staff, stood on the roof of his Kingsway HQ. Around him, German aircraft rained incendiaries on the nation's capital. The City was a sea of flame; only the luminous dome of St Paul's Cathedral rose from it untouched.

He called for Air Marshal Charles Portal, Commander-in-Chief of Bomber Command, to share the terrible sight. As the two men watched London burn, oblivious to the threat to their own safety, 'Bomber' Harris felt the first stirrings of vengefulness. 'They are sowing the wind,' he muttered.[4]

By March 1944, at least according to Harris, the German forces, and their civilian population, were reaping the whirlwind. He was now Commander-in-Chief of Bomber

Command and a fervent believer – along with Winston Churchill – in the effectiveness of area bombing. Harris believed the most efficient path to victory was to raze Germany's biggest cities to the ground, obliterate the enemy's capacity to equip its forces, and destroy the morale of its people.

He believed that the long-range bomber had fundamentally altered the nature of warfare. He had flown over the killing fields of the Somme and Passchendaele during his service in the Royal Flying Corps and had no time for those whose out-dated views he remained convinced would lead to a reprise of the mass slaughter of the First World War.

'If the ancient and ivory-headed warriors are permitted to have their way, another one to six million of the flower of the youth of this under-populated country, and of America, will be unnecessarily massacred in proving for the second time that these Ancient Soldiers and Mariners were wrong. It is but cold comfort to realise in the circumstances that not only is the Bomber the only thing that can win the War for us, but that it is going to win the War for us eventually, in spite of all the procrastinations and futile diversions which the old battle-horses are determining to stage in the interim.'[5]

Harris acknowledged the many dissenters: those who believed it was morally wrong to bomb strategic cities rather than focus on purely industrial and military targets. He was also acutely aware of the toll his strategy was taking on his young crews. But he knew too that since the Luftwaffe had killed thousands of civilians and destroyed vast swathes of London, Coventry, Liverpool and Bristol, the opposition to area bombing had become less strident.

Even though Harris's tactics were by no means universally popular, and despite the enormous losses they were suffering on a daily basis, the remarkable young men whose duty it was to carry out his orders had great faith in their Commander-in-Chief.

To them he was always 'Butch' and never 'Bomber' Harris. Dick Starkey, a Lancaster pilot, remembers a lecture he gave at a local school after the war: 'One of the children asked me if I regretted what I did. I said that I was proud of my contribution. I regret the death and the suffering, but I'm not sorry. I think the criticism of Bomber Command is terrible, because we were doing a job that had to be done at the time and there was nobody else to do it. We were fighting the Nazi enemy when no one else could.'[6]

Ever since Dunkirk, aerial bombardment was one of the ways Britain could signal to its allies and its own citizens that she intended to stay in the fight and carry it to the Germans. But by the winter of 1943 Harris was no longer interested in sending signals. He finally had the technology and fire-power at his disposal that he believed would bring hostilities to an end, in the shape of an aircraft designed to transport vast amounts of explosive over long distances while offering its crew hitherto unavailable levels of protection: the Avro Lancaster.

In 1942 Harris had inherited 400 front-line bombers, nowhere near enough to carry out his planned offensive. He increased production immediately and within a few months could call on a new range of four-engine heavy bombers such as the Stirling and Halifax, with a far greater range and ordinance than their twin-engine predecessors. But it was the arrival of the Lancaster that convinced Harris he could now press for a decisive victory.

The Lancaster boasted a 33-foot bomb bay which enabled it to carry the 4,000-pound 'cookie' bomb, capable of creating a shockwave that could devastate large areas of buildings. With further modifications, it would hold the 12,000-pound 'Tall-boy', capable of penetrating 100 feet into the ground before exploding, and, by the latter stages of the war, the 22,000-pound Grand Slam, the most destructive weapon available before the invention of the atomic bomb.

The Stirling, in the process of being phased out of frontline service, could only carry a 14,000-pound bomb load. After overcoming some early concerns about its performance, the destructive power of the Halifax was still hampered by its sectional bomb bay. And despite its huge payload, the Lancaster handled much more easily than its unwieldy predecessors, a telling advantage over heavily defended targets or when evading night fighters, especially for inexperienced personnel.

Lancaster crews felt they could rely upon their aircraft more than any other. The Mark I and Mark II Halifax had a tendency to go into uncontrollable spins at low speeds through a lack of rudder response, and though the Mark III was a fine aircraft, much loved by those who flew it, a new Lancaster was definitely a step up. The Lancaster offered reassurance. 'It was a beautiful aircraft to fly,' Dick Starkey says, 'a pilot's aeroplane. It handled very lightly, could reach 22,000 feet fully loaded, and even maintain height on two engines ... It had no vices, except for a slight swing to port on take-off, and was nearly impossible to stall.'

Rusty Waughman, a pilot with 101 Squadron, called the aircraft the Queen of the Sky. 'If the Lanc looked somewhat menacing and clumsy on the ground, she was quite a different picture in the air. Compared with modern machines she was rather crude, but efficiently laid out ... Aircrew, particularly the pilots, had every faith in the Lanc; very seldom did anything go drastically wrong due to faulty design. In fact, she was often flown in states of damage that were, I'm sure, beyond imaginable limits.'[7]

They were also equipped with the latest navigational aids, essential for deep, penetrative raids over heavily guarded German territory. Before the introduction of the Ground Electronics Engineering (GEE) system, navigators had to depend on 'dead reckoning' – following a set course and compensating periodically for the disrupting effect of the wind. But as wind speed and direction were often inaccurately forecast and fluctuated wildly during an operation, they regularly found themselves some distance from their intended target. The GEE system picked up electronic signals pulsed from England and displayed them on a small, black cathode-ray screen on the navigator's table. Though the curvature of the earth rendered the reading less accurate the further they got from base, interpreting these blips and entering them into specially created GEE charts allowed a navigator to fix their current position with greater accuracy.

At the briefing before his first operational flight with XV Squadron Mildenhall, Chick Chandler was told to 'throw out Window one-a-minute, then two-a-minute 40 miles from the target'. When he asked what 'Window' was, one of his engineers showed him the thin strips of foil designed to 'bugger up the enemy's radar'.[8] The metallic strips were designed to reflect German radar signals, disrupting the picture the operators received on their screens and making the bombers more difficult to track.

Once his Lancaster was high above the channel *en route* to Mannheim, Chick started to carry out what he took to be his instructions, but didn't realise that 'one a minute' meant one bundle. Instead he threw out one solitary strip – not even enough to register a single blip on the enemy screens, let alone turn them into an incomprehensible snowstorm, under cover of which the bomber stream could approach the target without detection.

And in order to concentrate the maximum amount of firepower in the shortest possible time, the bombers would leave their bases across eastern England and form up over the North Sea. They were each given a height and a time slot designed to minimise the chances of collision. The entire stream, once assembled, could be anything up to 70 miles long.

★　　★　　★

As January 1944 dawned, despite only having completed a third of their tour, flight engineer Jack Watson's crew was the second most experienced on XII Squadron. This was a bad omen: on recent raids the crew with the second highest number of ops to their name had gone missing. This sense of foreboding might explain why, as the snow crunched beneath Jack's feet on his way to a briefing in Wickenby for a raid on Stuttgart, he experienced 'the most uncanny feeling I have ever experienced in my life. I knew that if we didn't leave XII Squadron, we wouldn't survive. We went into the briefing, we did the trip, we got back and the next morning we were called into the flight office. The Flight Commander said, "You have got two options: you can either volunteer for the Pathfinder Force or we will send you," so we volunteered. From then on I was quite convinced that all the time I was with that crew we were safe.'[9]

To enhance the accuracy of the bomber stream, a special force had been created to find and mark the target. Manned by crews of the calibre of Jack Watson's, the Pathfinders flew ahead of the main force in Lancasters and Mosquitoes. Their very existence was initially a source of tension within Bomber Command. Harris feared that they would drain his squadrons of their best men, and thus also drain their morale – and he believed his bombers were accurate enough without them. His protests, however, failed to dent the determination of the forthright Australian, Air Vice Marshal Donald Bennett.

Bennett was a former operational pilot who had been shot down while trying to bomb the *Tirpitz*, the iconic German warship, but had escaped from Norway and returned to England to continue his war. His desire to be in the thick of it never deserted him. Even when he was appointed the Pathfinder chief, he sometimes waved his crews off and then took to the skies himself to orbit the target. When they returned from a raid to be debriefed, he would be waiting for them, often more aware of what had happened than they were.

Bennett's candour was as renowned as his brilliance as a pilot and navigator. Harris, who knew a thing or two about blunt speaking, once said of the Australian: '[He] could not suffer fools gladly, and by his own high standards there had been many fools.'[10] As his campaign wore on, Harris reassessed his earlier scepticism; the Pathfinders became a much-valued part of his strategy, and Bennett a loyal if perennially outspoken member of his command.

By March 1944 the Pathfinder Force under Bennett's control consisted of seven Lancaster squadrons, five Mosquito squadrons and the Meteorological Flight. Many aircraft had been fitted with two bespoke items of navigational equipment. Oboe, like GEE, was fed by electronic signals transmitted from England to guide the aircraft to the aiming point; H2S was a radar set that gave the navigator a rough picture of the terrain over which they were flying, giving the crew an even greater level of accuracy in position fixing and target location.

Emboldened by these technological and tactical advances, Harris launched an all-out attack on Hamburg in August 1943. During the course of four raids over 10 nights, Bomber Command dropped nearly 11,000 tons of bombs on Germany's second largest city and biggest port: 22 pounds of explosives for each of its 1.75 million residents. The last operation, code-named Gomorrah, caused a firestorm so severe that it was reported to have melted glass in windows, while 'sugar boiled in bakery cellars and people escaping from underground shelters on to the streets were trapped in quagmires of molten asphalt'.[11] The death toll was more than 40,000, and approximately a million people fled the city. Albert Speer, the Minister for Armaments, advised Hitler that another six raids of similar scale and destructive power on other major cities would lose them the war.

Harris was unaware of Speer's assessment, but he knew the raid had struck a severe blow to German morale. He increased the number and the intensity of their attacks, and turned his gaze in November 1943 towards Berlin. The series of raids he launched on the 'Big City' marked the start of a relentless onslaught designed to crush German resistance once and for all. He was so confident that a winter of ferocious bombing would bring the Germans to their knees that he set a date for victory: 1 April 1944.

The night of 18 November 1943 saw the first raid of what became known as the Battle of Berlin. It was swiftly followed by two more before the end of the month. Their combined death toll was 4,330, and more than 400,000 people were forced from their homes. 'Hell seems to have broken loose over us,' Goebbels wrote in his diary.

The Germans were forced to reorganise their defences and alter their tactics. On the first Berlin raid, 2 per cent of the bomber stream had been lost, only nine Lancasters. A month later, on 16 December, that figure rose to 9.3 per cent, a total of 55 bombers. Some crews began to dread the afternoon briefings – the revelation that the evening's target was to be the Big City. As the losses mounted, so did the demand for replacement crews. On 23 December, Harry Evans, a navigator with 550 Squadron, was sent there on his first operation. He was initially stood down that evening while his crew was shared across the squadron as stand-ins for members of other crews who had fallen ill or were unable to fly. An hour before take-off that plan was scratched; Harry and his crew were told they were going together. 'I'd missed briefing so I had to rush to get my pre-flight log and chart prepared. I raced to the aircraft, which was waiting at the end of the runway with its engines running.'[12] Harry tried to run across the tarmac, but his flying suit and boots, 'Mae West' lifejacket and parachute harness, large satchel, sextant and flying helmet (complete with oxygen mask and intercom lead) meant that he could barely walk.

Harry Evans (front left) and crew

He was almost blown over by the slipstream, then 'the pilot throttled back the two starboard engines and the mid-upper gunner helped to haul me aboard and we roared down the runway before I even had time to get to my desk'.

When they were finally airborne, one of their gunners saw a blinding flash of light to one side of them. Two aircraft from their squadron had collided – the two that most of Harry's crew would have been on if the original plan had remained in place. The margin between life and death in Bomber Command was small, and luck and chance were often the defining factors.

Harry and his crew flew on to Berlin. 'It was as black as black. The only light came from the odd flash of machine-gun fire as gunners tested their weapons, or the red-hot glow of an exhaust stub from one of the other bombers around us. Up front the phosphorescent dials on the engineer's panels cast a glow so bright that I feared it might be visible to enemy aircraft. No chance of that with the green blips on my GEE set. There were none. It had been jammed by the enemy.'

Few words were said as they flew over mainland Europe. All eyes apart from Harry's and his pilot's were scanning the night sky for fighters. Around 50 miles from Berlin a bank of searchlights swept across the sky, aiming to 'cone' a British bomber, so that it was caught in the beams of all the searchlights in a battery below. For the men on board it was as if they had moved from a dark room into blinding sunshine. The brightness over the target was intensified by the Pathfinders' marker flares and the fires rampaging where the leading aircraft had already dropped their bombs. Harry thought: 'This is like going down Regent Street at night.'

Their Lancaster started to tilt and vibrate, throwing the crew around 'as though we were travelling over a cobbled road at high speed'. This was the effect of flak – the relentless barrage of fire from 50,000 anti-aircraft guns which protected the skies around the major German cities. Often guided by radar, these ground defences blasted thousands of explosive shells skywards at the bombers as they flew towards their target. A direct hit could destroy an aircraft, and shells that exploded nearby caused them to veer and lurch as the murderous shrapnel smashed against – and often through – the fuselage. Harry thought of the 4,000 pounds of high explosive in the bomb bay just inches beneath him, and wondered what would happen if the flak scored a direct hit there. A few minutes later he had his answer: a nearby bomber erupted in a shower of flame. He watched, awe-struck, as the aircraft spun to the ground leaving a corkscrew-shaped trail of smoke behind it. Looking down at the city, Harry could see that the streets were burning too.

Once over the target, their bomb aimer gave a series of instructions to the pilot to ensure their bombs were dropped as accurately as possible. For the rest of the crew 'the next few minutes were agony' as they flew as straight and level as possible, desperate to give him the best chance, but feeling they were easy prey for the guns down below. The seconds felt like minutes, until the bomb aimer announced their load was gone and the aircraft lifted, freed of its burden. The pilot then brought the nose of the aircraft down and they turned and fled back into the welcoming darkness.

★   ★   ★

The New Year came and went with no pause in the offensive; there were six operations on Berlin in January alone. The only respite came when the moon was full; training exercises took the place of providing the enemy night fighters with little-needed target practice.

By February 1944 the RAF was averaging two heavy – 550 aircraft – raids per week. Their losses were beginning to increase, leading to renewed criticism of Harris's tactics. On 19 February Bomber Command experienced its worst night thus far during a Leipzig raid.

Rusty Waughman, with 101 Squadron, took off at 11.44 p.m. The first indication that things were not going as planned was when his navigator told him they were 20 minutes ahead of schedule. The wind was much stronger than forecast, blowing them towards the target before the allocated bombing time. There would be no Pathfinder markers, nothing to aim at, so they decided to 'dog-leg', flying in a zigzag fashion, to bleed time.

When they arrived, the sky was a riot of searchlight beams and flares dropped by enemy night fighters. Rusty watched as a Lancaster in the distance blew up in mid-air: another direct hit. Corralled by the winds, hundreds of their comrades had arrived prematurely over the target and started to orbit, waiting for the Pathfinders to arrive and illuminate the target. 'Like fish caught in an ever-shrinking net, the bombers were being picked off one by one.' There was a sound like a clap of

thunder as they started their bombing run. Two circling bombers had collided and were now just shards of burning metal
falling from the sky.

Rusty was able to drop his bombs, leave the danger area and
head back to England without damage, but 79 others were lost
that night. The brunt of the blame was borne by the Met
Office, but their job – to predict the weather on the way to
and over a target hundreds of miles away, based on very little
data – was unenviable.

Leipzig was a major setback and yet, even as criticism of the
campaign, both in the press and within the Air Ministry, started
to mount, Harris remained defiant. His critics claimed there
was no sign of deterioration in the mood or morale of the
German public. They remained 'apathetic' about the bombing
of their towns and cities. On 25 February, in a combative internal memo, Harris challenged his critics in typically robust fashion, giving those around him no doubt that his faith in the
heavy bombing of German cities securing an Allied victory was
as robust as ever. If anything, he was even more determined to
intensify the attacks. Under the heading 'Reactions of German
Morale to the Bomber Offensive as described in official documents and the Press', he wrote:

1. *I have the honour to refer to numerous accounts now current both
in official documents and in the public Press on the reactions of German
morale in heavily attacked areas to the Combined Bomber Offensive
and to state my conviction that these reports seriously misrepresent the
state of mind of the German populace at the present time.*

2. *I understand that incontestable evidence derived from Most Secret
sources exists to show that the continuance and probable intensification
of the Offensive is regarded in the highest Nazi circles as something
which, in the absence of unpredictable errors by the Allies, will certainly
ensure a German defeat comparatively quickly by producing a collapse
of morale as well as production on the Home Front.*

3. To my mind this belief, which is certainly confirmed by the efforts of the German propaganda machine to divert our bombing by any means from industrial targets in Germany and to convince the Germans that these efforts will shortly be successful, is inconsistent with the widely and officially disseminated view that the prevalent attitude to bombing in Germany is 'apathy'…

4…This view is manifestly false…There have been a vast number of indications that the attitude of the German population to the bombing, so far from being apathetic, is one of the utmost despair, of terror and of panic not always held in control by the authorities.

5. It is a depressing fact that this slogan as to the "apathetic" reaction of the German population should receive as it does the widest publicity in official documents and statements, whereas any impartial interpretation of the mass of information coming out of Germany, if it was properly weighed up, would inevitably show a condition of affairs such as I have outlined above and certainly no condition of 'apathy'.[13]

Despite his convictions, the brutal losses of that winter caused a change in attitude within the Air Ministry. The faith they had shown in Harris and his Combined Bomber Offensive was starting to waver. Harris was handed a new list of targets, centres of industry rather than of symbolic significance – Schweinfurt, Leipzig, Brunswick, Regensburg, Gotha and Augsburg – that should assume priority over any others. However, his obstinacy remained: there would be no immediate raids on any of the targets suggested to him. Harris still believed that his main offensive would bring the victory he had promised, even if the date by which he had predicted 'a state of devastation in which surrender was inevitable' was rapidly approaching.

The raids continued on his favoured targets – the largest so far on Stuttgart, with 116 sorties. On their return, Thomas Maxwell, an 18-year-old rear gunner on his sixth mission with

622 Squadron, was forced to bale out after his Lancaster was hit by enemy fire. He feared the flames would start licking at his turret, the most cramped and claustrophobic part of the plane, with only a Perspex shield between him and the 20,000-foot abyss below him. Like all rear gunners, he had to crawl into his 'cold hole', where there was so little room to turn that another crew member had to shut the doors behind him.

'I didn't have time to exit by the main door. I had to get my wits together quickly. First I needed a parachute. It was in the fuselage, an arm's length away. So I opened the turret doors and hoped they didn't jam. Then I dragged the 'chute carefully into the turret in case it deployed. Then I rotated the turret 90 degrees, otherwise I'd have baled out into the fuselage. But there was no room to put the 'chute on! With the turret now at right angles to the fuselage, the slipstream gale was grabbing, tearing and tugging at the flapping parachute backpack, the spewing fuel whipping past me. There was nothing now but Hobson's Choice: go back into the pitch-black fuselage or stick your rear end into this growling 120-knot wind.'[14]

Thomas managed to clip one parachute hook on, but as he was contorting his body to fasten the other he fell backwards into the night, his parachute under his left arm. 'I pulled the rip cord: Long John Silver managed with one hook, and one was better than none. Life is simplified when there are no options. There was a crunch as the drag-chute came out and the parachute woofed into its canopy above.'

Somehow, falling through the sky from 8,000 feet, Thomas managed to attach the other hook and within a few seconds was floating securely down to the ground. 'There was just a bit of moonlight now, and instead of landing on the spire of some French parish church, or drowning in somebody's swimming pool, I was dumped unceremoniously into a ploughed field and a relatively soft landing. The field was full of piles of manure. There is a saying: "It matters not whether you're in the s★★t or out of it, it's only the depth that varies." At this point, I was quite happy to be in it.'

Following Stuttgart there were two huge raids on Frankfurt, and a final onslaught on Berlin on 24 March, during which the weather forecast proved inaccurate once again. Chick Chandler had a ring-side seat once more. 'By some dreadful mistake we arrived early over Berlin. The rear gunner said we had no option but to circle. Circle over Berlin! What a disaster! We were only at 13,000 feet, so we had a bird's eye view of the whole thing. We saw at least four Pathfinder bombers blow up as they were going round. Seeing all those aircraft going down made me realise what we were doing. Although I was the baby of the crew, I knew just what the dangers were, and how easy it was to be shot down and killed.'

Strong winds had scattered the stream across a wide area and pushed many of them towards heavy flak defences they would otherwise have missed. Seventy-three aircraft were lost, an estimated 50 from flak. It was another bad night for Bomber Command.

By 30 March the Battle of Berlin was about to end, but Harris was determined to make one last attempt to score his decisive, symbolic victory. 'Yet, the March that had entered like a lamb was destined to go out like the proverbial lion. The ill-wind of death had still to be sated.'[15]

CHAPTER 3

The Fine Line

Ron Auckland

The average member of a Bomber Command crew had a 30 per cent chance of being killed before they completed their *first* 30-op tour. Of a total of 125,000 aircrew, 55,573 were killed: an overall death rate of 44.4 per cent; another 8,400 were wounded and some 10,000 taken prisoner. In no other branch of the armed forces were the chances of dying so high, or the combatants called into action night after gruelling night. Yet every one of the 125,000 recruits who took to the skies to wage war by night was a volunteer.

There were those whose fathers had fought in the First World War and who wanted to avoid the gruesome grind of trench warfare. There were others who were seduced by the glamorous modern image portrayed by the RAF, given added lustre by the glorious victory of 'The Few' in the Battle of

Britain. For many, such as Ron Auckland from Portsmouth, who had experienced the damage wreaked by the Luftwaffe earlier in the war, there was an element of revenge.

Ron had witnessed the first German raid on the docks of his home town, where he worked as a civil servant. On duty as a fire officer, he had carried out the dead and rescued the injured after an enemy bomb fell down the air vent of a crowded air-raid shelter. During another, he and his family were bombed out of their home. That was enough; he signed up. 'I'd seen a lot and knew just what the Germans could do. I was in a reserved occupation but I still wanted to join up. I wanted to be part of the war effort.'[16]

George Prince grew up in New Malden, Surrey, the son of a garage owner. He left school at 14 to work for his father as a mechanic, a job in which he learned many skills that would prove useful when he became a flight engineer. He coveted a green, four-seat 1934 MG PA in his father's showroom and was mortified when a German bomb shattered the windows and riddled the car body with shrapnel. George was only 15, but his father told him that if he repaired the MG he could have it.

'I mended the bodywork lovingly, and filled the holes in the radiator with putty. I couldn't drive it, but it became my pride and joy.'[17] George, like his near neighbour Cyril Barton, dreamed of being a pilot, but when he signed up his superiors decided that his experience in his father's garage was too valuable to sacrifice, so he became a flight engineer. The MG would come into use later, when he was operational and old enough to drive it. 'The whole crew would get in: two in the front, and the rest would squeeze in the back and hang out over the side.'

As a 16-year-old Londoner, Harry Evans had watched in awe as the night sky above his home city glowed red during the Blitz. That image and the sound of the Heinkel 111s were imprinted on his soul. One day a German bomb landed on his street. 'It demolished the house just to our right. The whole house shook like there had been an earthquake; all the windows were blown out and the ceilings came down. Some of the neighbours were killed. Once you've experienced something like that you never forget it. Shortly after my 18th birthday I volunteered for the RAF. My father had been in the Navy on submarines in the First World War and it didn't sound very appealing to me. I wanted to be one of the Brylcreem Boys!'

Bomber Command recruits also came from far-flung corners of the Empire. Ron Butcher grew up in Middle Sackville, a village near New Brunswick in Canada. He joined the RAF because all of his friends were doing it, even though there was no pressure for them to volunteer; just a sense of duty towards their ancestral home and ally. Britain needed their help against the Nazi terror, and to stand idly by seemed like an act of cowardice.

Andy Wejcman did not come from any corner of the Empire. He was born in Berlin in January 1923. When Hitler and the Nazis gained power in 1933 and revealed their virulent brand of anti-Semitism, his father, a politically active lawyer and intellectual Polish Jew, moved the family to Poland. In 1939, just before the German invasion, Andy was sent to England to learn the language. Despite having an American mother, the only English phrase he knew was 'Stick 'em up!' – from watching a cowboy film. Ironically, she insisted that he travel by train and boat because she believed flying to be too dangerous. On the day he left, his entire family came to wave him off at the station. It was the last time he saw his father.

Andy learned English at a school in Hampshire and proved to be such a good student that he was offered a place at Oxford University. He turned it down, even though he knew his mother would be appalled. 'I decided I would join the Air

Force, and if you're going to join the Air Force you might as well fly. I knew what the war meant; I heard the bombs and I'd seen the results of bombing and the destroyed buildings. I certainly wanted to help overthrow Hitler. I felt it was my moral and physical duty to do so.'[18]

★   ★   ★

Being a member of Bomber Command had benefits the Army and Navy couldn't offer. Even though most nights were spent dodging fighters and flak, the crews slept in a bed on British soil. It was a shorter journey home on leave. They could also enjoy their familiar comforts: pubs, dances, the cinema, and, for those who were single, local girls whose eye might be caught by a young man in uniform.

Once they signed up, the mundaneness of day-to-day training dispelled any notions that RAF life might be any more glamorous. Harry Evans joined in the summer of 1941, at the Yorkshire Grey pub in Eltham, where the ballroom had been converted into a recruiting centre. It was the end of the year before he was summoned to the Air Crew Selection Centre on the Euston Road, where he was tested, interviewed and given a thorough medical. Eventually he was accepted and kitted out as an Aircraftman 2nd Class, the lowest rank in the entire Air Force. When he was sent to digs near Regent's Park his spirits lifted; the airmen were billeted in luxury flats overlooking the park, where businessmen, bankers and diplomats once lived before the Blitz. Once inside, it became clear that this was just an accident of geography; it was the middle of winter, there was no heating, the interior doors had been removed and, despite the expensive tiles and fittings, nothing worked. The flats had become filthy and neglected, and the meals served to the airmen were in keeping with their surroundings.

A few days later, Harry was asked to report to another prestigious address. The Pavilion at Lord's Cricket Ground had been turned into a reception centre where new recruits were issued with uniform and equipment. There was one other test, of which few were aware. In the hallowed Long Room, with the great ghosts of the summer game looking on, each man was ordered to drop his trousers to be inspected for venereal disease by a medical officer. This was not the sort of thing Harry had in mind when he signed up to be one of the Brylcreem Boys.

The wait between signing on, being processed and starting training was interminable. Sam Harris,[19] a young Scotsman, had signed on in January 1941 at the age of 17, but his training in London did not start until November. He wanted to be a pilot, but his scores in the maths test were so good that he was earmarked as a navigator. Later that month he was sent to Babbacombe in Devon with 47 other trainees.

The life of a new recruit was no more exciting in the West Country than it had been in London. He shared a room with three others in a small boarding house with only enough hot water for a bath once a week. Every morning they paraded outside in their PT kit, 'gargled with some bluish purple mixture', and then went for a 30-minute run, followed by a splash of cold water, a change into uniform, and another parade before breakfast.

Their lectures were held in the windowless basement of what used to be a garage. 'There we wrestled with the mysteries of air navigation, including the triangle of velocities and the fact that straight lines on a Mercator navigation chart are not straight lines on the earth. In another building we learned to tap out Morse code and to send and receive messages by Aldis lamp. There were drill periods, a sports afternoon – which meant a long march to playing fields where we played football – and a long march back. We certainly became fit.'[20]

The recruits were free to spend Saturday nights as they pleased, as long as they were back at their digs by 10 p.m. Sam and his friends used to visit a pub in St Mary's, drink a few half-pints, go to the town hall dance and sprint back to their digs to beat the curfew. 'There were other perks – a bath on Sunday morning, Church Parade, and an afternoon walk to Cockington, followed by a free tea at a church in Torquay. Well, not quite free; we had to listen to a bit of a religious service first. Such was the glamorous life of the navigator under training ...'

Harry Evans was fortunate enough to be stationed at Ponca City, Oklahoma – a world away from what he had left behind. 'We were all volunteers and keen to learn to fly and there were no disciplinary problems – it was the life of Riley. Instead of a mess there was a cafeteria where we all queued to be served and rank was of no importance. The food was exceedingly good, especially compared to wartime Britain, and we tried such strange and exotic delights as peanut butter, sweetcorn and unusual mixtures such as bacon, griddle cakes and maple syrup.' But an ill-advised low-flying stunt over the local swimming pool to impress his fellow trainees and some local girls landed him in trouble. He and two other airmen were thrown off the course and sent to Canada to remuster. Harry chose to be a navigator.

After 28 weeks abroad – and a year since they had volunteered – the recruits were sent back to the Advanced Flying Unit in the UK, where they were taught to fly at night, and then to Operational Training Units, where they finally became part of Bomber Command.

Few of these young men – the average age in Bomber Command was 22 – would get near the aircraft they would eventually fly in combat until they graduated to a Heavy Conversion Unit. Even when the production lines were running at full capacity, the Lancasters were all needed for the main offensive. Raw, inexperienced crews were forced to learn on the older Stirling, Halifax and Wellington bombers, and even the lucky ones were only introduced to the Lancaster in the final moments before they became operational.

Harry Evans recalls acting as a pall-bearer at the funerals of fellow trainees three Mondays running. 'The crash rate was high, but this was bound to happen when you were training on old aircraft under operational conditions. I remember one of the most spectacular: a Canadian pilot flying a Wellington hit the runway hard, the aircraft bounced, he lost control and went straight into the side of the control tower, about 15 feet above the ground. It was still stuck there the next day. Four of the crew and three flying control personnel were killed, including two WAAFs. Only the rear gunner survived.'

The members of a crew risked their lives together, slept together, ate together and socialised together. The ones that gelled quickly were the lucky ones, and forged friendships that would last a lifetime. Those who failed to get along, or whose camaraderie faltered under the strain, often met with fatal consequences. Arguments or disagreements put the aircraft at risk. Total discipline was required on board; it was a fundamental rule of survival, and yet the process of 'crewing up' was surprisingly haphazard.

In July 1943 Sam Harris was nursing a pint with Sandy Clarkson, an Edinburgh-born fellow navigator, at The Golden Fleece in Loughborough. It was like the first day of school, but instead of making friends they and their fellow recruits were forming crews. As the afternoon wore on the number of unattached airmen grew fewer; it was time for Sandy and Sam to make a decision.

'What do you think?' Sandy asked.

Sam shrugged. 'Only two pilots left. It's a toss-up.'

Whilst Sandy's clannish instincts led him to opt for the Glaswegian of the pair, Sam and a bomb aimer who seemed to be at a loose end approached the remaining pilot, Ken Murray. Ken said that he had a wireless operator 'around here somewhere', and had spotted a couple of spare gunners lurking in a corner. A few minutes later the six of them stood at the bar, mugs of beer in their hands, toasting their new partnership.

Both crews were sent to Castle Donington. On 28 July, an eye-popping summer's day, Sam climbed aboard a Wellington, S–Sugar, a real bomber, for the first time. They were only practising circuits and landings, but Ken proved so capable that when they landed their instructor told him he could fly solo.

Sam sat behind his curtain, working on his charts, listening to Ken going through the checks and drills before they took off once more. Then he heard Ken's voice on the radio. 'This is S for Sugar. Aircraft in front has just gone in. Taking off …' Sam wondered what the hell he meant. He got up from his navigator's desk as they rumbled into the air and looked over the flight engineer's shoulder. The Wellington ahead of them had buried its nose in a tree. It looked like a nasty one.

As he watched, there was a vast explosion. The stricken bomber was engulfed in flame and choking black smoke billowed into the sky around them. Sam knew immediately that Sandy – his best friend for the past two years – and everyone else on board were dead. No one spoke. Air Traffic Control gave the order for Ken to land, and he circled the airfield, passing on the details of what he could see to the ground. The shattered bomber was still burning fiercely. Sam turned away.

Rusty Waughman's crew came together in a similarly haphazard fashion.

Idris 'Taffy' Arndell, a wireless operator, and his friend, Colin 'Ginger' Farrant, had fixed to meet two local girls in Loughborough the night they were supposed to find a crew. Knowing they would be expected to have a drink or two with their new mates, they decided to hide in the pub toilets until the selection process was over; they didn't want to miss their double date. Making for the exit as soon as they thought they were in the clear, they bumped into two pilots, one of whom was Rusty Waughman.

'Are you two crewed up?' Rusty's companion asked.

'Yes,' they lied.

'We don't believe you, and we're both short of a wireless operator. We'll toss for it.'

Rusty lost, and the other pilot chose Ginger; he appeared the more intelligent and dependable of the two, or as intelligent and dependable as you can appear when you've been caught hiding in a pub toilet. They were posted shortly after to XII Squadron at Wickenby and went missing on their first operation – a long haul to Stettin on the night of 5 January. It later emerged that Ginger had lied about his age; he was only 17 when he joined up.

Of the 55,573 men of Bomber Command who died during the Second World War, 5,723 were killed in training, and a further 3,113 were seriously injured. Like much bad news, these losses were downplayed at the time, in line with Charles Portal's decree that 'Statistical information regarding the chances of survival of aircrew should be confined to the smallest number of people; this information could be distorted and dangerous to morale.'[21]

The casualties also included men who had completed the full 30 mission tours and were then posted for six months as OTU instructors. It was often as hazardous to sit beside a nervous young pilot in a bomber he had never flown before as it was to be at the controls of a Lancaster in the night skies above Berlin.

Roger Coverley was a pilot with 76 Squadron at Holme-on-Spalding-Moor in March 1944, after completing 30 ops with 78 Squadron. He had been a pilot instructor on Halifaxes in the interim. 'I didn't enjoy it. It was boring and much too dangerous because you're teaching young kids how to fly. I was sitting in the right-hand seat, unable to get at the controls if anything went wrong. I had some very close shaves. I couldn't wait to get back on operations.'[22]

CHAPTER 4

In the Face of Death

Members of Rusty Waughman's 101 Squadron kit up prior to take off

Sam Harris and his crew travelled by train to Elsham Wolds, home of 576 Squadron, in early January 1944. They pulled up at a small rural station and Sam leaned out of the window to ask the lone porter on the platform if it was Elsham. He nodded and they lugged their bulging kitbags off the train.

As they looked around, wondering what to do next, the porter approached them. 'Are you boys after the airfield?'

Sam raised his eyebrows and surveyed the featureless Lincolnshire countryside. They were in RAF uniform, they were laden with kit. Did the man think they were here to enjoy the scenery? There wasn't any scenery.

'Yes,' one of the crew replied wearily.

'In that case, you need the next station. They'll pick you up from there.'

The train had sounded its whistle and was starting to pull away, but they managed to grab their stuff and climb back on board before it was too late. They flopped back into the seats they had left a few moments earlier. No one said a word.

Finally Ken spoke. 'Six bloody months to get here and we get off at the wrong bloody station.'

Though operational crews had little say in their immediate future, Rusty Waughman asked to be posted to 101 Squadron; Paul Zanchi, who had become a friend during training, was based there. He was told by a Flight Commander that 101 was a 'special' squadron, where only the best pilots were sent.

By the time Rusty arrived at Ludford Magna he discovered that Paul had become yet another casualty of the Battle of Berlin. On the night of 26 November, one of his first ops, he had been sent to bomb the Big City and never came back. 'It was a real shock, an eye-opener, an awakening; a realisation of what it all meant. I felt a sense of real sadness and I knew then that things weren't going to be as easy as they seemed to be in training.'

In November 1943 Reg Payne, a young wireless operator, had crewed up with two Pilot Officers, Michael Beetham (later Sir Michael Beetham, Marshal of the RAF and the Chief of Air Staff in ultimate command of the legendary Vulcan 607 bombing of Port Stanley runway during the Falklands War) and Frank Swinyard, and been posted to 50 Squadron at Skelling-thorpe. Shortly after he arrived, he was told that his mother had sent a telegram asking him to come home. His brother had been shot down. His new Wing Commander initially refused him permission to do so. He feared that Reg's parents, after losing one RAF son, would make him promise not to fly; they did not want a new crew of such promise to be broken up.

His boss relented when Reg promised that he would return regardless of his parents' pleas. 'As it was, my mum and dad didn't try to dissuade me. They just said, "Reg, whatever you do, just be careful."' A few months later they discovered that his brother was alive and being held in a prisoner-of-war camp; he was one of the lucky ones. 'We were always losing crews. There was a Canadian crew in our hut and they all got the chop. They used to have loads of cookies, cakes and biscuits sent to them from Canada. They would leave boxes open and say to us, "Just help yourselves to anything you want." One morning they didn't come back and we were left with all the cookies. A crew came and took all their personal stuff away. They didn't exist any more.'[23]

The introduction to squadron life was less sobering for others, but still disconcerting. On the advice of the Squadron Adjutant, Andy Wejcman had changed his name to Wiseman. His identity disc said he was Church of England. When Andy asked why, he was told that most recruits were C of E; changing the religious denomination to Catholic or Jewish meant stopping the machine that stamped the letters, a process the Women Auxiliary Air Force members found unduly laborious.

'I can get it changed if you want,' Andy was told.

'What's the difference?' he replied.

'You'll be buried in accordance with Christian rites when your charred remains are found on the continent of Europe.'

Andy didn't want to be labelled as difficult, and decided it didn't matter; he would be dead. The denomination remained.

He was posted to 466 Squadron Royal Australian Air Force at RAF Leconfield in Yorkshire – 'A Polish Jew, flying with the Australian Air Force!' – as a bomb aimer. 'I really enjoyed squadron. The camaraderie was lovely and the Australians treated me as an equal. If we argued, my pilot used to say, "Don't give me any airs just because you went to unifucking-versity!' But he didn't mean it seriously.'

When Sam Harris and his crew finally made it to Elsham Wolds on that icy January Sunday they were pointed in the direction of a Nissen hut in the corner of a field. Their living quarters was a room with 14 beds, six of which were surrounded by piles of clothes and books which two NCOs were putting in freshly labelled kitbags.

'What's going on?' Ken asked.

The men stopped what they were doing. 'We're the Committee of Adjustment,' one of them answered. 'We're collecting the property of the crew that were here. They're listed as missing; we look after their belongings in the meantime. If you give us some time we'll get the hut cleared and you can move in. I hope you have better luck than they did.'

The crew stood silent for a few seconds, watching as the two men cleared away the lives of their predecessors. Ken suggested they head to the mess for a stiffener.

The first crew member to experience the fire and fury of an operational raid was normally the pilot. As part of his training on base he was required to tag along with an experienced crew on a watching brief, a routine known as flying 'second dickie'. Some did not survive those flights; many a fledgeling crew lost their skipper before they had even started a tour.

Ray Francis (front row, far left), end of tour

Ray Francis, a flight engineer with 622 Squadron at Mildenhall in Suffolk, barely slept a wink the night their pilot, an Aussie named Ray Trenouth, went on his first op as second dickie. His crew just lay on their bunks praying for his return. Eight hours later, to their great relief, he walked back into the married quarter which was their home on base. He said nothing, kicked off his boots, sat on his bed, pushed his cap to the back of his head, lit a cigarette and inhaled deeply. His silence was more than the others could bear.

'What was it like, Ray?'

He blew out a cloud of smoke and chuckled. 'Just wait until you blighters go!'

Ray Francis had joined up after seeing his home city of Birmingham suffer under the weight of the Luftwaffe bombing. He wasn't going to be easily deterred. 'In the early days on the squadron we knew that people were being shot down and killed. But we never talked about it. We never related casualties to deaths. If 20 aircraft went up and two got shot down, you never said to yourself at that time, "That's 10 per cent gone, so we've got to do 30 ops, therefore we're going to get the chop three times." We were just keen to get in and take part. You never expected to finish a tour, but then again you always thought it'll happen to the other fellow and not me. Now that's a bit daft, isn't it?'[24]

Norman 'Babe' Westby was the youngest member of Rusty Waughman's crew. As a bomb aimer his role was to guide the pilot over the target and release the bombs at the right time. He spent most of the op next to or behind the pilot, but moved down into the nose during the bombing run, the point at which the aircraft was running the gauntlet of the enemy's most focused flak defences. He would lie down and look through the bombsight as shells exploded and shrapnel flew around him, to usher the bomber calmly into position.

It was not a job for the faint-hearted. In Norman's opinion, it guaranteed him the best view of the unfolding drama: the searchlights scouring the sky and the fires burning on the ground; the kaleidoscopic 'target indicators' released by the Pathfinders to mark his aiming point – or, when visibility was poor, the skymarkers, coloured flares attached to parachutes. And to round off the show, as he thought of it, were the 'fireworks'. 'Isn't it pretty?!' he would cry, surveying the flak-blasted stage. 'Isn't it beautiful?!'

'For Christ's sake, Norman, shut up!' the rest of the crew would chorus. They just wanted to hear that the bombs were gone and they could head for safety.

When another crew went missing, 'It wasn't worth thinking about,' Rusty Waughman says. 'We would raise a toast to them: "Here's to so-and-so, he's dead, and here's to the next one to die." Or: "Death put his bony hand on your shoulder and said – Live, chum, I'm coming." We were young and naive. We didn't have the mental capacity to truly understand the reality. The chaps who suffered most were the highly educated ones, who understood what was happening and knew they were likely to die.

'If the other crews in your hut didn't return, then the Committee of Adjustment arrived to remove all their personal belongings. One minute they were, the next minute they weren't, and then a new crew arrived to replace them. People just disappeared. You didn't see dead bodies, even though thousands of my colleagues died. People simply weren't there any more.'

Alan Payne remained an irrepressible optimist. He always thought there was 'a gap in the flak' where he and his crew would find safety under the heaviest fire. Roger Coverley was a fatalist. 'I knew I was going to get the chop because all my mates around me were getting it. So many aircraft were being lost that it felt inevitable. But it did not affect me. I thought, whatever happens, happens. No one shed any tears about it.

We laughed at it really. We thought, let's get on with it and then have a drink.'

Drink was not discouraged. Even Bomber Harris believed his men needed a release. 'I have always considered that the strain imposed by sustained bomber operations requires that aircrew personal should enjoy the maximum amount of freedom from restraint, and should be relieved, as far as can be done without loss of efficiency, of routine station duties.' He added: 'The last thing I would wish to do would be to impose on aircrew personnel an irksome regime of inspections, parades and spit and polish.'[25]

The focal points of the men's life became the pub and the mess. Any entertainment was welcomed which might take their minds off what lay ahead, whether it was the cinema or just a good sing-song in the mess.

Sam Harris and his crew were regular visitors to the Oswald pub in Scunthorpe on their free evenings. It had a gramophone; the barmaid would put on Bing Crosby singing 'Cow Cow Boogie', and on Saturdays there was a large back room where 'some of the aircrew would go on stage and do their party piece, usually when the night was well advanced and a quantity of beer had been consumed. A favourite was a Flight Sergeant from 576 Squadron who was in charge of "discipline"; he sang a rude song about a woodpecker. It was always greeted with applause and the crowd joined in the chorus.'

Not everyone could use these diversions to escape the feeling of impending doom. Chick Chandler's pre-war job – manufacturing parts for anti-aircraft guns – was a protected occupation, but everyone he knew had joined up and he didn't want to be left out. 'I can't say I really enjoyed life in Bomber Command. It was always in the back of your mind that tomorrow might be the day that you might die. Even when you were going out, there was always the thought that it might be the last time: that this would be your last pint, or this might be your last dance. I wanted to join up and be part of the war effort, but the reality wasn't quite as I imagined. Nobody told me they shot back!'

The other release was female company. The objects of their desire were the girls in the local town who might have an eye for a young man in uniform. There were also the WAAFS, members of the Women's Auxiliary Air Force who worked alongside the men on base, doing clerical jobs in operations and control rooms and working in technical, electrical and mechanical roles to free the men for flying duties.

Norman 'Babe' Westby had been a virgin when he joined Rusty Waughman's crew. 'Taffy, our mischievous wireless operator, took it upon himself to introduce him to the ways of the flesh. He knew of a full-bosomed woman in Grimsby called "Luscious Lil" with a penchant for revealing outfits, who'd be the ideal target for Norman's first operational sortie with the opposite sex.' He organised a pub crawl. 'By the end, Norman was rubbing his hands with excitement. The sight of her black stockings with the thin black lines at the back made it almost impossible to bear. Needless to say, the evening concluded satisfactorily as far as most parties were concerned, and Taffy took great pride in his achievement of turning a boy into a man.'

The married men worried about those they had left behind, and might leave behind permanently. When they were bombed out of their home in Portsmouth, Ron Auckland's family moved to Porchester. Another family who had also suffered the same fate lived two doors away, and Ron became friendly with Sheila, a friend of their daughter. 'As soon as I saw her, I knew she was the girl for me.'

She was equally smitten. 'I felt safe with him.'

They became engaged in 1942, shortly before Ron was posted to America for his pilot training. A year later they married. Ron's best man was Alan Barnes, another pilot whom he had met during the recruiting process at Lord's Cricket

Ground. Their group had been assembled in alphabetical order and the two men ended up next to each other in line – it was the chance start of a great friendship. They were soon stationed together as trainee pilots and became inseparable. Posted to different squadrons, they vowed to try and meet up every time they were on leave.

In January 1944 Ron called Alan's base to put a date in the diary for a pint. He was told Alan had gone missing on a raid over Berlin. 'I knew he was dead. It really brought home what we were all facing.'

Alan's body was never found.

Sheila had only met him at their wedding, but his last words to her were: 'If anything happens to Ron, I'll always look after you.'

Ron and Sheila Auckland's wedding

'It was a great shock,' Ron recalled. 'Of course people you knew were dying all of the time. In Portsmouth I went to a lot of the Navy dances and we lost many of our friends when one of the ships got torpedoed. We knew the war. We understood it.'

She and Ron never discussed the dangers. 'Sheila obviously knew what I was doing in Bomber Command but I didn't speak to her about the operations or the losses. I never wanted to worry her. She just expected me to turn up when we'd agreed.'

Sheila also did her best not to distress him. 'I cried every time he left but I never let him see me cry. When I saw him off at the railway station, he kept opening the door to say goodbye one last time. The porter shouted out, "Close that door and put that light out!" But Ron kept on opening it. In the end I said to him, "You've got to go, you've got to go." It was so hard. My sister's husband was in the Navy, so we both used to cry together.'

They ended up living together. 'I could talk to my sister about it. We would listen to the radio and some bad news would come on and we'd end up crying. She'd say to me, "Let's sleep together tonight," for comfort. But the men never knew about any of this.'

On one occasion Ron came back to the house unexpectedly to find Sheila in tears. 'I was upset because he saw me crying. I tried to be the brave girl because I didn't want him to worry. That was the wartime attitude. But it affects people on such a personal level – the fear that I had was being replicated by hundreds of thousands people across the country night after night, day after day. But you never showed it. No, we went dancing to take our mind off it.'

Each day Ron was away, Sheila lived in fear of the 'telegram boy' and what he might bring. 'One day he arrived with an envelope and I didn't want to take it. I thought it was telling me Ron was missing or dead. My aunt opened it. It was from

Ron. He was telling me he'd won the Distinguished Flying Cross. The silly man sent me a telegram!'

The unceasing tension took its toll. Rusty Waughman was forced to replace his first flight engineer. 'He was fine in training, but as soon as we were on operations he would just sit on the floor and quiver. He was incapable of carrying out his duties. I stuck with him for a couple of ops, but during one our starboard engine was on fire and the poor guy was unable to do anything about it. I had to take all the emergency actions myself. It reached the point where it was affecting our safety, so I reported him to the CO, and he left the station that afternoon so as not to affect the morale of others. I don't know if he was made LMF or not, but he should never have been because, although he knew of his condition, he never refused to fly on ops.'

LMF – shorthand for 'Lack of Moral Fibre' – was the label given to those deemed to have lost the will to fight, branded as cowards and removed from operations in disgrace. The threat of it was the sword of Damocles that hung over every airman's head. During the operation in which Chick Chandler had become confused about how much Window to throw out of the plane, their Stirling bomber developed a technical fault. The crew began to argue over whether they should turn back or continue to the target. 'We were facing mortal danger, but we were more worried about what would happen if we returned. I knew we didn't have a chance of surviving, but someone said: "They'll say we're LMF." It was an ever-present fear in Bomber Command. They were more scared of being called a coward than they were of flying. People were willing to risk their lives to avoid being branded LMF.'

Any early return from an op came under the kind of scrutiny that induced many to press on regardless. One can only speculate upon the number of aircraft which might have perished because the crew decided that dealing with any mechanical problems was a less daunting prospect than the disgrace of being labelled cowards. Bomb aimer Campbell Muirhead recorded an account in his diary of the treatment of a sergeant who had refused to fly: 'There he was standing out in front, all on his own, in full view of every person in the unit, to be stripped of his wings and then his sergeant's tapes. They had all been unstitched beforehand so they came away easily when they were ripped from his uniform. He was immediately posted elsewhere.'[26]

Alan Payne was sent to find and bring back his mid-upper gunner, who ran away after two operations. On the return journey, once he had assured them he wouldn't try to escape, they attempted to lighten the mood by taking him to a dance hall in Nottingham. It only provided a temporary respite, however; once they got back to Lincolnshire, the gunner was stripped of his stripes and brevet and posted to a camp in Sheffield to be 'retrained'.

Alan and his crew were sympathetic, but didn't dwell on his fate. Once gone he was barely mentioned; there was always another operation, and life in Bomber Command was hazardous enough without having someone on board who might be incapable of carrying out his job at a critical moment.

Andy Wiseman had the misfortune to see what went on in an 'LMF camp', though as a visitor and not an inmate. 'I remember seeing one of the bases they used for people who were branded LMF. They were allowed to be drilled for 55 minutes, and they had cold showers in the morning in winter. It was terrible. LMF was one of the great unfairnesses of the war. Though I suspect that some of the LMF people *were* cowards, most of them were just deeply affected by their experiences and couldn't cope any more. I think it took more courage to admit you were afraid and couldn't go on. Bravery only lasts for so long ...'

Men could serve on so many operations before the bank of courage from which they had drawn was empty. Some found the will to carry on regardless, perhaps because they were too ashamed to admit to their fear and dreaded the accusations of cowardice that might follow. Harry Evans served his early ops with a mid-upper gunner, 'a proper Jack-the-lad', who soon found it difficult to cope. 'The crew didn't tell me till much later, but he went to the Gunnery Officer and asked to go. The officer talked him out of it. On ops he would have panic attacks, especially if we were being shot up. He'd start shouting: "We're all going to get killed!" or "There's holes in the tail!" We'd just say, "Shut up, you ..." But he got stuck in from then on. I look at it in two ways: he wasn't the best mid-upper gunner because of the panic. On the other hand, he was too scared to doze off at his position ...'

Rusty Waughman believed the mental scars were worse than any physical wounds. 'I know one airman who pressed on. When they were damaged by flak during an op, he blacked out, left his seat and wandered to the back of the aircraft. The rest of the crew tried to talk to him, but he couldn't speak and he had no further recollection of the op. He was transferred to the hospital at Matlock, where he was unconscious for several days until a nurse dropped a metal dish. He woke up screaming, "There's another poor sod going down. Look at the flames! Look at the flames!"' The man was eventually invalided out of the service.

When men suffered a nervous breakdown because of the stress and exhaustion of incessant ops, they were given medical and psychiatric treatment rather than punishment – and given the relentless nature of life in Bomber Command it is surprising that so few men suffered psychological problems. Only 0.3 per cent of aircrew were officially classified as showing a Lack of Moral Fibre, though countless more suffered from a spectrum of what we would now term post-traumatic stress disorders.

Jack Watson's crew was joined by a Mosquito squadron on base at Upwood. Jack was in his room in the old married quarters when a Mosquito which had become lost in the fog careered into one of the adjoining buildings. 'The house was ablaze, and as we were running towards it we could see three of our lads who had just come back from a raid sitting on the bed. We could see them sitting there; they still had their uniforms on. They couldn't get out and we couldn't get in to help them – and there wasn't a thing anybody could do about it. Suddenly the house crashed down and collapsed on them and they disappeared into a cloud of flame and smoke. One of our mates tried to get in to help them out, but he got badly burnt and in the end he had to jump out.

'At the end of the terraced houses there was a little brick wall and I went down there to find the navigator and pilot of the Mosquito. They had come straight through the top of the aircraft canopy and had hit this wall. They were just lying there. That's something which shook me. They were a real mess, but they were still completely in their flying kit, which virtually held them together. And when they put them in a blanket it just folded up into a ball ... I have never seen anything like it.'

The next morning was warm and sunny. A group of airmen sat on the lawn ruminating on the events of the night before. Jack Watson was among them. One of the men turned to another. 'You know, I could see you sitting there in that house burning like that last night.' It was crass thing to say, but it had been meant as a joke. 'We used to say stupid things like that,' Jack explains.

They were young and gauche, and gallows humour provided another release. But the recipient of the comment did not see the funny side; he stood up and walked away. They never saw him again.

CHAPTER 5

30 March 1944

Sam Harris (front row, right) and crew

At the end of March 1944 Britain had yet to emerge from a long and harrowing winter, but the newspapers were still trying to kindle optimism in any way possible. The front page of the *Daily Mirror* led with the story of the Russian Army's progress across southern Poland under the headline 'Soviet Racing for Czech Border', while '"Eat Your Words" challenge to MPs' reported a piece of political brinksmanship by Winston Churchill on the home front to help shore up his coalition government. The *Daily Express* also found time to report the story of Harry P. Mclean of Windsor, Ontario, who threw $1,000 into the street from his fourth-floor window. 'I like to see people happy,' he said.

Happiness on the home front was still in short supply. The British people were enduring their fifth year of war, and rationing had bitten deep. Londoners had just come through a 'Baby Blitz', Hitler's attempt to repeat his terrorisation of the capital four years earlier by dropping 2,000 tonnes of explosive, and feared further attacks. One story that was not reported was the recapture of 73, and subsequent execution of 50, of the 76 Allied prisoners-of-war who had escaped through a tunnel at Stalag Luft III.[27]

Against this backdrop, Sir Arthur Harris made his way to his operations room in an underground bunker at RAF High Wycombe just before 9 a.m. on 30 March. As he did each day, he greeted the officers of Bomber Command's Air Staff with a brisk 'Good morning, gentlemen,'[28] sat down at his desk and lit the first in a chain of cigarettes. Peering over his half-moon glasses, he would then growl, 'Did the Hun do anything last night?' before taking his opening drag. He would occasionally substitute 'Boche' for 'Hun', but his dislike of the enemy was never less than clear.

Harris was driven; he took his responsibility so seriously he never dreamt of delegating it, and didn't take any leave in three and a half years. He was determined to carry out his job to the best of his ability and bore the enormous strain that accompanied it without complaint. Those who worked with him lived in fear of his thunderous roar whenever they were late or failed to answer a question, and he made frequent enemies of politicians and Air Ministry civil servants. But he did not care. Winning the war was what counted.

The three children from his failed first marriage might have found him similarly uncompromising. They were cut from his life – or at least the version of it he gave to his biographer, Henry Probert. Yet the man who made the most combat-hardened Wing Commanders tremble melted at the sight of his five-year-old daughter. Jackie was a regular visitor to High Wycombe, and Joan Dally, a WAAF Corporal in the HQ Met Office, was occasionally asked to look after the little girl when her mother went shopping. 'Others might have been in awe of him, but I saw a different side of Harris – a kindly father of a little girl. I would sometimes go into his famous office and Jackie would be playing there. I could see by the way he looked at her that he adored her.'[29]

Once his question about the activities of the Germans had been answered, the morning conference followed a set pattern. Harris read out the report of the previous night's operations. That March morning there had been no major raids for three nights because of poor weather conditions, so it was brief.

He was followed by Magnus Spence. Making predictions about the weather over a distant patch of Europe based on scant information was a challenge that Spence and his meteorologists faced daily. Harris took a special interest in the forecasts. Joan Dally remembers his frequent visits to the Met Office. 'He would come in and say things like, "Now, when are you chaps going to find me some decent weather so I can send my boys out?" He always referred to the aircrew as "my boys". You could tell by the way he spoke about them how much he cared for them. He'd say, "I don't want my boys to run into bad weather tonight."'

Spence's report encouraged Harris to believe in the possibility of some cloud cover towards the south of Germany, and a half moon at its height between an hour past sunset and the small hours of the morning – when the bomber stream would be reaching its target.

Next to speak was a representative of the US Eighth Army Air Force. At the beginning of this offensive Harris had promised a decisive victory with the help of US bombers, but the Americans remained committed to daytime raids and, in public at least, rejected the concept of area bombing. Their heavily defended B-17s – each had six gun ports – flew in tight formations and sought to destroy the Luftwaffe on sight rather than hide from them in the dark. And they boasted that their Norden bombsight was the best in the world.

Though it also brought heavy losses, daylight – in theory –

would allow them to locate their targets without the need for Pathfinders. Even though cloud cover regularly obscured their objectives, they steadfastly ignored the facts and maintained that their methods were more accurate, and that their only targets were military sites, factories, docks and other strategic industries. The reality was very different, though; as historian Anthony Verrier points out, precision bombing was a myth, 'an aspiration which some crews in certain conditions occasionally achieved'.[30]

After hearing the morning's reports, Harris's conclusion was swift: there would be a major raid that night. The target would be an industrial city which had not been bombed for seven months, with factories producing tanks, armoured cars and diesel engines, a large engineering works, two Siemens electrical factories and an aircraft repair facility on the outskirts. It was also a major administrative and communications centre, and the iconic location of huge pre-war rallies filmed by Leni Riefenstahl and screened across Germany. *Triumph of the Will* both charted and enhanced the rise of the Nazis and the creation of the personality cult around its leader, imbuing the city with symbolic as well as strategic importance.

Nuremberg was a beautiful city with a rich history. Its medieval quarter still boasted an imperial castle which dated back to the twelfth century. Its darker side was reflected in the Nuremberg Laws of 1935, which formally reduced the status of Jews in Germany to that of non-humans. Hitler had described it as 'the most German of German cities', and championed the building of a host of monuments there, designed by Albert Speer, to celebrate the Thousand Year Reich. Destroying these, the railway lines and army barracks, scrambling the lines of communication and obliterating the factories where many of the 426,000 population worked, would strike a uniquely damaging blow.

Harris presented his plan to his senior staff and advisers in the operations room at High Wycombe later that morning, advocating a straight run to Nuremberg. His Deputy Commander-in-Chief, Robert Saundby, kept his concerns to himself until the meeting was over. His boss was not a man to cross in public; many even questioned the wisdom of doing so in private. 'He was generally acknowledged to be a grim man who could freeze an Eskimo with a look; a man of explosive temperament; a man of few words – all of them forceful.'[31] Saundby also knew that Harris did not take his decisions lightly, only too aware that each time he signed off on a raid it meant thousands of men would be risking their lives.

When they managed to speak, Saundby expressed his reservations about the 'straight run-in' to Nuremberg, though whether this refers to the long leg or the bombing run after the turning point is unclear. Harris 'thought for a moment, then grunted – and those knowing him will appreciate how effective those grunts could be. He said he would wait to see the result of the afternoon's Met Report.'

Saundby remained uneasy, but on his shoulders fell the task of finding the best route to and from the target. A straight route meant easier navigation, shorter flying time, less fuel and more bombs, though it also gave the Germans a better chance to plot their course and ambush the bomber stream. An indirect route increased the chances of aircraft going off course and meant more time in the air and a lighter bomb load.

Air Vice-Marshal Donald Bennett, chief of the Pathfinder Force, was also concerned. He called Saundby to propose a more deviating course. Saundby listened carefully and canvassed the opinions of the other group commanders before coming to a final decision: the direct route it would be. The order was sent to Harris for approval, and once that was gained it was transmitted by telex across 39 air bases throughout eastern England, from North Yorkshire to East Anglia. Approximately 1,000 aircraft and 6,500 men would be part of the operation, which had been given the codename Grayling.

The bombers would take off at approximately 10 p.m. to make use of the forecast cloud cover and avoid being caught in moonlight. The stream would assemble over the North Sea, then fly over the enemy coast and into Belgium, going west of Brussels. Charleroi marked the start of the perilous 265-mile straight leg south of the Ruhr.

Four 'spoof' raids involving 162 aircraft would be launched as diversions, and to camouflage the primary target for as long as possible. Fifty Halifax bombers would head for the North Sea, to give the impression of a much larger force threatening Hamburg or Berlin, then drop mines in the Heligoland Bight, a bay at the mouth of the River Elbe. Three separate forces of Mosquitoes would head for Aachen, Cologne and Kassel, where they would drop target indicator flares as if for a full-scale attack, designed to draw the enemy fighters away from the main stream.

At the end of the straight leg, the stream was to take an abrupt southerly turn 79 miles north of Nuremberg. Within 19 minutes of altering course it would be over the target, giving the Germans little time to react. Until then, Frankfurt, Stuttgart, even Munich, might still be the target.

The aiming point was a railway goods depot south of the centre of Nuremberg, to compensate for any 'creep back' – the fires started by the first bombs to be dropped were often used as the aiming point by subsequent crews; they would release their load as soon as the blaze below came into their sights, and as each successive wave bombed the nearest 'edge' of the fire it crept further away from the target. The setting of the moon would give them the cloak of darkness for their five-hour return journey against the forecast headwinds.

Zero Hour was set at 1.10 a.m. on 31 March. Five minutes before that the Pathfinders would start marking with flares to illuminate the area, so their fellow Mosquitoes and Lancasters could release their target indicator bombs on the aiming point, and the last bomber would drop its load at 1.22. The entire 68-mile-long stream, arriving in five waves behind the opening Pathfinder force, would have 12 minutes to carry out the attack – at a rate of 57 aircraft per minute. If the winds *en route* held up the progress of the stream, Zero Hour could be adjusted.

In those 12 minutes the objective was to drop 2,600 tonnes of explosives on Nuremberg, half of which were incendiaries. In later raids the bomb load increased – 3,900 tonnes would be dropped on Dresden in February 1945 – but it was still significantly more than the 500 tonnes the Luftwaffe had rained on Coventry in November 1940.

★　★　★

As Sam Harris woke that morning in Elsham Wolds, a warm spring still seemed a distant promise. Two of his crew, Eric and Mac, had already gone for breakfast. He and the others sat in bed smoking cigarettes, summoning the will to exchange the warmth of their beds for the chilly floor of the hut and the freezing dash to the ablutions hut to shave with cold water. No one had lit the coke stove around which they had chosen their beds on their arrival in January. The stove usually warmed the whole hut; they even used the outside of it to toast bread 'obtained' from the mess. One night it got so hot that it ignited Chalky's blanket.

Their hut nestled in the corner of a field, down a narrow dirt track, a bike ride away from the mess and the other squadron buildings. This seclusion had its benefits; nipping under the coke compound fence to steal extra supplies for the stove was one. Otherwise, their meagre ration only gave them an hour or so of heat. But on mornings like this the squadron office and the NAAFI wagon with its delicious sticky buns and steaming mugs of tea seemed a long way away.

Eventually they climbed on to their bicycles and set off, their breath billowing in the cold air as they pedalled. The morning cuppa and bun had become an essential part of their routine over the course of the last three months and 10 completed ops. That morning Ken Murray decided they should practise a few drills aboard their aircraft. The idea was not universally popular, given the weather, but they all knew that preparation was as important as luck in determining their chances of survival. They cycled grudgingly across to their Lancaster, G–George, eager to get back to the warmth of the mess before all the newspapers had been claimed and the crosswords completed.

Lancasters were never warm, and as they went through their drills that morning it felt even more arctic inside their plane than it did outside. They had come a long way with G–George since the January morning when they first encountered her. First impressions had not been promising. Someone had painted 84 yellow bombs beneath the pilot's position on the port side to mark each completed trip, and the rest of the ageing veteran's outer skin was crisscrossed with patches covering the plethora of holes, gouges and scrapes from the flak. Inside it was dirty, scruffy, unkempt and unloved. She had been inherited from 103 Squadron, who shared Elsham, because no one wanted her.

As a member of the ground crew first showed them around, he announced with a grin that because they were a new crew no one expected them to last long, so there was little point in wasting a new aircraft on them. No one laughed. Ken had bristled. 'We'll show you what a new crew can do,' he said.

Their first couple of ops hadn't endeared the plane to them. She was slow to climb, her auto–pilot was unreliable and she needed a longer take-off distance than any other Lancaster on the squadron. Mac called her 'horrible, ancient', and Ken was so fed up that he complained to their Commanding Officer. The response was similar to the line they got from the ground crew, minus the humour: 'A sprog crew doesn't expect to get a new Lancaster. You'll be lucky to last five trips.'

Against the run of the dice they had survived the ill-fated raid on Leipzig; they overshot the target because of the winds and flew back with bombers being shot out of the sky all around them. At that point it occurred to them that, for all its discomforts, this old girl knew how to get back from an op, and from that moment they started to love their creaking but reliable Lancaster. They lived with the constant awareness that an aircraft could be their coffin, but they knew a good one could be their saviour.

While the night veiled many of her flaws, G-George always looked older and more frayed in the cold light of dawn, and this morning was no exception. She looked like a blown rose next to the sleeker machines alongside at dispersal. They climbed aboard via a small ladder to an entry hatch forward of the tail. Prior to an op they had to squeeze along the fuselage, trying to avoid banging their heads on the roof, their flying suits and kit snagging and banging on the sides of the cold metal frame. It was less of an obstacle course on a drill, but they missed the warm gear. The smell of fuel hung heavy in the air, together with the mustiness that attested to the bomber's age, and at times like this they still envied crews who had been treated to one fresh off the production line, its cockpit pristine, without the slightest hint of a scratch on the Perspex or the dials, a complete absence of oily smears or dust, and the delicious, leathery scent of factory goodness in the air.

They took up their positions for the drill. Bert Winn, the rear gunner, turned left, the only man on board to do so. He crawled through the tail on hands and knees and slid his legs through the doors to his cramped Frazer Nash turret. Once in, that was it: facing away from the direction of travel, he would barely move for the rest of the flight, his gloved fingers gripping the twin triggers of his four Browning machine-guns.

The rest of the crew made their way through the fuselage. Eric Page, the mid-upper gunner, took his station just forward of the main entrance. His ceiling turret was armed with two Browning machine-guns. When he and Bert swung into action the staccato rattle of their weapons could be heard throughout the aircraft, and the lingering smell of cordite would mingle with the Lancaster's perpetual cocktail of hot oil, glycol and sweat.

Roland Luffman took his position at the wireless operator's desk on the port side of the cabin, forward of the wing. Next to the inner engine, it was the warmest part of the plane, and so where the crews often kept their 'pee can'. On one raid, Rusty Waughman, of 101 Squadron, remembers a bomber below them exploding, 'which rolled us a half roll over'. As he fought to regain control of the plane, Taffy, his wireless operator, started to scream 'Blood! Blood!' over the intercom. He thought he had been hit. In fact the pee can had been turned over during their dive and emptied on his head.

Sam Harris eased himself behind the navigator's table, hidden behind a curtain on the starboard side, just behind Ken and flight engineer 'Mac' Mackenzie, and lit by an Anglepoise lamp. Chalky White, the bomb aimer, slid down the steps into the nose and lay flat on the ice-cold floor. Things would get a damn sight hotter for him when the flak crackled around him and the aircraft lurched and veered its way on the final run in to the target.

Once at their posts, they went through the usual drills. After cries of 'Prepare to abandon aircraft', then 'Abandon aircraft! Abandon aircraft!' they threw open the escape hatches and slithered over the wings to practise a ditching at sea. Nothing could mimic the real challenges of trying to escape a bomber in a vertiginous spin, pinned to the sides or the roof by massive g-forces, unsure which way was up and which way was down. But it was something – certainly better than surrendering their fate entirely to chance – and it might buy them the precious seconds that could separate life from death.

They paused for a smoke and a chat, ran through a final crash landing drill, and headed back to the mess for those newspapers. After lunch there were no rides into town because there was no definitive word on whether there would be an op that night. No word meant staying on camp, idling away time, catching a nap, playing cards, stealing some coke for the stove or writing a letter home.

Then the base Tannoy sprang to life.

'All crews to report to their squadrons.'

★   ★   ★

The poor weather had seen three successive operations cancelled, which meant that Rusty Waughman and his crew had just enjoyed their third good night's sleep in succession – all except their rear gunner, Harry 'Tiger' Nunn. The previous night's op had been scratched just prior to take-off, and by then Harry had taken a 'wakey-wakey' pill, the methamphetamine cocktail intended to make sure he would be alert for the whole flight. As his mates got their heads down, he had spent the whole night pacing the floor of their hut, talking to himself, too manic to even lie on his bed.

Rusty Waughman, the 20-year-old son of a Durham colliery worker, had worked hard to become a pilot. Like Cyril Barton, he had been a sickly child. He had suffered bouts of diphtheria and tuberculosis and had a heart murmur, and his mother, a Royal Red Cross-winning matron at a military hospital during the First World War, constantly had to nurse him back to health. He missed out on many things as a result, football and swimming amongst them, so he always felt an outsider – and when he was old enough to join up he seized his chance to be part of something rather than feel left out once again.

Like the Bartons, his parents worried about him constantly, but when he told them about his plans to follow his father into the Navy they weren't unduly concerned, confident that his childhood illnesses would render him unfit to serve. When Rusty filled in the medical form at the recruiting centre, he omitted to mention his tuberculosis but included everything else. Then, on the spur of the moment, he decided to try his luck with the RAF instead. Their medical examination was less stringent and he was accepted immediately.

While Harry Nunn finally caught up on some rest later that morning, Rusty made his way across the base. Ludford Magna was a difficult place to warm to. It was built on farmland as a temporary installation by the construction company George Wimpey in 90 days, and its first Commanding Officer had described it as 'a joke in very bad taste played by the Air Ministry at our expense'. Under a steel-grey sky and a bone-numbing wind, after several days of heavy rain, it was living up to its nickname: Mudford Stagna. Rarely had the 101 Squadron motto, *Mens agitat molem* (Mind over matter), seemed so appropriate.

Rusty expected to be stood down yet again that evening, or assigned a training flight at most. His surprise when told at the squadron office that there would be an op gave way to unease when he walked past the aircraft at dispersal. Having primed them for the cancelled raid the night before, the ground crews were now winching down some of the bombs to make way for additional fuel. Whatever their new target might be, it was clearly a long distance away. And that was never a good sign.

Rusty kept his concerns to himself. He didn't even share them with the eighth member of his crew, Special Duties Operator Ted Manners. The Lancasters of 101 Squadron were fitted with a device known as the Airborne Cigar (ABC) that disrupted the enemy's radio broadcasts between their night fighters and ground control stations. When it was introduced in the autumn of 1943 the first words heard through its air-waves during a raid over Hanover were *'Achtung! English bastards coming!'*

Ted had become a popular and much-valued member of the crew, even though he was billeted elsewhere – in case he divulged any secrets in his sleep that his crew-mates might give up under enemy interrogation. There was nothing secret about the three large aerials that picked up the radio signals which Ted tried to jam – two protruded from the top of the fuselage and one from beneath the bomb aimer's position – but they also never asked him about the things he heard during an op as he sat, headphones clasped to his ears, in his own closed-off area behind the navigator and wireless operator.

Ted had spent three years learning German at grammar school, and so was selected for special duties when his training as a gunner was complete. His objective was to tune in to the radio exchanges between enemy controllers and their airborne fighters, which showed as vertical 'spikes' across a horizontal base on a cathode ray screen. As soon as he recognised a German voice he switched on his jammer, emitting a high-pitched shriek – which the enemy called *Dudelsack* (bagpipes) – to interfere with their communications traffic.

With three transmitters at his disposal, Ted could target three frequencies simultaneously, constantly monitoring the enemy's shifts of frequency to counter his interference. The downside was that his own jamming signals made the aircraft vulnerable to tracking; 101 suffered the heaviest losses of any squadron as a result, and since some of the Special Duties Operators in 101 Squadron were of German birth or heritage they could expect no mercy if they were captured.

While Rusty waited for more news, the crew tried to kill time. Some wandered off to the local farmhouse in search of a fry-up; others went to dispersal to chat with their ground crew. Harry Nunn had slept off his amphetamine high and was now sitting on his bed in his long johns with his clarinet. His mates did not always enjoy listening to him practise.

He had recently lost a reed, and eventually found it sliced in two. He had been smarting and determined to punish the culprit ever since.

The call came just after lunchtime. Crews were to report. The waiting was over.

★   ★   ★

Chick Chandler

Flight Engineer Chick Chandler did not need wakey-wakey pills to keep him alert. His drug was fear. He was responsible for everything mechanical during a flight. From his position beside his pilot Oliver Brooks, he monitored the instruments, as well as a second panel that told him the health of the aircraft's four engines and its fuel status. There was a bucket seat for him to perch on, but Chick didn't think it gave him the best view, so he sat on his toolbox.

When he joined XV Squadron at Mildenhall in October 1943, his technical knowledge was sorely inadequate. He was told his training would take two years to complete, but he was activated after six months, nowhere near ready for combat.

Much of his time had been spent playing football, and Chick injured himself so frequently that he was more often in the sick bay than at lectures; he managed to miss a lesson on propellers that left him clueless about how they might work or be repaired, but losses had become so great and replacement crews in such demand that Chick was deployed to Suffolk despite his lack of competence.

His early experience with Bomber Command had done little to bolster Chick's courage. On a Berlin raid he had watched in horror as countless bombers were shot from the sky, with no billowing parachutes to indicate that anyone on board had managed to escape.

At Mildenhall he and his crew had been moved from a wooden hut into the relative luxury of bricks-and-mortar married quarters. By that time they had completed 13 ops; barely halfway through their tour, they were the most experienced members of their squadron. As they lugged their kit through the door, a map of mainland Europe was being ripped off the wall. Chick moved closer to see that it was covered with pins. The previous occupants had marked every one of their targets. Now they were missing and the Committee of Adjustment was removing their belongings, pins and all. Chick realised that the berth he had been looking forward to with such enthusiasm was probably a dead man's bed.

On every op, as a lucky charm, Chick carried a grey silk scarf with black markings which his mother had given him. As the order came through that cold March day, he made sure his scarf was close at hand.

CHAPTER 6

The Red Line

Cyril Barton (back row, centre) with 78 Squadron

By the middle of the afternoon, to the surprise of many in the upper echelons of Bomber Command, the Nuremberg raid was still on. The first meteorological report of the day was handed to Harris and his team at 1 p.m.

'Bases fit for take-off with only a possibility of a few scattered showers. Over N. Sea broken convection cloud mainly below 12,000 ft, but there may be some isolated tops to 15,000 ft or above. Over continent convection cloud is expected to break up appreciably.'[32]

There would be no need to call off this raid. The breaking cloud over the continent would offer the bombers a clear view of the target and enable the main force to mark and bomb effectively. A Mosquito was sent over mainland Europe to assess the weather the bombers might encounter on their outward route. The flight returned at 3.25 p.m., its navigator suggesting that the earlier reports were inaccurate. There was little prospect of cloud cover on the way out; the bombers would be exposed. And the sky above Nuremberg appeared to be overcast, the enemy of accurate bombing.

Meteorological officer Magnus Spence issued another briefing: 'Nuremberg: Large amount of strato-cumulus with tops to about 8,000 feet and risk of some thin patchy medium cloud at about 15-16,000 feet.'

In a letter to the historian Martin Middlebrook, written on 14 September 1971, just 12 days before he died, Bomber Harris's deputy Robert Saundby confirmed that both he and his chief saw that forecast. 'I can say that, in view of the met report and other conditions, everyone, including myself, expected the C-in-C to cancel the raid. We were most surprised when he did not. I thought perhaps there was some top secret political reason for the raid – something too top secret for even me to know. But now I do not think that this was so.'

Saundby gave three reasons why he thought Harris still chose to go. Churchill wanted to hit Nuremberg for symbolic reasons; he wanted one last heavy bomber raid before they switched to French targets in preparation for Operation Overlord; and because summer was on its way, the shorter nights meant that long-range ops were increasingly hazardous.

'Harris was under pressure to make the attack,' Saundby said. 'He took a chance and he backed a hunch.'[33]

Whatever the reasons, Harris would not be swayed. The preparations were complete. The target had been selected; the route had been finalised; the aircraft were being primed; the squadrons chosen to take part had been notified, and their commanders had selected the crews to carry out the raid.

Owing to the cancellation of several previous raids – and thus no recent losses and no fatigue – there were more crews than usual available, but an operation deep into the heart of enemy territory that gruelling winter meant that experience was at a premium.

The battle orders were posted, listing the crews that would be involved by the name of their pilot. The minutes before the main briefing were often long ones. The atmosphere on base became yet more highly charged. Life in the nearby towns appeared to grind to a standstill. Ground crews checked the aircraft at dispersal. Fuel bowsers and bomb trailers went into overdrive. Some airmen would try not to think what might lie ahead. Some spent their time writing to loved ones.

Before his first op, while the rest of his crew smoked and paced around him, Cyril Barton had sat on his bed and opened his writing pad. 'Dear Mother,' he wrote, 'I'm hoping you never receive this but I quite expect you will ...'

Nine months and 18 operations had passed since Cyril had written that 'last letter' and entrusted it to his younger brother Ken, only to be opened in the event of his death. There had been near misses. A piece of flak flew through the roof of the plane during their sixth raid, on Leverkusen, and fractured Len Lambert's skull, but he still managed to navigate the return journey home. He missed two months of ops but rejoined them after a bone graft in January 1944, in time for the crew's move from Snaith to Burn. 'After I was wounded, I wondered if I was good enough to get us back every time. I seem to remember worrying not so much whether I would survive myself, but whether I was good enough to get the crew as a whole to survive, because it's a nasty feeling getting lost in the air. A lot of people lost their lives because their navigators got lost.'[34]

The crew did everything together. Cyril and Len were tee-total, more likely to be found in the NAAFI having a cup of tea than in the pub with a pint, but when they did go to their local, even if he was only having lemonade himself, Cyril always made sure he stood his round. The Websters' farmhouse was another regular port of call. They used to be invited there for supper after church on Sundays, and the family always gathered at the end of the runway to wave off Barton's Barmy

Bomber Boys, as the family knew them, before each raid. 'Mrs Webster would make these big apple pies,' Len remembered. 'She had the pastry cut out: BBBB.'

Cy's crew had a book in which they jotted down observations of each other and life in Bomber Command. 'My introduction to a Fraulein,' wrote Wally Crate, the crew's Canadian bomb aimer, of how he might chat up a young German woman. 'Excuse me, miss, when did I bomb you last?'[35]

March had not been easy, however, and not just because of the intensity of their operations. They had also been plagued with mechanical failure. At the beginning of the month the brakes on their Halifax Mk III had become unserviceable. Cy's new aircraft had developed a problem with its oxygen supply on its first raid over Stuttgart. Two nights later the bomb doors failed to open over Frankfurt. They eventually managed to open them and ditch their load over Darmstadt, but had to land at their base in North Yorkshire with the bomb doors still wide open.

The next three raids, on Frankfurt, Berlin and Essen, had gone smoothly, and their faith in their new Halifax was renewed. Yet Cyril was troubled. The crew had as little idea of the strong feelings stirring beneath his normally jovial exterior as his family did on his last visit home. They knew he was a church-goer, but no one realised the importance of his faith, or how sorely it had been tested since becoming operational.

His father's prediction – when granting him permission to sign up – had not been too wide of the mark. Cyril revealed his inner conflict in a letter to a friend and fellow Christian in mid-March. He confided that the vigour of his prayer had suffered because he was worried about offending or upsetting Jack and Wally, with whom he shared a room on base, by ostentatious shows of faith. On 28 March, just two days before the Nuremberg raid, he wrote again; he had taken the opportunity to pray properly, in front of his crew-mates, rather than furtively, as if it was something he should be ashamed of. Jack had been listening to the radio, but turned it down out of respect to his skipper, though he forgot to turn it off when he got into bed, which perhaps showed how shaken he was by Cyril's behaviour. It seemed to resolve Cyril's turmoil, though. 'The Lord was very real to me for a few minutes and I was very thankful to Him for bringing me through, whatever the consequences might be,' he wrote. 'I have now done 18 ops and am looking forward to finishing within a reasonably short time.'[36]

That March afternoon in Burn, Cyril's correspondence was rather less profound, but no less important. It was his youngest sister Pamela's 10th birthday on 5 April and he had bought her a card with an illustration of 'Hush-a-bye Baby'. The nursery rhyme was reprinted inside, prompting Cyril to add, 'PS: Hope the nursery rhyme isn't too babyish for you!' He scribbled the address on the envelope and put it back in his locker. He would post it tomorrow.

At RAF Leconfield with 466 Squadron, Andy Wiseman had written a 'last letter' to his girlfriend Jean. They had met before the war, when Andy was at school in Hampshire and her mother was a friend of his headmaster, whose son was suffering from polio. Jean and her mother used to visit, to try and cheer the boy up. On one occasion they stayed so late that they needed an escort home; Andy was given the job. 'It was love at first sight. She was the first girl I'd ever come close to. I think I had a novelty value for her. I was a foreigner; I could speak languages; I'd travelled. I kissed her hand and I clicked my heels when her mother came in – I was different.'

They stayed together throughout the early part of the war but had not married because Andy feared he might be killed. 'I knew what the odds were. Jean said, "Oh, I'd love to marry you and have a child," but I wouldn't, because I didn't think I'd survive. It was a conscious decision.' In his 'last letter' Andy told Jean he loved her and apologised for dying, but he couldn't resist a joke. 'I wrote: "You'll never find anybody quite as good as me, but you'll find somebody almost as good, and good luck to you both."'

In New Malden the Bartons were not the only family wondering whether a loved one would be at risk that evening. Jocelyn Norfolk was concerned because Flight Engineer George Prince had not come back on leave from 50 Squadron in Skellingthorpe. They had been friendly, nothing more than that, since before the war, though during his last visit, when she saw him in full uniform, she admitted to having 'a sparkle in my eye'. She and a friend had made a foursome with George and a mate of his, and they had been for a few drinks. 'We were enjoying life as much as we could.'

Jocelyn worked in the West End of London and knew all about bombing raids and warnings. She had become so blasé that when the sirens sounded she didn't go down to the shelters because her office was four floors up. But when George failed to appear at the end of March, she called a friend to ask if she had heard from him. She hadn't either. Jocelyn wondered if she was mistaken about his leave, but she wasn't. It had been cancelled because of the Nuremberg raid, and the need to have as many aircrew in the air as possible.

*   ★   ★

At 3 p.m. Sam Harris made his way to the squadron navigation briefing room. Navigators and pilots were normally the first to be told that night's target at an afternoon pre-briefing, which allowed them time to draw up the necessary charts.

Ranks of wooden trestle tables and fold-up chairs faced a wall draped with sheets concealing a map of Europe marked with the details of the operation. Sam and Chalky sat in the front row, as they always did. 'You could always tell the newer crews because they made straight for the back of the room, as if trying to hide, while the older hands headed for the front.'

Ken arrived with a group of other pilots, navigators and bomb aimers and came to stand behind them. Harry and Chalky lit up their Capstans and the room steadily filled with cigarette smoke, small talk and nervous laughter.

Harry fished his chart of mainland Europe out of his bag and spread it across the table. He had prepared it a few days before, with anti-aircraft positions marked in red, the territory covered by searchlights in blue. Almost all of the Ruhr, great swathes of the rest of Germany and chunks of France, Belgium and the Netherlands were vibrantly coloured. As they waited for the briefing to begin, Sam shaded in a few more areas, then sat back and admired his handiwork.

The Squadron Navigation Officer bustled in, followed by the Meteorological Officer, and walked to Sam's table. He picked up the Capstan pack, tapped one out and lit it, inhaling deeply. Then he turned, the cigarette dangling from his lips, and pulled the sheets away.

A line of red string stretched from Elsham, over the North Sea and across much of Germany, then veered south to the target and looped all the way back to base.

'Gentlemen,' the Navigation Officer said. 'Tonight your target is Nuremberg.'

Sam was dismayed. Not because of what Nuremberg was, or what it represented, but because he could see one long, straight red line that passed south of the Ruhr before turning towards the target. An interminable, undeviating leg that would give the German ground radar operators ample time to track the route of the bombers, and give the enemy fighters plenty of chance to vector in on them. 'The night fighters will be laughing tonight,' he thought. He prayed for some cloud cover; without it they would be sitting ducks.

The briefing continued. It may have been his imagination, but it seemed longer that night, and to cover every detail of the operation, no matter how minute. Once it ended, he and

Chalky sketched out the flight plan while Ken joined the rest of the pilots to discuss tactics.

★   ★   ★

Navigator Harry Evans was also given advance notice of the raid. A 21-year-old South Londoner, he had been sent to join a new Squadron, 550, at first based at Waltham near Grimsby, then moved a few miles to North Killingholme. His first seven operations were all to Berlin; by March they were battle-hardened and battle-scarred.

Harry had been nominated for an immediate Distinguished Flying Cross for an act of valour during the course of one of those raids, the memory of which was still blurred. The rear gunner had failed to respond on the intercom 20 minutes before they were due to change course. Harry volunteered to weave his way through the cramped bomber in his bulky flying suit, lifejacket and parachute harness, squeezing over the main spar, ducking past the mid-gunner and then crawling on his hands and knees to the doors of the rear gunner's turret.

When he opened them he found the gunner semi-conscious through lack of oxygen. Harry managed to drag him back through the fuselage and hook him up to an oxygen point. As he did so, the aircraft came under attack. He scrambled back to the rear turret, climbed in and fired a salvo at the marauding Focke Wulf. The attacker wheeled away, according to the mid-upper gunner, with a plume of smoke pouring from his engine. But by this time Harry was suffering from oxygen starvation himself; he staggered back into the main body of the plane and lost consciousness. By the time he came round, after being hooked up to a portable oxygen bottle, and made it back to his desk, he discovered they had gone way off course. When they eventually made it back to base he was able to record one of the few 'scores' ever made by a navigator.

At his pre-briefing, Harry's first reaction when the curtain was drawn back and the target was revealed was relief. At least it's not bloody Berlin again! Then the more alarming details of the plan were outlined; the straight leg, which was going to take at least an hour, prompted the most concern. Bloody hell, he thought, this looks a bit dodgy ... They never flew on an undeviating course for that length of time. 'Looking at this ruddy great long straight leg,' he recalled, 'it immediately struck us as dangerous.' Then he learned that they were to fly at 18,000 feet rather than the usual 20,000 or 22,000, because there would be thick cloud at that height. Harry still felt uneasy, but as he buried himself in his charts and began planning the route he became more philosophical. They had been here before. There was no such thing as an easy op.

★　　★　　★

At Linton-on-Ouse in North Yorkshire, Ron Butcher, a young navigator in an all-Canadian crew, shared Harry's sense of dismay. He had learned to trust his misgivings. During a short break from ops, his roommate, friend and fellow navigator Gord Schacter had gone down with flu and Ron was detailed to take his place on a trip to Essen. He knew from Gord – and from their number of early returns – that the crew had 'personality and co-ordination difficulties'. 'I can truthfully say I was never more scared! Thankfully, there was an engine problem and the crew did an early return – again! I certainly had no desire to fly with a crew other than my own, and certainly not that one.'[37]

Ron had arrived in the UK in January 1943 and became operational in December. Six of their first 10 ops had been raids on Berlin. They had survived; many others they knew had not. It did not take long for the dangers of air warfare to tone down their youthful swagger. They had witnessed death during training, of course; aircraft crashed all the time, taking young lives with them. The realities of combat were even more sobering. Ron and his mates had become quickly accustomed to the idea that their lives might not be long ones.

While they did their best to shrug off their fears and skirt around the subject of mortality, their bluff veneer fell away one evening and the worries poured out. 'We had not talked about the dangers we faced until the beginning of February. There had been some very heavy casualties. Then one night we were all together in our quarters and someone said, "Maybe I won't see tomorrow." It prompted a big discussion. We talked about the possibility of dying, and the prospect that we might never see Canada and our loved ones again. It was quite a stark conversation: we were young men acknowledging how close death was and how grim the reality of our situation was. I think we all acknowledged we were scared, but we decided that we'd soldier on as best we could. There simply was no other choice. Once you'd committed to the training in Canada, there was no way back. Being scared wasn't going to help much.'

Ron had expected the op to be cancelled because of the full moon right up until the moment the target was unveiled. But the order to stand down never came. The main briefing was at 6 p.m.; Ron and his companions were there, drawing anxiously on their cigarettes, wondering what lay behind the curtain.

The main briefing followed a similar pattern at every base, although each briefing officer would gauge how best to present the objectives, depending on his sense of how the morale of his crews might be affected. He might accentuate the iconic significance of the target, and emphasise the degree to which a successful strike would puncture the enemy's national spirit. He might point to the number of factories, small and large, that had been turned over to war production.

Ron Butcher

Ron waited patiently through the roll call until the briefing entourage arrived. 'When the curtain was drawn back to reveal that night's target there were gasps around the whole room, followed by a stunned silence. I thought, what the hell are they doing now?'

Despite his unease about the route, Ron knew there was little he could do to alter the course of events, so he made sure he paid attention to every scrap of information they were given: the location of German defences, the spoof and diversionary raids that would hopefully distract German attention from the bomber stream, radio codes, Pathfinder marking strategies, the method of attack at the target, and the designated Zero Hour. Then it was time to synchronise watches and the briefing was over.

Ron Butcher and his crew were veterans of 17 operations. Number 18 looked to be as tough as any that had gone before.

★   ★   ★

Rusty Waughman scanned the battle order for that night in the squadron office at Ludford Magna. He saw his own name on the list of those taking part; he also noticed 26 others, more than the squadron had ever sent on one op. They were making a special effort, involving a total of more than 200 men.

Later that afternoon he and his crew gathered at the briefing, swapping the usual, slightly brittle banter, then falling silent when the senior commanders entered the room. Finally the Intelligence Officer mounted the rostrum. There were some groans, even a few catcalls, when Nuremberg was revealed as the target. Rusty, like most others, remained impassive. On first appearances, there seemed to be nothing unusual about it, other than its unfamiliarity. But soon all eyes were drawn to the red ribbon strung across the centre of the map, passing close – uncomfortably close – to the flak- and searchlight-defended areas near Liège, and squeezing through a narrow corridor between the even more intensive ones around Cologne and Frankfurt. There were also four German night fighter squadrons stationed close by the route of the longest leg.

Rusty's navigator, Alec Cowan, was as precise as you would expect a London office clerk to be. But Rusty knew he would need all his skills that night to avoid drifting off target and into the Luftwaffe's lethal aerial embrace, or into a swarm of flak from the ground. Alec had already completed his charts, and his calculations made for disturbing reading; a 'long leg', more than 250 miles, through one of the best-defended areas of the Reich. Rusty consoled himself with the met officer's assurance that they would have the comfort of cloud cover most of the way to the target, and that Norman, their bomb aimer, would then have a clear view of the Aiming Point.

Rusty listened as the specialists took to the rostrum. His worry gave way to an almost supernatural calm; regardless of the cloud cover, he still believed the presence of the moon would make them reconsider the whole enterprise. It just seemed too risky. 'We believed the op would be cancelled and we thought that right up until the point we were told to start up the engines.' The Commanding Officer closed by wishing them good luck. He did so before every raid, but for some reason it had extra resonance that night. If the op were to go ahead, certainly they would need it.

★   ★   ★

Dick Starkey, a pilot from Barnsley, South Yorkshire, and his crew had spent much of the day in an unsettled state, uncertain as to whether they would be going that night. This had nothing to do with moonlight or weather forecasts. They were one of four crews in their squadron at Metheringham, Lincolnshire, who were coming to the end of their tour of operations. If they all flew every raid, their Flight Commander risked losing his most experienced crews in one fell swoop. To make sure that didn't happen, he had decided to stagger their remaining ops. Dick and his crew had been told to stand down for the previous night's raid on Brunswick, and that they would stand down the following night as well.

His crew had been dissatisfied all day. No one wanted to sit out an op which might take them closer to the holy grail of 30; they wanted to finish their tour as quickly as possible. They got into a huddle and agreed that Dick should ask the Flight Commander if they could be put on the battle order. It wasn't their fault the Brunswick op had been cancelled; they had been the stand-down crew for that one, and a different crew should be stood down now.

At first Dick's request was turned down, but he continued to beat the drum and the Flight Commander eventually changed his mind. They were going to Nuremberg.

Unlike elsewhere, the target map in the Nissen hut which doubled as a briefing room at Metheringham wasn't concealed.

As soon as Dick and his men walked in they could see a 'nasty red line of tape' stretching from the east of England to the heart of Germany. His first reaction too was relief that it wasn't Berlin. He was not alone; some of his crew members were grinning openly, thankful they wouldn't be going anywhere near the Big City. The fine detail of the raid was more sobering – especially the length of the direct leg that would skirt some areas of heavy defence.

As they left the briefing room for the ritual pre-op meal of eggs and bacon – the eggs were deemed important ahead of a long flight because of their binding properties in the bowel – a few of Dick's crew were regretting their earlier ebullience. Perhaps being stood down from this one might not have been a bad idea after all.

★　★　★

Lesley 'Scouse' Nugent, a mid-upper gunner with 78 Squadron, knew the feeling. From the moment he heard the words, 'Gentlemen, your target for tonight is Nuremberg,' a nagging voice in his head told him, 'Don't do this one, Scouse – you won't make it back.'[38] He was only 23, but this was to be his 27th op, making him a veteran. If he had not taken a spell of compassionate leave earlier in the tour, he might already have finished and been enjoying six months of non-combat duties, rather than being crammed into a small fetid room with 118 other blokes. Regardless, he had seen and heard enough not to be duped by the emollient words of the briefing officer.

'It will be bright moonlight over Europe on both the forward and return journeys,' the met officer told them.

Who's he bloody kidding? Scouse thought. What return journey?

The end of the briefing was met by silence, only broken by the scrape of a chair as someone finally stood up.

'This is a bloody big one,' Scouse heard someone mumble.

'The brass must be mad to fix this attack without cover,' added another.

Not everyone experienced the same sense of foreboding. Chick Chandler focused solely on getting the job done; his only concern was how much fuel he needed to get his crew there and back. They were going with a full load, 2,145 gallons, so he knew it was going to be a long one, but he would be scared wherever they might be heading, regardless of the length of individual legs or how much cloud there was likely to be.

CHAPTER 7

Enemy Coast Ahead

Alan Payne

For bomb aimer Alan Payne it was a similar story. He was thankful they wouldn't be going back to Berlin. The direct leg and the moon were causes for concern, but so far it seemed to be just another op.

He found his girlfriend Pat in the mess. He wasn't able to talk to her about where they were going – not that he wanted to. The possibility of it being the last conversation they would ever have didn't alter the fact that Alan just wanted to exchange small talk and pretend nothing was different. When it came time to leave she handed him the flask of coffee she made for him before each raid.

★   ★   ★

Pilot Officer Jimmy Batten-Smith, a colleague of Rusty Waughman at 101 Squadron, was courting a WAAF who serviced their flying kit named Patricia Bourne. Like Cyril Barton, he had written a letter for his parents, who lived in India, in case he did not return; he gave it to his girlfriend before every raid, together with his writing case. That night, after briefing, he did something different. 'Think of me tonight at one o'clock, will you?' he asked. Patricia agreed and made a mental reminder to set her alarm clock for that time.[39]

Rusty Waughman and his crew made for the mess. Curly and Norman, in particular, liked to flirt with the WAAFs who worked there, a last touch of normality before the tension was ratcheted up and they headed to dispersal. The girls knew, of course, what the boys were heading into, and they made it their business to smile and be as friendly as possible. Over the course of three months Rusty and his mates had got to know them well. Sometimes they even managed to bag an extra pre-op egg.

After lingering over each mouthful of their dinner, it was time to get into their flying gear and collect their kit. The temperature at 20,000 feet was rarely forgiving, so most would wear as many layers as possible, including thick woollen stockings and thermal underwear. Rusty Waughman had two pairs of long johns for operations, but only ever wore one 'lucky' pair. He never washed them, which guaranteed him all the room he needed in which to get changed. The rest of the crew reckoned that when he peeled them off after a raid they would be able to stand up in his locker by themselves.

*   *   *

Sam Harris's locker room was unusually crowded, but few spoke; everyone seemed subdued that night. Men fought for space as they climbed into whatever they needed to keep warm. The gunners were the best insulated. Their first layer was an electrically heated flying suit, with a pair of electrically heated slippers that clipped to it. They didn't always work; sometimes they would be left with one hot foot and one frozen. The next layer was the regulation flying suit, then a canvas fireproof suit. Some found them too restricting and went without, but most wore one: fire was the biggest fear of those on board, and with some justification. If the bomb load went up, the suit was inconsequential, but 2,000 gallons of fuel could burn quickly and fiercely. Once aboard the aircraft, the gunners also wore electrically heated gloves and leather gauntlets, and Mae West life jackets. It was a wonder they could move a muscle.

In the middle of this smoke-filled chaos, Sam and his crew were handed their flying rations: chocolate, sweets, sandwiches or an orange, with a flask of tea or hot chocolate for warmth.

Once dressed and ready, rations packed, they trudged off to collect their parachutes. Each man was responsible for his own harness, but the parachutes had to be signed out before flying and back in after the flight. They were serviced, packed and handed out by WAAFs, who also checked the dinghies and Mae West life jackets the crews would need if they were forced to ditch at sea. 'It was all rather nerve-racking, particularly when you saw how large the parachutes were,' says Liz Bond, a WAAF in the parachute packing section. 'It had to be put in a small bag correctly, as it might save a man's life.'[40]

As the last friendly faces the crews would see before take-off, Liz and her colleagues developed a strong bond with the airmen. She had an autograph book which she asked the men to sign when they returned their equipment. One 'cheeky little cockney' called Peter Booth wrote: 'Thanks for some of the best moments of my life, spent with you and the gang of the para section. I go, I come back.' He went missing on the next op he flew.

Clutching their 'chutes, Sam and his crew were finally ready to be taken out by truck to dispersal, where G-George stood vast and silent, silhouetted against the night sky.

★   ★   ★

Like Ron Butcher, Roger Coverley was based at Linton-on-Ouse near York. These short trips on the 'meat wagon' were always the same, as far as he was concerned. He was an officer and had already completed a full tour, but seized the opportunity to step in when the pilot of an inexperienced crew was branded LMF.

Roger was delighted to be back in the front seat, and the crew was delighted to have an experienced hand at the controls. He treated them all to lunch at one of York's best hotels after every op. Some army officers Roger met frowned upon such fraternisation with the ranks, but he ignored them; in his opinion rank ceased to have any significance once they were off duty.

By the time they were on their way to dispersal, the usual black humour abounded.

'If you get the chop tonight, can I have that pair of slippers you keep in your locker?'

'OK.'

'Can I have that in writing?'

An IOU was swiftly penned.

Roger was happy to encourage this kind of banter among his crew. There was no point dwelling on their fate. 'The attitude was rather like a game of rugger – you might get knocked over and knocked out, but you'd pick yourself up again. Nobody wanted to let anybody down. We were more terrified of being branded as LMF than of being shot down.'

Once they had swapped messages of good luck with the others on board the lorry, they were dropped at dispersal. Their usual Halifax was unserviceable that night, so they had been given a replacement. It belonged to the Squadron Commander and was known to the men as The Royal Barge. Roger gazed admiringly at its sleek lines, thinking, I hope I don't bring it back with any holes in it.

⋆   ⋆   ⋆

The time between arriving at dispersal and boarding the aircraft was more solemn for Ray Francis, a flight engineer, at Mildenhall. His crew had endured a torrid introduction to life in Bomber Command since becoming operational in February. By the end of March they were survivors of raids on Leipzig, Schweinfurt, Stuttgart and Frankfurt. Their experiences had bound them 'closer than any family'.

One afternoon they had been sitting on the grass at dispersal, waiting for the signal to board from flying control. 'The usual jokes and light-hearted chat began to dry up.' Each of them had been pulling up daisies from the damp ground and threading them into chains. There was complete silence.

'This is bloody silly,' one of them said, flinging his flowers into the wind.

Ray looked down and realised that they had been making their own wreaths. He followed suit, and then they all did. The banter and off-colour jokes returned, a crucial part of any crew's attempts to remain sane. Ray's contained three Australians, who liked to bewitch their Pommy mates with stories of bronzed, long-limbed Sheilas parading on the sun-kissed Sydney beaches. It took Ray and the others a while to discover that not one of the threesome had even visited the place. Still, the images they had conjured up were nice to cling to in the middle of an arduous English winter.

⋆   ⋆   ⋆

Scouse Nugent continued to feel pessimistic. The thoughts that accompanied every mission crowded his mind. Will our crew be the lucky ones? Is this it? Will I ever see my wife again? It all came down to one simple question: Will I live or die? He could tell the rest of his crew was thinking the same way; the atmosphere had become quiet and tense. No one said a word as they gathered at their aircraft.

Some of the boys took this chance to exchange a few words with their ground crews, for many the unsung heroes of Bomber Command. Men like Eric Howell, whose job it was to service, maintain and prepare the Halifax and Lancaster squadrons up and down the country and keep them flying at any cost. Eric was based at Dunholme Lodge in Lincolnshire and had been servicing bombers since 1942. His day had started at 7 a.m., when he made the first checks on the aircraft in his care. A full three-hour inspection followed, which would not finish until the crews were safely up in the air. In his two years he had spoken with many crews, struck up good friendships with most of them, and suffered the anguish of not seeing them return.

No matter how many times he heard it, his pulse always quickened at the sound of the bombers revving up at dispersal, and the throb of a heavily laden Lancaster reverberating through the night air. He had once sat in the NAAFI when the planes took off; cups, glasses, doors and windows rattled and shook in time with the beat of the Merlin engines. Then came the strange silence as the red and green navigation lights faded to black, before the everyday sounds of the base asserted themselves once more – the hoot of an owl, the bark of a dog or a wireless blaring from one of the billets.

In warmer weather, Eric would stretch out on the grass and watch the crews depart. 'Can you imagine? Lying amongst the sweet-smelling grass and clover, peering through the distractions of the low overhanging branches of a massive old English oak at the silhouette of a Lancaster in the moonlit distance, knowing that hundreds of miles to the east death and destruction was taking place.'[41]

As the aircrew truck loomed out of the darkness, the ground crew would extinguish their cigarettes, remove the giant oilskin covers that protected the aircraft wheels and give the Perspex in the cockpits and turrets a final polish.

There was some conversation before take-off, but rarely

about the matter at hand. They would help the crew, clad in their bulky flying gear, on board, and then take away the ladders and finally close the doors and hatches as the engines coughed into life. One of the ground crew scrambled along the now cramped, crowded aircraft and asked the pilot to sign the 700S, the aircraft's engineering and serviceability log. Finally, on the pilot's signal, the chocks were removed and the aircraft moved slowly away.

After take-off, when Eric was on duty, he would go to the dispersal hut and wait an anxious, fitful seven hours, hoping and praying that those good men might return the next morning. The night of 30 March was no different. Eric waved off 16 crews, including one brand new Lancaster, C-Charlie, piloted by Trevor Charlesworth. Eric had lost three such aircraft since the beginning of 1944, an average of one a month, and he didn't want to lose another. Back in the hut they stoked up the stove to create a warm fug, and settled down for their vigil. The next day was Eric's birthday; he wanted to see as many of his Lancasters and his lads as possible make it back, and preferably all of them.

★   ★   ★

Jack Watson, a member of the Pathfinder force for the operation, was one of the first to take to the sky that night. He had become increasingly preoccupied with the aircraft he was assigned to fly, M-Mother, and decided that the omens were not good. M was the 13th letter of the alphabet; this was to be their 13th trip, and the business end of the op would be taking place on the 31st, the inverse of 13.

During these last moments on the ground, before the orders came through for take-off, superstition was quick to take hold. While most crews recognised the importance of preparation, training and vigilance, even the best and most experienced were aware that sheer good fortune often played the most crucial role in the unfolding drama. Many put their trust in keepsakes and charms, or went through often elaborate rituals to try and keep Lady Luck on their side.

Reg Payne's crew gave their aircraft a careful pat before they climbed aboard and whispered their wife's or girlfriend's name. Frank Swinyard, the navigator, would say 'Good old Brenda,' and Reg would follow with 'Good old Ena,' and so on. After every completed op, when the engines were shut down after landing, the voices of the crew would sing out the same mantra over the intercom. They believed it was the aircraft that helped preserve their lives and would continue to ensure their safety.

Reg made particularly sure to give the plane a pat that night. He had been unsettled by the briefing, and not just because the raid was due to go ahead despite the moonlight. At the conclusion of his address, the Wing Commander would normally single out a crew member to come to the front and recite its most significant details. Unless he could do so accurately, he would be scrubbed from the op. That night he had simply bid them goodbye and good luck; they obviously needed all the crews they could muster for Nuremberg, whether attentive or not.

Ray Francis's charm was a lucky whistle. Every crew member carried one, in case they had to ditch in water and call for help in darkness, but his wasn't RAF issue; it was a boy scout's whistle, even though he had never been a boy scout. He also carried a silver bracelet given to him by his dad, engraved with the words: 'Happy Landings, Father'.

Alan Payne had a St Christopher. Like Chick Chandler, Alan's skipper Geoff Probert wore a lucky scarf. He had been warming their aircraft's engines before one op when he suddenly realised he didn't have it, so he climbed out, got on his motorbike, shot back to the billet and returned, scarf in place, only seconds before take-off.

Dick Starkey had a pair of miniature flying boots, which he used to stand above his instrument panel. He knew deep down that they didn't bring him the slightest bit of luck, but had reached the stage where he didn't dare risk leaving them behind. Their mere presence gave him reassurance.

Andy Wiseman always took a doll knitted by his girlfriend Jean; he hung it from one of the pilot's instruments. Some months earlier, he and his crew had stretched out in front of their plane to enjoy a last cigarette before take-off. The Station Commander arrived to wish them luck. As the 'L' word left his lips, Andy suddenly remembered Jean's doll.

'What's the matter with you?' the Station Commander asked.

Andy felt his cheeks burn. 'Nothing.' There was no way he was going to admit something like that to the old man.

The Station Commander was having none of it. 'Come on, what's the matter with you?'

In the end, Andy confessed.

Without saying another word, the Station Commander got back in his jeep, drove to Andy's billet and retrieved the doll from his locker. It was the last time he ever forgot her.

Andy Wiseman

Andy was the only member of Bomber Command for whom it was a return to Nuremberg. Before he and his family fled for Poland, he had been there on a school trip. He had no memories of the visit; perhaps just as well, given that he was going back to flatten it.

He disliked the wait before take-off. Unlike the rest of the crew, as a bomb aimer he had no instruments or equipment to check once their bomb load had been winched into the bay and he had given one of the projectiles a gentle pat. For the rest of the time, he stood and smoked and chatted, always about the most trivial things. He looked upon this phase of the proceedings as a dry run for the way things would unfold once the op was underway. He would have to bide his time for seven hours, buffeted by flak, his life in peril, at the end of which his job would be all over in seven minutes. That night he had every reason to doubt whether he would be called into action at all. The red line that separated them from the target suddenly seemed impossibly thin.

★   ★   ★

When he was six, Rusty Waughman had been forced by his mother to kneel by his bed and say his prayers. 'Now I lay me down to sleep I pray the Lord my soul would keep. If I should die before I wake, I pray the Lord my soul would take.' He had not even mumbled the words since, until he found himself doing so during one particularly perilous op when the flak was so thick 'I could have got out and walked on it.'

For the more religious amongst them, it often paid to keep their prayers to themselves. Rusty knew of one skipper who took a senior officer out over Germany. Their aircraft came under heavy fire from a night fighter. When the rear gunner shouted, 'The bastards are everywhere!' their guest replied, 'Never fear, rear gunner, never fear – the Lord is with us.'

'He might be up your fucking end,' the gunner replied, 'but there's no sign of him back here.'

The crews climbed into the Stygian gloom of their aircraft, hauling their kit and equipment with them, to complete their final checks. Hidden from sight by his curtain, Sam Harris unpacked his navigation gear and tested his instruments and lights. Everything was in working order.

Then it was back outside for one final ritual. Sam's crew gathered at the far side of the dispersal and reached for their smokes. Mac normally brandished a pipe, but on these occasions he always had a cigarette. Eric wouldn't touch the things, but stood with them while they had their final nicotine fix. Take-off time was fast approaching. They formed a line at the edge of the tarmac, fought their way into their multi-layered flying suits and peed into the adjoining field.

Some relieved themselves on the aircraft wheels for luck – and sometimes to hide their modesty from the well-wishers who had come to wave them off from dispersal, among them several members of the WAAF. Harry Evans and his crew had stopped doing so after they were told the urine might weaken the metallic undercarriage and cause it to collapse. It was a worry they could live without.

By this time the thick cloud and gusting wind which had made the day so miserable appeared to have eased. The sky was now alarmingly clear. The conversation among the crews began to falter, leaving each man alone with his thoughts. A few anxious eyes turned from the heavens to the flight control tower, still half expecting to see the red light which would indicate that the decision had finally been taken to scratch the raid.

The light turned green.

It was time to go.

The rain started to fall as the men scrambled aboard. The Lancaster and Halifax engines coughed into life as the chocks were removed from their wheels. All across a vast swathe of eastern England they lumbered out of their dispersal bays. The process began at the airfields of North Yorkshire, furthest away from the point where the stream was to assemble over the North Sea, then south to Lincolnshire and finally East Anglia. The taxiing aircraft formed a line of looming silhouettes as they trundled towards their runways and prepared for take-off. This would be the last chance for many of the crews to swap jokes, or idle chat; once they were airborne many of their skippers forbade any kind of conversation and reserved the intercom for important information only.

The piercing cold had done little to deter the crowds who had gathered at the end of the runway to wave them off: WAAFs, ground crew, idle crews, anyone else on base who wanted to show their support – at Dunholme Lodge the station commander made it his duty to salute each aircraft as it left the ground. The departing crew might scour the faces in the crowd for a familiar or an unwelcome one. That morning, a flight sergeant from 50 Squadron at Skellingthorpe had been approached by a notorious 'chop girl' – the name given to those WAAFs who had dated more than one man who had gone missing on an op. After a brief chat he had beaten a hasty retreat but, as they made their turn at the end of the runway, he glanced across at the assembled onlookers and noticed, with a sense of dread, that she hadn't taken no for an answer.

In his bed near East Kirby, Fred Panton listened to the sound of the bombers taking off from the airfield at the bottom of their hill. His father was a stickler for a punctual bedtime, and there was school tomorrow, so there was no chance he and Harold could run down to watch them take off this late. He lay snugly beneath his blankets, wondering what it would be like to lumber off into the darkness with a full bomb load. Was Chris going tonight? From the number of planes he'd heard take off, he guessed it was a big raid, so it was likely.

Their father sat downstairs, as the last of the day's fire crackled in the hearth. He had his own ritual: as soon as he heard the engines roar into life, he grabbed a piece of paper and put a mark for each aircraft he heard leave the ground. He would count them back in the next morning and compare the tallies.

From the northernmost base, RAF Dishforth, in Yorkshire to the furthest south in Wrattling Common, Cambridgeshire, the night air was filled with the thunderous sound of the 795 aircraft – 572 Lancaster bombers, 214 Halifaxes and nine Mosquitoes. The 75 members of the Pathfinder Force carried amongst them 120 clusters of illuminating flares and 336 target indicator bombs, along with 116 skymarkers in case of dense cloud over the target. Each of the Lancasters in the main force was carrying one 4,000-pound 'cookie' bomb and somewhere between 5,000 and 6,000 pounds of incendiaries. Some of the Halifaxes carried a lighter but still potent bomb load, in order to leave room for extra fuel. They shuttled to the end of the runway, or stood in line, waiting for the green light to flash for take-off.

Sam Harris and his crew had the privilege of being the first of their squadron to take off because G-George was setting out on her 100th trip. This would be their 10th operation together, and their early indifference to their aircraft had been replaced by great warmth. 'It was slow and it was messy and battered, but we kept bringing it back. After the first trip the ground crew who looked after it were amazed, and more so after the second. A sort of *esprit de corps* grew between those who flew it and those who serviced and maintained it. The aircraft seemed to behave better and the ground crew would always be there to greet it, even if they had worked for 24 hours non-stop before it went and it came back in at some unseemly hour in the early morning.'

A small crowd had gathered around the caravan parked alongside the tarmac that doubled as a control tower to see the venerable bomber off. Paraffin lamps flickered and guttered in the wind at the edge of the runway. Once the checks were completed, Ken Murray put on the brakes and opened the throttles. The Lancaster started to strain like a dog on a leash. The brakes were released; there was a pause, then, with a cacophonous roar, the plane began to move. Slowly – too slowly, it always seemed to those on board when it was fully laden – they gathered momentum. At last the tail was up and the speed increased, 80 mph ... 90 ... 95 ... 100 ... 105 ... and it was still on the ground. 110 ... 115 ... and then the noise became a touch quieter as the pilot eased back the control column and the wheels left the ground.

'Undercarriage up,' Ken's voice rang out across the intercom.

Mac cut in: 'Gear up and locked, lights out.'

'Flaps a quarter ...' Ken's mantra continued until the wing flaps were fully retracted and throttles and boost were set to climbing speed. G–George was airborne at 9.37 p.m. GMT.

Scouse Nugent sat in his turret listening to the routine exchanges between pilot and control tower, running through the instrument checks, before thundering down the runway and slowly lifting off. He had forgotten to do up the chinstrap of his helmet, but that did not bother him. Instead he was thinking about the operation and how, with a heap of luck, he would be back kissing the tarmac, just as he had done after every single one of his 27 previous ops.

Once they hit a speed of 100 mph there was no turning back. Using every ounce of their skill, the pilot and his engineer sought to keep their vast machine steady until the time came when, under immense strain, some 68,000 pounds of metal and fuel and explosives would wrestle their way into the air. One mistake or small mechanical failure and the consequences could be devastating.

That night, only two aircraft failed to get airborne. The flaps rose on one Lancaster at Coningsby as it hurtled along the runway. By the time the pilot noticed it was too late to abort take-off. Once the wheels were up he tried to coax it into a climb, but the aircraft refused the invitation. It struck a post beyond the end of the runway, ripping open the tailplane and a fuel tank in one of the wings. Astonishingly, the pilot still managed to land safely and no one was hurt.

A second accident, at Skellingthorpe, provided another miraculous escape. A Lancaster burst a tyre as it accelerated, careering off the runway and badly damaging one of the wings. Despite its full fuel and bomb loads, there was no fire and none of the crew was harmed.

For the other 793 the perils of the night had only just begun. They climbed steadily to their assigned flying height – vitally important, since more than 800 of them were due to rendez-vous over the North Sea and collisions were a genuine risk. As they ascended at approximately 100 feet per minute, the land beneath them faded to black. When they reached 17,000 feet the crews switched on their oxygen. If it failed, they only had a few minutes to find another supply or lose consciousness.

Looking around from his pilot seat – 'like a throne' – Rusty Waughman saw a bank of illuminated cloud, a vivid backdrop against which the shadows and silhouettes of the other bomb-ers stood out as they made their way towards the assembly point. Rusty had never noticed this before. Knowing they were not alone was a great source of reassurance. He just hoped they would be less visible once they were over the European mainland. At 11.15 p.m. they left the Suffolk shores behind them and headed for a deadlier coast.

Rusty was flying a Lancaster Mark III coded 'W', known to them as 'A Wing and a Prayer'. It was the first Lancaster he had ever flown, but it had already seen them through some sticky situations, which is why they named it after a patriotic song written in 1943 about a damaged aircraft returning home. After every op, as they approached the airfield at Ludford

Magna, everyone on board would join in a rousing – and highly relieved – rendition.

> *What a show, what a fight,*
> *We really hit our target for tonight.*
> *How we sing as we limp through the air.*
> *Look below, there's our field over there.*
> *With our full crew aboard*
> *And in our trust in the Lord*
> *We're comin' in on a wing and a prayer.*

Rusty's gunners tested their weapons. Curly, his flight engineer, had synchronised the engines so they were running in perfect pitch, and maintained a close eye on the instruments while Rusty engaged the automatic pilot. It would be a long flight and a long night, so he welcomed any opportunity to ease the burden. Ted Manners switched on the ABC equipment, making sure it had warmed up before they crossed the Belgian shores, where he and the other ABC aircraft, spread out among the stream, would activate their jamming signals once they picked up the radio transmissions between the enemy fighters and those on the ground.

As Dick Starkey climbed towards the Norfolk coast, there wasn't a cloud in sight. As they reached their allotted height, he registered the low temperatures and something else he had never witnessed before, streaming from the tails of the bombers around him: vapour trails.

Fifty-two bombers failed to make it to the meeting point, forced to turn back through mechanical failure, mostly engine problems, but also failed oxygen supplies, problems with intercom or the GEE navigation sets. Few crews were keen to return to base prematurely, partly because of the stigma attached to early returns – the suspicion that you might be considered LMF – and partly because it meant the operation did not count towards a tour, so some pressed on if the problem was not deemed insurmountable.

Cy Barton's Halifax left Burn at 10.12 p.m. Back home in New Malden, the Barton family, oblivious to the dangers he was about to face, took comfort in their nightly routine: Dad sitting in his armchair in front of the hearth doing his cross-word; mother knitting on the sofa beside him; Cynthia, Joyce and Pamela upstairs in the front bedroom with the porridge-coloured wallpaper and small open fire. It was a cold night, so they would have removed the fire bricks and wrapped them in an old cloth to warm their beds. After reading stories to each other, they turned off the light and swapped tales in the dark before drifting off to sleep.

There was little talk in Cy's Halifax as the broken cloud swirled off the wing tips. He insisted on a minimum of chat over the intercom, and swearing was forbidden, but his crew, like his family, idolised him, reassured by his calm demeanour and lack of panic at the helm, even under the most intense fire. Freddie Brice marked him down as 'a fine judge of men. I had little fear flying with him; never any panic, and his calmness seemed to reach us all.'[42]

Nuremberg was their 19th mission. As the plane climbed, Freddie stared through his Perspex turret with increasing concern. A good night for the night fighter, he thought. Len Lambert had misgivings about the whole raid, which the brightness of the moon did little to dispel. But he set those doubts aside and gave Cy the course to meet up with the bomber stream.

From the coast of England to the assembly point was approx-imately 15 minutes' flying time. The first wave consisted of around 100 aircraft, including the Pathfinder 'openers' who would be dropping their marker flares for the rest; it was less concentrated than those that followed, spread across the first 20 miles of the stream. Behind them were five more waves of around 138 aircraft each, each approximately 10 miles long. The theory was that if the bombers managed to stick to their allotted height and course, the stream would remain compact enough to ensure that their firepower would be as concentrated and severe as possible over the target.

The front of the stream was nearing Belgium. Across the intercom three words rang out:

'Enemy coast ahead.'

CHAPTER 8

Jazz Music

Bruno Rupp

As they crossed the North Sea, Ron Butcher had been mesmerised by the moonlight shimmering on the water beneath them, but now that his Lancaster was forging its way over mainland Europe he turned back to his charts.

His brow furrowed as he plotted their position, using the stars. They had been told to expect 80-knot winds, yet his recordings told him they were between 40 and 50 knots faster. To add to his disquiet, there was no sign of any turbulence from the slipstreams of their fellow bombers. Ron started to feel intensely vulnerable. 'It made the crew feel terribly exposed to realise that other aircraft were not in close proximity.' He began to worry that his estimates were incorrect and they had been blown off course. Should he continue to rely on the forecast? If he was right, and the winds *were* stronger than predicted, they would be propelled towards Nuremberg at a far greater speed than they had anticipated.

Sam Harris and his crew had encountered light flak as they passed over the enemy coast, but managed to fly through it unscathed. It was bitterly cold outside the aircraft – minus 31 degrees centigrade – and not much warmer inside, which might have been the reason Sam muddled his calculations. He had meant to add 17 minutes to the time on his chart, but added 14 instead. As a result, Ken began his turn for the long leg at the wrong point. Sam frantically checked and rechecked his charts according to the information transmitted from England and realised his mistake in time to direct his pilot back on to the right course.

Four minutes later the German city of Aachen appeared on their port bow. The whole sky was ablaze with searchlight beams and great arcs of flak, but Sam and his crew somehow avoided the worst of it.

Further back in the stream, Rusty Waughman and his crew approached Charleroi, 18 minutes away from the German border. 'Turning point coming up, skipper,' Alec, his navigator, called out. 'Steer new course ...'

They flew due east from Charleroi. As they reached Aachen they were rocked by flak and the air around them filled with the pungent smell of cordite. Rusty gripped the controls more tightly, bracing himself, but it soon subsided. His main concern remained the moon rather than the anti-aircraft fire. The Germans wouldn't need radar to find them, he thought. There was simply nowhere to hide.

A series of 'spikes' appeared on the cathode ray set of Special Duties Operator Ted Manners. The radio broadcasts to enemy fighters had begun.

'They're on their way,' Ted said.

★   ★   ★

Feldwebel Bruno Rupp was stationed at Langendiebach, near Frankfurt. The 23-year-old Luftwaffe pilot's breath billowed in the crisp night air as he walked out of the station common room. He glanced towards the rows of idle Heinkel and Messerschmitt fighters as he pulled out his cigarette case. The moonlight glinted off the Perspex canopy that shielded each cockpit. There was little chance they would be taking off tonight, he decided.[43] The enemy preferred to launch their 'terror raids' with ample cloud cover.

Since 4.15 that afternoon they had done little but play cards and wait. He puffed away absent-mindedly, wondering when they would be stood down. When the cold started to seep into his bones he tossed the butt to the ground and killed it with the heel of his flying boot.

Back in the warmth, the card school was still going strong. He pulled up a chair. The men who sat around the table with Bruno Rupp, or dozed fitfully elsewhere in the room, were members of a ferocious and rejuvenated fighting force. Until the summer of 1943 the Germans believed they possessed the defences to repel even the heaviest of Allied raids. But when Harris sent his bombers *en masse* to Hamburg in August 1943 their response, both on the ground and in the air, had proved inadequate.

Until the Hamburg raid they had had night fighters stationed at every route into Germany. They had divided their airspace into a grid, each box patrolled by one aircraft, guided to its target by ground radar – ground radar that was now being disrupted by Window, the thin strips of aluminium chaff thrown in bundles from Allied bombers.

Until recently, the Luftwaffe had stationed groups of night fighters around the major cities bombed by Allied forces. As a raid progressed, they would wait as long as possible to assess the location of the stream's final target, before sending them in. Codenamed Wild Boar, this strategy obviated the need for radar and reduced the confusion caused by Window. But it had one major disadvantage. The scores of circling fighters all needed to land at the same bases when their fuel ran low, and there were frequent crashes and collisions.

A new approach was needed, and so Wild Boar was replaced by Tame Boar. The Tame Boar fighters were divided into five divisions, each with their own underground operations room, known as 'Battle Opera Houses'. Once the fighters were airborne, control passed to the best-positioned operations centre, from where a lone radio-operator would give each pilot constant updates about the location and course of the invading force – the running commentary that Ted Manners and the other Special Duties Operators of 101 Squadron sought to jam.

The Battle Opera Houses co-ordinating the night fighter response were sophisticated affairs. Information gleaned from intelligence reports, listening posts and pilots in the air was fed on to giant glass maps which plotted the position, height, course and strength of the British bomber stream and the location of their own night fighters. 'The whole [scene] was reminiscent of a huge lighted aquarium, with a multitude of water-beetles scuttling madly behind the glass walls.'[44] Even accounting for the disruptive effects of Window, they were capable of plotting the action so concisely that the picture displayed in the bunkers was rarely more than 60 seconds behind the events unfolding in the skies.

The anti-aircraft batteries were as much of a threat to Allied crews as the night fighters. There were 50,000 guns stationed across Germany and the North Sea coast, ready to attack any aircraft that entered their airspace, of which 15,000 were heavy artillery pieces with a range of 25-30,000 feet. The lighter guns had a more modest range but, like their heavier counterparts, they all fired explosive shells which scattered shards of molten shrapnel, easily capable of destroying an aircraft's control systems or slicing through its fuselage to kill or maim those on board.

These vast defensive systems stretched German manpower to its limit; women, veterans, even schoolboys and Russian PoWs were recruited to fire them. When they were concentrated over a target, the sky became a seething mass of exploding shrapnel. Every time Harry Evans and his crew flew into the maelstrom of red flashes and orange explosions from the defences around Berlin, he felt he would never make it through. 'There's nothing you can do except hope. The aircraft is being thrown and bumped around, and the shells are exploding all around you. The worst thing is to turn back prematurely because you have to get in and drop your bombs. It was absolute terror.'

Some anti-aircraft guns were guided by radar, others by an array of radar-guided searchlights. All crews feared being trapped in the beams of all the searchlights in a battery, which formed the shape of an inverse cone. 'Being 'coned' was a terrifying experience,' Harry Evans says. 'It was like being caught in a spider's web of powerful beams. To try and escape from their clutches, the pilot would throw the aircraft into sudden and violent manoeuvres, many of them involuntary because until the pilot's eyes had adjusted to the brilliant light he couldn't see the instruments.'

Fighters, flak and searchlights were a constant nightmare, but the Luftwaffe had developed another even more lethal weapon. Their traditional method of attack was to approach from behind at speeds of up to 300 mph, clearly visible to all but the most unobservant of rear gunners. A Lancaster pilot's most common escape tactic was to execute a series of steep diving and climbing turns to port then starboard, a flight path similar in shape to a corkscrew, after which the manoeuvre was named.

Michael Beetham threw his Lancaster into a violent corkscrew during a training sortie which still haunts Reg Payne. 'The immense strain broke one of the glycol plates and the glycol caught fire. The first thing I heard was "Prepare to abandon aircraft." The flames died, but all of a sudden the fire reignited, only this time burning far more furiously. Because it was a training exercise there were 10 of us on board and four didn't get out – our rear gunner, Fred Ball, and flight engineer, Don Moore, were among them. Don hadn't even taken his parachute because it was a training flight and he didn't think he'd need it. As I jumped I could see him frantically looking for one. Fred Ball didn't want to jump out; he was too scared – and that was the death of them both.

'It was my first parachute jump and that was a real eye-opener too. We had a very lucky escape. Now we knew how dangerous and difficult it was to get out of a Lancaster. As I was coming down in the parachute, I looked back and saw the wing was flopping back and forwards like a leaf. I had been the last one to make it out.'

Though the corkscrew was disorientating for those on board and rendered them vulnerable as the plane levelled out between its twists and swoops, Rusty Waughman swore by it. 'Corkscrewing placed tremendous strain on the airframe and called for a super-human effort from the pilot, but it was nearly always successful in throwing a night fighter off the scent.'

Now the night fighter pilots had discovered a more fundamental area of weakness: it was possible to fly beneath any bomber without being seen. The Luftwaffe's engineers fitted their aircraft with two upward-firing machine-guns. The Lancaster crew's first and often last indication of their enemy's presence was when his shells slammed into the belly of their aircraft, laden with fuel and explosives. Those fortunate enough to parachute to safety could only discuss these 'invisible' attacks from behind the wire of their PoW camps.

The Germans had given an ironic codename to the new weapon, inspired by the angle of its elevation and the sound of its often fatal gunfire: *Schräge Musik*. Translated literally as 'slanting music', it was their slang for jazz – the decadent rhythms of the culture that the Nazis most detested.

Gerhard Wollnik, based at Stendal, 125 km west of Berlin, with the 1st Fighter Division, scored his first kill to the tune of *Schräge Musik* in his Messerschmitt 110 on the night of 19 February, during the infamous raid on Leipzig. 'At last, our Wireless Operator, Fischer, identified a clear blip on his SN-2 radar set. It flew at our height and some 300 metres in front of us; we could already feel the turbulence from its propellers. Slowly we approached the enemy aircraft.

'We thought it was a Lancaster, judging from its green exhaust flames, which were clearly visible. If it were a Halifax, the flames would have been more reddish. Our pilot Reschke pushed our Me 110 down to about 100 metres under the Lancaster. It was a giant bird, with gun barrels protruding from its defensive turrets. The Lancaster crew had not yet spotted us. Complete silence reigned in our machine. Our pilot had decided upon carrying out an attack with his obliquely mounted guns, from a position underneath the bomber. The two 2 cm cannons had been installed very close to my gunner's position. The barrels of the guns pointed upwards and forwards at an angle of 80 degrees. At this time, *Schräge Musik* was still top secret, and in the case of being diverted to a strange airfield we had orders to hide them from view.

'The moment of the attack was now drawing near: Hauptmann Reschke slowly approached the enemy bomber from underneath. Our Me 110 now hung some 50 metres underneath the Lancaster, and still we had not been spotted. Then a short burst from the oblique guns; in all, Hauptmann Reschke only fired nine 2 cm rounds. The shells struck home between the two engines in the right wing, and immediately the bomber started burning fiercely. It trailed a long sheet of flames, which covered almost the complete fuselage.

'The aircraft lost height at once, and plunged towards us in a right-hand turn. Hauptmann Reschke swerved to starboard to avoid a collision. The flames burned bright in a yellow-red and trailed back towards the blue-white-red roundel. They clearly illuminated the squadron code on the fuselage too; I could make out the capital letters AR, and made a note of this. A few minutes later, we watched how the Lancaster hit the ground in a sheet of flames ... Not one of the seven-man crew had been able to bale out of their doomed Lancaster. We had no idea why, as Hauptmann Reschke had deliberately not aimed at the cockpit area.'[45]

Bruno Rupp remembers that he aimed for the fuel tank rather than the bomb bay or the cockpit to give those men on board the bomber a reasonable chance of escape from their stricken aircraft. 'My countrymen were badly affected by the large number of aircraft attacking their country and the bombs they dropped which destroyed so much of their towns and cities. There was a lot of anger towards the aircrews. But personally I certainly didn't feel any satisfaction when shooting down enemy aircraft. I had too much respect for them and their bravery.'

Most of the Junkers 88, Focke Wulf 190 and Messerschmitt 110 pilots were young men, not unlike those they were hunting down. Some had already become heroes among the German public. The highest-scoring night fighter ace, Major Heinz-Wolfgang Schnauffer, had achieved legendary status as the 'Night Ghost of St Trond' (after the name of his Belgian base). He was to be credited with 121 kills, most of them in a Me 110.

Schnauffer had honed his combat skills during daylight sorties early in the war. Men with the skills to pilot a night fighter in pitch darkness in all-weather conditions were in short supply by the time of the Nuremberg raid. The elite campaigners with dozens of scores to their name were increasingly outnumbered

by untested newcomers who would be lucky to survive a handful of missions.

Many of the less experienced Luftwaffe pilots were killed
in accidents. Those who survived to face the firepower of the
Allied bombers were often shot down whilst striving too
eagerly for their first kill. Others were less keen to stray into
the sights of the British gunners. When Josef Scholten, a radar
operator, signed a form 'voluntarily' joining the Luftwaffe,
eight of his companions refused to do so. They were marched
ceaselessly, day and night, around the square until they came to
see the wisdom of devoting themselves to the service of the
Führer, the Fatherland and its people by taking to the skies.

At 'blind-flying' school in Belgrade, Josef and his fellow
recruits were made brutally aware of the dangers of training
over occupied territory when a Heinkel 111 went missing
with four trainees and two instructors on board. They spent
two days searching the countryside without success. When the
wreckage of the plane was eventually found, so were the men's
bodies. All six had survived the landing, but had their throats
cut by the local Resistance.[46]

Reg Payne

The fighter crews were also handicapped by the lack of an aircraft designed for their particular environment. The Messerschmitt 110 still led the way, but the new technology – such as the upward-firing guns and SN-2 radar – increased its weight and made it less easy to handle. The Heinkel 219 had these features incorporated into its design, but had only just started to roll off the production line.

The high death toll, especially amongst new recruits, poor training, ageing aircraft and the danger and stress of flying at night, still failed to dent morale. 'It was more of a family than a military unit; [it had] an air of relaxed informality not seen in any other branch of service, with the possible exception of the U-boat crews, who also lived in close proximity and shared the dangers of their work.'[47]

The night fighter crews were the last line of defence against the devastating destructive power of the Allied bombers, the last hope of survival for the men, women and children in the cities beneath them. As the men of Bomber Command drew strength and courage by remembering the Blitz, the night fighter crews were desperate to prevent more of the carnage that had been inflicted on Hamburg or Berlin.

During the first three months of 1944 they had shot down more than 750 Allied bombers and accounted for most of the 78 that failed to return from the ill-fated raid on Leipzig. During the Berlin raid eight days earlier, Martin Becker had recorded the most kills in a single night: six Lancasters in the space of 38 minutes.

An Oberleutnant with 1st Division, Becker was so highly rated that he was permitted to operate in challenging weather conditions that meant others were grounded – but like Bruno Rupp he believed the chances of a raid that night were minimal. In the Battle Opera Houses across Germany, however, the mood was changing. The German listening posts had picked up a mass of radio activity in England during the course of the afternoon, usually a good indicator of an impending raid.

Only a year before, General 'Beppo' Josef Schmidt had led Goering's Panzer Division in Tunisia, but he was now commander of 1 Fighter Corps, south of Berlin – the man in charge of the night fighter divisions. Late in the evening Schmidt was informed that a substantial force was heading across the North Sea. Despite the moon, the British were coming. He and his staff had spent the last few hours poring over the incoming intelligence reports, determined to identify their target.

Further reports indicated that the bomber stream was forging a route that would take it to Hamburg or Berlin. For the time being, at least, the 'spoof' diversion – the force that would be dropping mines in Heligoland – was working. Then news came through at 11 p.m. of another stream gathering off the south-east coast of England. Schmidt and his team had to decide which of the two provided the real threat.

Generalmajor Walter Grabmann had received the same intelligence in the operations room of the 3rd Fighter Division near Arnhem. He was in no doubt: the southerly stream heading towards him and the Ruhr valley was the main force, not the one to the north.

★   ★   ★

At 23,000 feet the bomber stream was making steady progress. The first wave had reached the German border untroubled by enemy fighters. Despite the occasional spikes appearing on Ted Manners's ABC screen, 'uneventful' was the word on Rusty Waughman's mind. The moonlight was now so bright that he could read his instruments by it – but maybe this was not going to be a bad one after all.

Then the infrequent spikes on Ted's cathode ray screen became a mass.

*   *   *

Bruno and his comrades continued at the card table late into the evening. Their stomachs well lined with sausage and potatoes, they remained convinced that the order to stand down was imminent.

'Bereitschaft!'

Readiness! The scramble alert banished further thought of sleep. In an instant they gathered their caps and gloves, headphones and microphones and hurtled across the tarmac. Bruno and his two radio operators, Hans Eckert and Gerd Gerbhardt – who shared his birthday – and their mechanic, Albert Biel, quickly took their positions in the Junkers Ju 88 G6 and waited for take-off.

The signal came at 11.25 p.m. All Bruno Rupp knew at that point was that a vast RAF bomber stream was heading for Germany, its target unknown.

Generalmajor Grabmann had ordered every available night fighter to gather at the Ida beacon, south-east of Cologne. After he'd shared his assessment with Schmidt, the rest of the Tame Boar groups were sent to join them as soon as possible. Those too far from Ida were instructed to head for another beacon north of Frankfurt, codenamed Otto.

*   *   *

Ten-year-old Friedrich Ziegler was getting ready for bed in Kleingeschaidt, a small village near Lauf, nine miles from Nuremberg. It had been a long day. As usual, lessons had started at eight and finished at one, but several hours of gymnastics had followed, to satisfy the school's commitment to developing healthy young people for the future strength of the Reich.

When Friedrich got back to his father's farm, he had to carry out some odd jobs and run errands for his father before he was allowed to play with Lux, the family Rottweiler. The dog talked a good fight, but whenever the air-raid sirens sounded Lux was the first to seek shelter in the basement. Twelve of them lived in the house: Friedrich's family, his grandparents, some farmhands and four French prisoners-of-war who worked the land instead of being confined to a camp, and displayed enviable culinary skills whenever they were presented with a freshly killed rabbit. They all had to share the shelter, too. Friedrich hoped that night would be quiet and he could sleep in his bed. He did not want to have to cram into the sweaty, fetid cellar.

Seven miles east of Nuremberg, in Eschenau, Fritz Fink was also thinking of getting some sleep. Thirteen-year-old Fritz was prohibited from going to school because his parents were not Nazi party members, so he helped out on the farm instead. In private both his mother and father spoke disparagingly of their leaders. A relative of theirs, a police captain named Friedrich Fink, had been shot during Hitler's attempted putsch of 1923. As far as they were concerned, the Führer and his acolytes were obsessed with their own power and cared little for the wellbeing of the people. But these were words and thoughts Fritz dared not repeat anywhere else.[48]

Unlike Friedrich Ziegler, Fritz Fink was not too disturbed by the raids. His family's farm was near the Schlossberg, a 50-metre hill with a panoramic view of the surrounding area. When the air-raid sirens sounded, he and his family would race up the slope to watch the flak and flares light up the sky. As their bombs never fell anywhere near his house, Fritz felt little hatred towards their British opponents. At least they worked by night, unlike the Americans, who bombed by day and appeared to relish targeting trains and vehicles filled with people.

If anything, Fritz felt sympathy for the bomber crews, especially the poor souls trapped inside the balls of flame he saw spiralling to the ground. Like most German boys, he had visited the crash sites; he had seen the mangled wreckage of the enemy aircraft and the broken bodies of the airmen and felt nothing but compassion and sadness for their families.[49]

CHAPTER 9

The Long Leg

Harry Evans's crew

Harry Evans peered from behind his curtain at the streams of vapour pouring from the bombers' exhausts. The moisture in the smoke and fumes emitted by the aircraft cooled rapidly as it met the freezing air and formed condensation trails as visible as tramlines across the velvet sky. What a silly lot of bastards ... He cursed those behind the decision to send them up on such a clear night.

To rid themselves of the trails that would lead the night fighters straight to them, Harry knew they needed to alter their height. They descended to 12,000 feet, even though that was where the flak was likely to be fiercest. Still the contrails billowed from the rear of the plane, a clear invitation to attack, so they started to climb instead, and finally reached an altitude where they were less visible.

Harry had already decided to overshoot the turning point at Charleroi; when they changed course they would be between five and 10 miles south of the track, and so avoid the heavy defences around Aachen. This was no time to follow their brief to the letter.

John Chadderton of 44 Squadron was ahead of Harry Evans, near the front of the stream. His crew's job was to record the wind speed and feed it back to base, where it was processed and retransmitted to the rest of the pack. His flight engineer nudged him and pointed below them, to where a fellow Lancaster was 'leaving four long white fingers which were twisted into a cloudy rope by the slipstream'.[50]

Over the intercom, his young Canadian mid-upper gunner asked if their engines were working. There was smoke streaming from them, he said. The answer came from the rear gunner, a dry Scot who provided the perfect antidote to the Canadian's over-excitement. 'Wheesht yer bletherin' – they're contrails!'

The dose of crisp Scottish realism did little to soothe John's nerves. 'We had never made them before, although we had often admired the pretty patterns left by the USAAF on their daylight raids 10,000 feet above us.' Chadderton had no doubt the cause of the problem was the absence of cloud. For the previous five months they had flown blind through a range of different densities. 'Despite the constant anxiety of icing and flak, this damp cloak of darkness was just what we burglars needed to enable us to creep in and creep out again.'

The first skirmish of the night took place almost by accident. A German fighter pilot on his way to the beacon near Cologne was alerted by his gunner, who had spotted the outline of a bomber before the crew had even activated their on-board radar. As they started to turn they saw another. The radar immediately picked up three more targets. They headed for the nearest and delivered a blast of *Schräge Musik* which set the wing ablaze. The stricken Lancaster – the first British victim of the raid – crashed in a ball of flame five minutes later, but the crew managed to bale out before they hit the ground.

Jack Watson was at the front of the stream with the Pathfinder force, tasked with supporting those who were marking the target. As they reached German territory, three Mosquitoes peeled away on a spoof raid. It was soon clear they would not be completing this operation undetected; the moon above and the searchlights below them formed an alleyway of light. Their gunners scoured the sky behind them.

'I can see an attack,' said the first to break the silence.

'I can see another,' the rear gunner echoed.

Jack and his crew had been fortunate enough to slip through before the enemy had a chance to scramble. Now more than 200 night fighters were in the air, heading towards Otto and Ida to await further orders – orders which did not have time to materialise before the British bombers had flown straight into their deadly embrace.

★　　★　　★

Between crossing the German border and passing the Rhine, the stream had lost 10 Lancasters and two Halifaxes. One Lanc, on its 29th and penultimate op, had been mistaken for the enemy by the rear gunner of a 'friendly' Halifax. A long burst of tracer strafed the unfortunate aircraft's engines; only four of the seven men on board escaped before it hit the ground. The winds blew a second off course, towards the heavily defended town of Coblenz; it was struck by flak and went down with all hands near the village of Rübenach at 12.15 a.m. Both were from Rusty Waughman's 101 Squadron.

★　　★　　★

Oberleutnant Martin Drewes, one of Germany's finest pilots, was among the first in the air that night. The son of a pharmacist, he had been through officer school with the army before switching to the Luftwaffe. Since then he had won an Iron Cross and, more recently, a German Cross in Gold for repeated acts of bravery in combat.

He took off from Loan-Athies in France shortly after 11 p.m. with two other crew members crammed into his twin-engine Messerschmitt 110. Directly behind him was his radar operator, Georg Petz. The pair had 38 kills to their name. Their air-gunner was huddled to Petz's rear in a small glasshouse with two 2 cm drum-fed cannons at his knees, each holding 75 rounds of ammunition, built into the back of the cramped cabin and aimed upwards: *Schräge Musik*.

Drewes pointed his aircraft across Belgium and headed for the Ida beacon. Ground Control's running commentary told him to take an easterly course. He saw a bomber above them almost instantly, but their relative speeds were such that he was unable to turn and give chase.

'Not to worry,' he said to Petz. 'Where there is one, there will be others.'

Petz switched on his radar screen. Drewes was right. Three clear blips appeared on the screen. A few seconds later they could see a Lancaster silhouetted in the moonlight. As it flew on, heedless of the threat, Drewes manoeuvred into position beneath its massive belly. Mindful that the full bomb load only metres above his head could destroy them as well as their prey, Drewes delayed their attack until the air-gunner could target the bomber's engines. After a prolonged burst of *Schräge Musik* he dived away to safety as flames started to consume the wounded Lancaster then tore it apart.

Ten minutes later Drewes slid his Messerschmitt beneath a second Lancaster. His gunner's cannon jammed, but he still managed to score a hit. The bomber tried to dive to avoid further damage, but its starboard wing was soon ablaze. Georg Petz watched as its nose started to fall. 'As Drewes pulled away, the Lancaster blew up, showering the sky with thousands of fiery fragments ... Around us, bombers were dropping like flies sprayed with an insecticide gun.'[51]

★   ★   ★

Chalky White, down in the bomb aimer's position in Sam Harris's aircraft, saw fire in the sky. The night fighters and the main waves of the bomber stream had reached the radio beacons simultaneously.

'Bomber going down in flames off the port bow,' he called.

'I've seen that too,' Mac said. 'There's another going down on the starboard side.'

Sam switched off the tiny light perched on his desk and looked out from behind his curtain.

'I've just seen two more get hit on the port side.' Eric moved through the aircraft to get a clearer view. The moonlight glanced off the crisp, snow-laden peaks below them. Then there was a blinding flash, the sky turned blood red, and he could see the clear outline of a bomber in flames.

'Do you want me to log these, Ken?' he asked, overcome with a profound sense of helplessness. It was the navigator's job to record and note the approximate position of aircraft losses.

Ken shook his head. 'It's just a Scarecrow.'

Rumours had spread amongst the crews that winter of a new type of flak designed to undermine the morale of the raiding crews. The shells burst in a shower of debris at the height of the stream to mimic the appearance of an exploding aircraft. Some were even said to release a succession of small parachutes, to create the illusion of escaping crew. After the war Scarecrows were discovered to have been a myth, and what the men were seeing really was an exploding bomber, but many of the men clawing their way towards Nuremberg that night may have found it easier to believe in it than to accept that they were witnessing the violent death of friends and fellow aviators.

Ken's crew remained unconvinced.

'It's a Scarecrow, I tell you,' Ken insisted. 'Now I want you all to shut up about it.'

Sam had to admire what Ken was trying to achieve. The situation was dire; aircraft upon aircraft were being ripped out of the sky; he just wanted them to forget about it, focus on the job in hand and give them all the best chance of survival.

Exploding Allied bombers continued to light up the sky as they fell victim to the feasting night fighters. There was nowhere to hide. Sam returned to his position and closed the curtain, doing his best to banish any thought of what might be happening out there, praying that they would be spared. They climbed to 23,000 feet. Nuremberg was still 55 minutes away.

From the cockpit of his Lancaster towards the middle of the stream, pilot Dick Starkey watched tracers stitch wild patterns across his path. In a matter of minutes – time seemed to have lost all meaning – he counted 30 bombers falling from the sky. 'I had never seen anything like this, and certainly not with as much clarity. The brightness of the moon meant that you could see it all in great detail. Fire would rip through the aircraft until it reached the bomb bay, which would blow up and shower debris around like flaming confetti. The flames died as what remained of the aircraft plummeted to the ground; then there would be another massive explosion on impact.' So many bombers had fallen that the earth was ablaze.

To give them the best chance of seeing and avoiding the night fighters, Dick turned into a 'banking search', veering steeply to port for 15 seconds and then banking to starboard to regain course. He had been on bad trips before, including Leipzig, but this was already turning out to be one of the worst.

With the help of his navigator, Dick had edged 10 miles north of the track, constantly banking and searching for safety, when a shadow appeared at their side.

'Corkscrew!' The warning came from one of the gunners.

Dick thrust the bomber into a turning dive then hauled back on the controls and reversed into a climb in the opposite direction. He kept repeating the manoeuvre, sweat pouring off him from the sheer physical effort of throwing a heavy, bomb-laden aircraft around the sky. The rear gunner tried to fire at the enemy fighter as the g-force slammed his head into his chest.

When Dick brought them level again, the intercom was silent apart from the rasping breaths of his crew as they tried to re-inflate their lungs and regain their bearings.

The rear gunner finally spoke. 'All clear …'

The words had barely left his lips when another fighter was at their heel. Dick hurled the aircraft into a corkscrew once again, twisting down and then back up. They resumed course when the sky was clear. Dick started to bank, eyes peeled, hoping for some remission. But it was never long before the rear gunner cried out and the whole frantic, coiling manoeuvre would begin once more.

They were now 60 miles short of Nuremberg, and the endless, energy-sapping evasive action seemed to have worked. They were off course, but they were safe. Dick dared to believe that they *would* make it to the target. The bombing run always presented its own set of potentially lethal challenges, so in this brief moment of respite he tried to catch his breath and regain some strength.

The next night fighter attacked without warning. Muffled by his helmet and the drone of the four great Rolls-Royce Merlin engines, the noise of its shells piercing the fuselage was like that of a peashooter pelting an overcoat. Then Dick saw vivid flashes of tracer flash across the space above his bomb aimer's head.

The shock only lasted a few moments, but that was long enough for the port wing and engines to burst into flames. The Lancaster's nose fell and it started to plummet. Dick's flight engineer tried to feather the engines and help him with the controls, but their dive became steeper with every passing second.

'Abandon aircraft!' he yelled across the intercom.

He heard the bomb aimer acknowledge the order. The rear gunner was trapped in his turret. The port engine was no longer supplying it with power, and he was unable to swivel round and scramble back into the fuselage. His only chance of survival was to reach the manual controls which would allow him to turn and fall straight out into the night sky. Dick had no idea if the gunner even had a parachute within reach.

The mid-upper gunner and the wireless operator did not speak. Both would have been in the direct path of the incoming rounds.

The controls went limp in Dick's hands. The blazing aircraft was hurtling towards the ground at 300 mph. His only concern now was to buy every precious second he could, to give his crew a chance to leap to safety. His flight engineer appeared at his shoulder and snatched a parachute from the rack at their side. The g-force glued Dick to his seat, but he struggled with his 'chute and managed to connect one of its hooks to his harness.

Peering through the canopy, he was unable to distinguish ground from sky. The engineer and navigator were at the escape hatch, ready to go, but Dick couldn't move a muscle; he didn't even fumble with his parachute. He had felt no fear in the time since they had been hit, but now he was truly terrified. The plane was going to crash and he wasn't going to get out. In the blink of an eye his life would be over.

He sat waiting for the impact. I haven't even had a chance to pray, he thought.

There was a mind-numbing explosion as the Lancaster's full bomb load and 1,500 gallons of high-octane fuel detonated. Dick's head was forced back into his shoulders. He felt as though he was being lifted from the cockpit, through the Perspex canopy in front of him, soaring upwards.

Then he lost consciousness.

★   ★   ★

Scouse Nugent was a mid-upper gunner with 78 Squadron. He and his crew were approaching Marburg, halfway between the north-west German border and Nuremberg, when a Junkers 88 catapulted towards them, guns blazing, shells slamming relentlessly into their airframe.

'Bandit at rear port – dive to port!' Scouse screamed.

Harry Hudson acted immediately, throwing the plane out of the path of the attacking fighter before he started to corkscrew.

When he had corrected their course once more, Harry checked that everyone was OK. His voice was supernaturally calm. The fighter appeared to have gone in search of another target, but Scouse did not relax. He could see aircraft being blasted from the sky all around them. Their safety depended on his vigilance.

Knowing an attack was most likely to come from behind them, he encouraged the rear gunner to watch the sky below them whilst he scoured every inch of the space above. For five long minutes they maintained their vigil. No one spoke; the only sound was that of the Merlin engines and the blood rushing in their ears.

Another fighter swung into view and Harry repeated the corkscrew. When they resumed course Scouse could see the port wing was on fire. There was no time to panic. He turned his attention back to the sky. Another Junkers, slightly above and to the rear, was heading straight towards them. Scouse wrenched his guns around, cursing himself for not spotting it sooner. In a split second the enemy was in his sights.

He squeezed the trigger. Nothing happened. He followed the fighter as it passed them. Pressed the trigger. Nothing.

Had the guns frozen, Scouse wondered? Or had the earlier damage caused an electrical fault?

He glanced at the port wing. It was now burning fiercely. The nose of the plane had dipped. It was starting to go down.

'What's happening, Skipper?' he said over the intercom.

There was no answer.

He asked again. Complete silence. It was like the *Marie Celeste*.

He slipped off his helmet; forgetting to do up the chinstrap on take-off saved him a crucial few seconds. He dropped it on the floor and headed for the cockpit. As he did so, he started to feel light-headed. By taking off his helmet he had removed his own oxygen supply. He slumped to the floor, unable to see, using his outstretched hand to try and work out where he was. His fingertips brushed against a parachute and, despite his grogginess, he managed to clip it on to his harness.

He forced open his eyes and peered along the fuselage. The others must all have been killed by the ceaseless onslaught of the Luftwaffe. The port engine was still burning. Smoke caught in the back of his throat and the intense heat of the flames seared his skin.

He felt himself getting weaker and weaker, but somehow forced himself to his knees. He scrabbled for the escape hatch between his turret and the rear gunner's but was sent tumbling backwards along the plane. He slammed against the rear turret and shook his head, trying to clear it. What was he doing there? It dawned on him with agonising slowness: the plane was in its final dive, plunging vertiginously to earth, and he was pinned to the rear turret doors by the enormous forces created by the aircraft's 300 mph plunge. But Scouse refused to give up. He summoned every last ounce of his remaining strength and willed himself forwards.

At last he found a handle: the door to his turret. What he thought was the floor was in fact the ceiling. One twist and he was sucked from the aircraft 'like a vacuum cleaner picking up a fragment of dust'.

The cold, fresh air brought him round. A different kind of panic kicked in. Was his parachute working? He started to tug frantically on the ripcord. He glanced upwards, desperate to see a mushroom of silk billowing above him. Nothing. He wrenched it again. It wouldn't open. He was terrified, unable to believe that he had escaped from a burning plane only to find his parachute couldn't save him.

'God, it won't open!' he shouted over and over, in increasing panic, as the ground rushed towards him – a plea to a deity in whom he didn't believe, but whose help he urgently needed.

Amid the panic, a moment of clarity: he had been tugging the carrying handle. Now he found the ripcord. There was a jolt as the 'chute opened and slowed his fall. In the distance he could see a burning plane spinning to the ground.

Scouse smashed through a tree. Branches clawed at him as he tumbled towards the ground. The force of the impact broke his ankle. But he was alive.

CHAPTER 10

One Hour of Death

Roger Coverley

In all of his flying days Roger Coverley had never experienced such relentless attack, or witnessed such devastation. As the sky raged with fire and combat, and he flew through the thick of it in his Halifax, Roger started to hum 'Paper Doll', a popular ballad of the time. Tracer ripped into a nearby plane and it fell from view, leaving a trail of fire and a cascade of scorching debris. But Roger carried on. 'And then the flirty, flirty guys with their flirty, flirty eyes / Will have to flirt with dollies that are real —'

The voice of his rear gunner over the intercom cut short his song.

'Fighter on our tail! Corkscrew!'

Roger reacted immediately, in tandem with his gunners. With a few well-aimed salvos they drove the Ju 88 away, but not before the fighter had scored a hit on the starboard engine and their mid-section had started to burn.

As a precaution the flight engineer passed Roger his parachute before he went aft and checked the damage. In the process of shaking off the fighter, they had lost height and speed. Roger set about getting them back on course.

As they sighed with relief, Otto Kutzner's Messerschmitt 110 stole unseen beneath them. His upward-firing cannon blew a hole in the Halifax's starboard wing, ruptured its fuel lines and started a furious blaze. There had been no warning calls over the intercom, no flashes of tracer; only the vibration of the shells tearing into their airframe.

'I've been hit,' the rear gunner yelled.

Roger wrestled helplessly with the controls, fighting to keep them level and airborne. The aircraft was not responding to its rudder and was losing speed. It had started to climb and, no matter what he did to try and force the nose down, it refused to respond. The fire rampaged along the starboard wing and began to consume them. 'It all happened in seconds; there was nothing I could do. The aircraft was in flames and it was uncontrollable.'

'Get out!' Roger shouted. 'Abandon aircraft!' He stayed at the controls, trying to keep them level to give the crew the best chance of baling out. They only had seconds before the plane fell into a fatal spin or blew up. Strangely, Roger felt no sense of panic as the heat in the cockpit grew. He just thought: the CO is going to be pretty annoyed when he finds out I've lost The Royal Barge ...

A piece of debris struck him in the face, knocking off his oxygen mask and temporarily blinding him. Roger managed to unstrap, haul himself from his seat and clip on his parachute. As he did so, he tumbled backwards down the steps towards the escape hatch in the nose.

It must have been open. All Roger felt was the sensation of falling, the wind rushing past his ears and the cold air on his face. He fumbled for the handle of his parachute, but couldn't find it. It was on upside down. His first instinct was not fear but anger. 'Here I was falling through the sky towards German soil and I couldn't open my bloody parachute!' He scrabbled around, trying to find the handle. There it was. He gave it a tug and felt the jerk of the parachute, and the sudden blissful sensation of floating rather than falling.

After the fire and the fury of the preceding moments, the sky was deathly quiet.

The surviving members of Roger Coverley's crew had his bravery to thank. He had bought them time. Meanwhile on another crippled Lancaster the mid-upper gunner and the pilot sacrificed the chance to save themselves by choosing instead to try and free the rear gunner from his turret. It cost them their lives. The bodies of the three men were found in the wreckage of the crashed aircraft.

Tom Fogaty's Lancaster was intercepted by a fighter as they crossed the German border, but he decided to fly on to Nuremberg. The 115 Squadron pilot initially believed that his aircraft was still functioning normally, but then quickly realised that the damage was worse than he had thought. The heady stench of fuel and oil filled the cabin and they had descended 5,000 feet in 10 minutes. Every passing second cost them height.

He ordered the bomb aimer to release his load and felt the control column push back against his palms once the explosives were gone. He asked his navigator for a homeward track and started his turn. The aircraft had stopped losing height, but because of the head wind they were now losing air speed.

A blast of flak turned the night sky ochre around them. Tom felt the aircraft pitch and roll as the shrapnel struck their flank. Once they were clear he asked the engineer for a report on the damage. The news was good: a few holes in the airframe but, once again, none fatal. Tom wasn't convinced; the controls were becoming increasingly unresponsive. Suddenly they went limp in his hands.

The aircraft fell into a steep dive. Tom wrestled with the controls but the bomber was already down to 2,500 feet and he knew there was no way they would make it back to England. He ordered his crew to clip on their parachutes and bale out.

The rear gunner was stuck in his turret. The mid-upper gunner crawled along the fuselage and turned the turret manually until his mate was facing him. He gave him a thumbs-up before he fell backwards into the night. Once he had gone, the mid-upper joined the navigator and wireless operator at the rear hatch.

Only Tom and his flight engineer were left. The plane was down to 1,000 feet; if they were going to jump, they had to do it now. But the flight engineer's parachute was jammed under his seat. 'Quick, take mine,' Tom said. 'There's no time to lose.'

The engineer paused; if he took it, there was virtually no chance that Tom would survive.

For a moment the two men just looked at each other. 'Go,' Tom insisted.

The engineer hesitated briefly, then clipped on the 'chute and nodded his farewell. He crouched down and disappeared through the hatch.

Tom struggled back to the cockpit and turned on his landing lights. The snow-covered ground loomed out of the darkness; only 500 yards away and closing in. He grabbed the controls, but there was still no response. The only sound he heard above the shriek of the Merlins was his own breath over the intercom. He was down to 200 feet and the trees and the hedgerows were rushing towards him. He cut the engines, closed his eyes and mumbled a prayer. As the plane smashed against the unyielding earth he felt a fierce pain in his forehead, a sense of floating, then darkness.

When he came to, he was lying in the snow 50 yards from the wreckage of his bomber.[52]

★   ★   ★

Cy Barton and his crew flew on 'unmolested'. The sky was a tangled web of tracer fire, but he kept their Halifax straight, entreating all on board to keep their eyes peeled for enemy fighters. Two searchlight beams appeared in front of them, so bright they were temporarily blinded. They all held their breath as, with almost surgical precision, Cyril managed to find the narrow gap between the beams.

There was no let-up, though, as they emerged on the other side. The sky above them was lit by flares dropped by German fighters, marking the position of the stream for their comrades. Cy called for absolute vigilance once more. Two bombers ahead exploded, but their Halifax remained untouched.

The danger had become relentless; even those with no belief in God asked for His protection. Frederick Taylor, pilot of V-Victor, had never been a religious man, but that night he heard himself reciting the 23rd Psalm. For hours on end. 'The Lord is my Shepherd / I shall not want ...'

Behind him, Sidney Whitlock's radio went dead. A series of small explosions buffeted the aircraft. Sidney switched over to intercom and heard Taylor give the order to bale out. He could see smoke and flames rising from the bomb inspection panels on the floor. The front escape hatch was stuck fast, so he and the navigator scrambled to the back of the plane and hauled themselves over the main spar, trying to clip on their parachutes as they went. The tail gunner wrenched open the rear hatch and jumped. The mid-upper gunner followed.

Sidney sat down on the step and rolled out into the night. Falling, he pulled the ripcord and offered a prayer of thanks when the parachute opened above him. As he floated down he saw his aircraft hit the ground. Everyone had escaped apart from a new pilot flying second dickie and a stand-in flight engineer. Their usual one had been taken ill. Lucky bugger, Sidney thought. [53]

★   ★   ★

Bruno Rupp could hardly believe his eyes. Locating the stream was more often than not a question of luck; it was usually cloaked by cloud. It was not uncommon for him to return to base without firing a single shot, having used half his fuel in the search. Yet here they were, bombers everywhere, lit up like Christmas trees. The radar screen was swarming with blips: if one bomber managed to escape, they would soon find another.

Bruno slid under one Lancaster. A burst of *Schräge Musik* was followed by a series of small explosions. Soon the aircraft would fall from the sky, but not, he hoped, before those on board had a chance to parachute to safety. He scored two kills that night.

Leutnant Wilhelm Seuss was enjoying even more success. He still could not quite believe they had been scrambled. Based at Erfurt, near Weimar in Saxony, he was due to go on leave the following day, and he had been so confident there would not be an enemy raid that he had already packed his bag.

Sent to circle the Otto beacon, he saw the bombers going down 'one after the other'. The trail of burning wrecks on the ground led them directly to the bomber stream. 'I flew along, following the crashes on the ground, and I saw a Lancaster in a searchlight, and I shot it down. I could have picked up bombers on my SN-2 but it wasn't necessary. The stream was tightly concentrated and I shot down two more very quickly.'

Seuss eased beneath another Lancaster. His *Schräge Musik* guns were out of ammunition, but by mirroring each move the bomber made he remained unseen until the drum was changed. When the Allied pilot finally saw him and attempted to corkscrew, he only succeeded in flying directly into a cannon burst. A few seconds later the aircraft was consumed by fire. When it exploded, Seuss only narrowly avoided being hit by the blast. He turned for home. There was little enjoyment for him in such easy pickings. 'I could have stayed in the stream and shot down even more, but I had simply had enough. My nerves were completely gone, and I thought if I carried on I would be endangering my crew.'[54]

The most successful German pilot that night was Martin Becker, the hero of Leipzig. Encountering the stream early, he managed to shoot down three Lancasters and three Halifaxes in the space of half an hour. He landed, not yet content with his night's work, refuelled and took off once more. The ease with which a pilot of his skill could find and destroy the enemy that night devalued his success, he believed, even though Hitler was to personally award him a Knight's Cross of the Iron Cross for his efforts. 'There were such a lot of British bombers around that we could have knocked them down with a fly flap.'[55]

Walter Heidenrich was the radar operator for a Junkers 88 crew led by Oberleutnant Günther Köberich. Based at Quakenbrück, north of Münster, they had 12 kills to their name, three on the Stuttgart raid. They were heading south when Heidenrich noticed something strange about the shape and size of the blip that had appeared on his screen. As they closed in on their target he discovered why: two Lancasters were flying so close that they had registered as one.

Köberich flew below them and fixed the nearest in his sights. His opening burst of *Schräge Musik* blinded him and his crew; for some reason, tracer had been loaded into the drum. When he regained his night vision he could see their first target in flames. He turned his attention to the second. Another short burst and that Lancaster too was mortally wounded.

Heidenrich watched the whole eerie episode unfold. 'For quite a time, the two of them went straight ahead, both on fire. One went off to the left and crashed on the right-hand bank of the Rhine, while the other crashed on the opposite bank.

When they hit they seemed to burst in all directions, with all sorts of colours, reds and greens and yellows. I think they were Pathfinder machines ... I don't know whether they were found, and I don't know whether any of the crews managed to get out, but I think they probably had time to.'[56]

In fact, only one Allied airman survived: a wireless operator, blown out of his Lancaster with his parachute miraculously intact.

Not every German ace was able to add to his tally. Major Wilhelm Herget had 49 kills to his credit and was unable to reach his half-century. 'I got into the stream and I could see bombers going down to my left but I could not find one of my own ... I could have kicked myself; it was obvious that the other fighters were doing well.'

Diverted to the Otto beacon, he just managed to avoid pulling the trigger on a particularly aimless Junkers 88 which flew across his sights. 'I was furious. I nearly put a few rounds in front of his nose to wake him up.'[57]

★   ★   ★

Those watching the massacre unfold from the centre of the stream knew they would be haunted by the sight for ever more.

'Gunners, keep your eyes open; there's two aircraft just been shot down right in front of us ...' Reg Payne's pilot, Michael Beetham, warned his crew of the danger ahead.

'Three more have gone down behind us ...' the rear gunner added.

Another bomber blew up on their port side. Reg went to see what was happening. 'I darted up to the astrodome and saw the smoke and the shower of flames as an aircraft died in front of my eyes. Seven people in it; gone in an instant.'

He gazed at the burning trail on the ground ahead. We're flying into that, he thought. Their rear gunner reckoned he could also see blazing wreckage stretching back for 60 miles behind them. Reg was stunned by the brightness of the moon-light above them and the fires raging below. He could see the other Lancasters and Halifaxes so clearly that he could read their squadron codes.

They flew alongside another Lancaster for a few moments, then watched helplessly as a string of cannon shells tore into its belly and transformed it into a ball of fire. Reg didn't see the fighter that shot it down. All he knew was that it could have been them; for some reason fate had decided some other poor buggers' number was up.

Les Bartlett, Michael Beetham's bomb aimer, thought they were only seconds away from being hit. The situation appeared calamitous. 'I looked down on the port beam at the area over which we had passed. It looked like a battlefield. There were kites burning on the deck, all over the place – bombs going off where they had been jettisoned by bombers damaged in combat, and fires from their incendiaries across the whole area. Such a picture of aerial disaster I had never seen before and certainly hope never to see again. I suppose it was just the same on daylight raids, except that the spectacle of a kite on fire at night is much more terrifying.'[58]

Ray Francis, a Lancaster flight engineer on 622 Squadron, reckoned they were only 50 miles into the raid when he saw his first aircraft burn: a furnace-like blaze spiralling downwards. Nuremberg was only his fourth op: he wondered if this level of destruction was normal. Aircraft after aircraft fell from the sky. I hope to God I get out of this, he thought.

Streams of red tracer streaked across the sky, seeming to hang in an endless arc while the planes ahead continued to disappear in lightning flashes. Driven by the need for self-preservation, the pilot, Ray Trenouth, tried to climb above the main stream. The gunners swivelled constantly in their turrets in search of enemy fighters while the skipper and flight engineer scoured their port and starboard flanks. Even the wireless operator was detailed on watch, standing in the astrodome, staring at the unforgiving sky.

The mid-upper gunner saw the fighter first and ordered a starboard corkscrew. He tried firing a defensive burst, but his guns had an automatic cut-out to prevent him from destroying the tail of his own aircraft. The rear gunner squeezed off a salvo as they dived and turned and his tracer mingled briefly with the enemy's.

They shook off their attacker and resumed course. Now it was the rear gunner's turn to issue the warning: another enemy fighter was at their heel. Trenouth reacted instantly and vigorously, almost throwing their aircraft out of the sky. Hemmed in and immobile because of the g-forces generated by the spinning plane, the rear gunner was unable to fire, but it didn't matter – the fighter had gone. The violence of the manoeuvre, however, had caused a blockage in the guns.

Trenouth sent the wireless operator back to take a look as they flew on. When he didn't return and the guns were still inoperative Ray went back to check on him. After clambering through the fuselage, hoping that another corkscrew wasn't in the offing, he found his crew-mate slumped unconscious from lack of oxygen. He managed to drag him back to the main supply before returning to finish the job himself. The guns were soon in working order. For now, they had survived.

As Ray Trenouth climbed higher, others left the stream altogether. Those who remained in the formation took some comfort from the idea of safety in numbers, but that was in the process of being fatally undermined that night. The night fighters were drawn relentlessly to where the pickings were richest; as the enemy feasted on the main stream like vultures on carrion, those who struck out on their own reckoned they stood a greater chance of survival.

Pathfinder Jack Watson and his crew, at the cutting edge of the stream, had almost reached the end of the straight leg when a bomber blew up beneath their Lancaster. They saw no fighter, and no evidence of one once the sky had cleared; there was a chance they were the intended target, and had that unfortunate bomber not flown underneath them at that exact point they might have become another victim of *Schräge Musik*.

Chick Chandler, a flight engineer with 622 at Mildenhall, had never witnessed destruction on this scale. He could not tear his eyes from the cauldron of fire in the sky. There were explosions all around them; aircraft with fire streaming from their wings battling to stay in the air, and then finally going into a flat spin. Each time, Chick willed the crew to bale out before that point. He knew that if they were still on board, the colossal g-forces and the speed at which the plane fell would mean there was little chance of escape.

Whilst others strove to distance themselves, focus on their jobs, forget there were men just like them on those burning planes, Chick felt more scared than ever. There are people dying out there, he thought, and wondered when it might be his turn.

Ray Francis's crew

The gunner's voice crackled over the intercom. 'Fighter low on the port side.'

For the moment, there was no order to corkscrew and the pilot held the same course. All eyes were on the night sky. Chick turned, eyes unblinking, peering out at the night sky for an oncoming shadow, aware that a moment's lapse could lead to their death.

A Junkers 88, 'bigger than life', was boring in from the starboard quarter.

Chick screamed, 'Corkscrews starboard go!' and ducked, as if that would help. As the bomber corkscrewed, the Junkers strafed the underside of their port wing. The skipper continued his defensive move, and when he levelled out the fighter had gone. 'When we'd straightened up, I did a visual check and I could see petrol coming out of the outer fuel tank on the port wing. I thought, Oh my God! Then I realised that the fighter had hit a tank with just a tiny bit of fuel remaining. We had been lucky.'

The tension eased a fraction. 'Who gave the order?' the pilot asked.

No one spoke. Chick's voice had been so high-pitched that it had been unrecognisable. But his panic had saved them. A second later and the enemy shells would have blasted into the body of the aircraft and transformed them into a flaming Catherine wheel. Chick had never seen a German fighter before. He prayed he would never see one again.

Even now, more than 65 years after that night, Chick Chandler's eyes grow wide as he recalls the sight of that enemy aircraft tearing out of the darkness towards him. 'The whole thing was so vivid I can still see it quite clearly,' he recalls, sitting in his favourite armchair in his Hampshire cottage. He holds his hands out in front of his face. 'It's *there!*'

There were so many men parachuting from stricken planes that navigator Ron Butcher was forced to alter course and gain

▼ Sir Arthur 'Bomber' Harris, centre, in the Bomber Command bunker.

▲ Alan Payne in 2012.

▼ Andy Wiseman in 2012.

► Members of Rusty Waughman's crew relax before an operation. Rusty is above the tea urn with a flask and cigarette. On his left wearing a forage cap is his rear-gunner, Harry Nunn. On Harry's left, wearing the gloves, is navigator Alec Cowan.

◄ Rusty Waughman's crew during a reunion in 2003. From left to right: Norman, Ted, Curly, Rusty, Alec, Taffy.

▼ Alec Cowan, Rusty Waughman and Norman Westby at the Bomber Command Memorial unveiling ceremony.

▼ Ron and Shiela Auckland in 2012.

▲ Focke Wulf 190 fighters in action.

▼ Roger Coverley, 2012.

▲ Reg Payne, 2012.

▼ The ruins of Nuremberg, following the bombing.

▲ Chick Chandler, 2012.

▼ George Prince, 2012.

▲ Harry Evans in 2012.

▼ Tony Hiscock at a squadron reunion in 2008.

▲ Messerschmitt 110 fighters in formation.

▶ Avro Lancasters in formation above the clouds.

▼ A Lancaster bomber flies over Hamburg during a night raid.

◀ The author in the cockpit of Lancaster *Just Jane* at the Lincolnshire Aviation Heritage Centre.

▼ *Just Jane* – the Lancaster Fred and Harold Panton maintain as a memorial to their brother and his thousands of colleagues, killed whilst serving on Bomber Command.

▼ The giant bomb bay of Lancaster *Just Jane*.

▲ On board *Just Jane*, looking back from rear door into tail gun turret. The cramped conditions are plain to see.

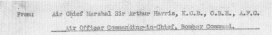

From: Air Chief Marshal Sir Arthur Harris, K.C.B., O.B.E., A.F.C.

Air Officer Commanding-in-Chief, Bomber Command.

27th June 1944.

My dear Mr Barton

    I write to inform you that His Majesty The King has been graciously pleased to confer upon your son the Victoria Cross.

    I ask you on behalf of Bomber Command, and for my own part especially, to accept our sympathy in your loss.

    I hope, however, that this loss will be to some extent mitigated by the manner of your son's passing and by his high award, so well deserved, so hardly won.

    Your boy set an example of high courage and, finally, of extreme devotion to duty towards his crew, which will go down to history in the annals of his Service and shine as an inspiration for all who come after him.

    I hope indeed that a rightful pride in his achievements and his conduct will be of some consolation to you and yours at this time.

                                    I am very sincerely

                                    Arthur T. Harris.

F.J.Barton Esq.,
171 Elm Road,
New Malden,
Surrey.

◀ The letter sent by Sir Arthur Harris to the parents of Cyril Barton informing them that their son had been awarded a posthumous Victoria Cross.

▼ Joyce and Cynthia Barton, Cyril's surviving sisters, discuss his life with the author.

▲ Her Majesty Queen Elizabeth II with Air Commodore Malcolm White, chairman of the Bomber Command Association, at the unveiling of the Bomber Command Memorial statue in London, June 2012.

height to avoid hitting them. As far as Ron was concerned, 'fear was inevitable, death was near', even at 23,500 feet. Below them the moonlight framed the airborne version of Dante's *Inferno*. Nimble night fighters spun the cumbersome bombers around in an endless dance of death.

Ron usually stayed cocooned at his station but that night the gasps of incredulity and horror from other members of his crew brought him out to watch. Never before had he seen a plane going down in flames, or the ghostly shapes of parachuting airmen. His initial reaction was 'Thank God it's not us', followed quickly by a rush of guilt. The guilt was fleeting, though. What could they do about it? he asked himself. Not a thing. There was no point dwelling on the fate of others.

Towards the back of the stream, bomb aimer Andy Wiseman had been waiting as patiently as ever to carry out his job. To keep himself occupied on the journey to their target, he maintained a ceaseless vigil for fighters. They were still an hour from Nuremberg and the seven minutes when he would be called into action.

Without warning, there was a burst of cannon fire; tracer shot past their starboard wing. Another burst struck home; flames blossomed from a port engine. There was a curse over the intercom, and another, louder, when the wounded propeller started to rattle. A starboard engine had also been hit. The bomber started to dive. Andy was at the pilot's side, watching him wrestle with the controls, doing everything in his power to keep it level. For a few seconds their lives seemed to hang in the balance. Andy's thoughts turned to his girlfriend Jean. She would be in bed, asleep, blissfully unaware of the trouble he was in. Maybe his last letter would be delivered after all.

By a stroke of luck the fire went out, but the engine died with it. With only two out of four working, there was no question of continuing. The flight engineer reported that the fuel tanks were intact. The pilot shouted to the navigator for a reciprocal course. There was nothing for it but to turn back. They would jettison their bombs to lighten their load for the return flight, but a long way short of their target.

There were so many marauding fighters on that long leg that luck was often all that stood between life and death. Leonard Dack, a wireless operator with 106 Squadron, boasted one of the most remarkable tales in a night that was already studded with them. His Lancaster had been struck in the bomb bay. 'The Skipper said, "It's time to get out, everyone." I was a careful sort of bloke and I always kept my parachute underneath my seat. I put it on, but then she went down with all four engines flat out. It went through my mind that it was just like a scene from one of those American films; the aircraft going down, screaming out of control. Once that started, I knew we couldn't get out. I was thrown on top of the navigator and we were rolling about together. I remember my face being pressed against two dials which I remembered were in the roof so I knew we were upside down. I tried to prod the navigator up towards the front to get out of the front hatch. All the time I had the awful thought that we had a Blockbuster on board which went off on impact. I forgot that we wouldn't have survived the impact ourselves.

'Then there was an almighty explosion and I was sent spinning. I thought we had hit the ground but it eventually dawned on me that I was still in the air. Then something whooshed past my face and I was sitting nice and peacefully up in the sky under my parachute. I remember shouting for my wife – I was apologising because I had promised to be home on Saturday.'[59]

Leonard and the flight engineer were the only two of their crew to survive.

★   ★   ★

Rusty Waughman was in the later waves of the stream. The tension mounted inexorably as he flew further into German territory. He was unaware that two crews from his squadron had already gone down, but had no illusions about what lay ahead. He called for silence and asked his gunners to scan the sky for night fighters. Only they were allowed to speak over the intercom.

Before either gunner said a word there were two explosions to their starboard side. Rusty could see ice-blue tracer trails arrowing towards a target and then disappearing, consumed by the explosion they had triggered. It was a new experience for Rusty; he had never seen tracer like that before. 'Usually they were a sort of pinky-scarlet, things which float up towards you then whip past. It was certainly alarming because there was such a mass of it. But in a strange way it was quite spectacular.'

One of his gunners broke the silence. 'Lancaster in trouble on port beam ...'

'There's another one on fire. Jesus, look at that ...'

The intercom was soon crowded with disbelieving voices. Alec the navigator tried his best to note the positions of each fallen aircraft as accurately as possible. Rusty had counted 16, Alec even more. Every fatal hit was relayed across the intercom in astonished detail.

'I don't want to hear any more,' Alec said. 'I can't log them all.'

Everywhere they looked, smoke and fire streamed from shattered fuselages. Some bombers rolled and dived towards the ground. Others just fell from the sky like stones.

As quickly as Ted Manners could jam one frequency broadcasting a running commentary to German fighters, another appeared on his scope. He was doing his best to 'stop a rout from becoming a slaughter'; to give the battered bombers some respite from the relentless attacks. But it was a futile task. The transmissions between the ground and night fighter crews were too powerful, spread across too many frequencies; his disruption was having little effect.

Despite the carnage, Rusty flew on, almost detached from what was happening around him. The aircraft that had gone down were mere machines; he banished the thought that there were men aboard; men like him, dying in their droves. He needed to stay at the helm, concentrate on his job, and hope they made it through a hole in the sky, or that if a fighter locked on to them they would be able to shake it off.

The commentary from his crew had died down now, even though bombers were still being plucked from the sky all around them. As Rusty flew on, almost oblivious, through the trail of destruction, it was finally replaced by a stunned silence.

Alec's voice echoed in the void. 'Two minutes to turning point.'

Almost 60 bombers had been lost during the 220-mile leg from Belgium to the turning point north of Nuremberg – one every minute. There had never been such a concentrated period of devastation in RAF history. There has never been one since.

Ahead of them lay the perils of the bombing run.

CHAPTER 11

The Turning Point

Tony Hiscock

The bombers at the front of the stream reached the end of the long leg at 12.45 a.m. Nuremberg was 75 miles to their south.

Lancaster and Pathfinder pilot Tony Hiscock,[60] with 156 Squadron at Upwood, had been tasked with dropping four red and yellow flares, one 4,000-pound cookie, five 1,000-pounders and one 500-pound bomb. The Pathfinders were due to arrive at the target first, to release their illuminating flares and highlight the area into which the other 'Openers' would drop their target indicators. Tony's role that night was to be a 'Blind Backer-Up' and renew those markers for the main force. They were so far in front of the rest of the stream that his rear gunner had seen only dark skies and tufts of clouds, and no signs of the massacre that others had reported.

Zero Hour remained unchanged; the Pathfinders were still on course. Those behind, however, had been scattered; any notion of a compact stream had been abandoned. Its constituent parts were now strewn across a 50-mile area. While the night fighters were mainly responsible, some crews felt that those back in England were too. It was they who had failed to take heed of the updated winds calculated by 'windfinder' aircraft at the front of the stream. When John Chadderton's navigator learned that the information they were sending back was being ignored, he made his displeasure known. 'Nav to pilot. Group has done it again, Johnny. They're still using the forecast winds; it'll put everybody north of the track.'

As the bombers turned for the target above the snow-blanched Thüringen forest and its ancient mountains, they were met by a canopy of cloud – precisely the opposite of what had been briefed. Cloud cover on the outward journey would have made their trip considerably less perilous, but shrouding Nuremberg it would make accurate bombing almost impossible.

The cloud presented the Pathfinders with an immediate challenge. Their red and yellow target indicators might not be visible through the two miles of thick cloud that cloaked the city. Not all of the Pathfinders had been loaded with skymarkers – flares attached to parachutes, so they hung in the sky when ground visibility was poor – and of those aircraft which had, a number had been blown off course. To compound the problems, some of the parachute flares drifted quickly away from the target.

The 'Openers' had done their best in testing conditions, but their marking, like the whole bomber stream, had been scattered. Behind them, Tony Hiscock and the Backers-Up not only re-marked the target area, but also the flares which had been incorrectly positioned or had drifted eastwards. The confusion grew exponentially for those following.

The Tame Boar tactic – the German night fighters gathering around a beacon for the stream to fly directly into their path 'like the gentlemen guns in a partridge shoot waiting for the coveys to sweep over them'[61] – had wrought havoc on the stream. Now four Wild Boar groups were poised on the ground, waiting to hear which target they would be ordered to defend. Should they be sent north or south of the bomber stream's track?

The Luftwaffe's decision gave the RAF their first and only break of that night – the Wild Boar groups were sent north towards Berlin instead of south to Nuremberg – but it offered little breathing space to the battle-weary Lancasters and Halifaxes of the main stream. The Tame Boar fighters still had enough fuel in their tanks to follow as they turned for the final run to their target – or were able to land, refuel and take off again in search of their quarry.

John Chadderton 'had managed to slip through the deadly gap before the wolves had gathered'. At the turning point for the bombing run their concerns switched focus from the winds to the thick cloud. They managed to find Nuremberg, or somewhere near it, on a course of their own choosing and drop their bombs, but how accurate they had been was anyone's guess. 'I felt the exhilarating twang under my feet as Easy surged upwards, like a tired hunter taking the last fence after a muddy chase. I held the course for 30 seconds for the obligatory photo flash and camera run, both useless tonight, but which one day would earn the crew an aiming point photograph and a 48-hour pass.

'In the middle of a normal raid this always seemed the longest half-minute of my life, with searchlights and flak all around and a hideous inferno below, but here at Nuremberg it was quite unreal: a bit of flak about, the odd skymarker still drifting on a reciprocal underneath us, and the occasional bump of a slipstream passing at 90 degrees to us ... Tongue in cheek,

I asked Jack if he was sure we had bombed Nuremberg, and got the expected forceful reply ...'

Cyril Barton was completing the sharp turn to port that would set them on course for the target. As they banked, he calmly reminded his crew to keep a sharp lookout. A voice shouted over the intercom, but was drowned out by a series of loud bangs that made the whole aircraft shudder. As it dropped into a shallow dive, Freddie Brice thought he saw the shadow of a night fighter swoop over the rear turret.

Cy threw the plane into a corkscrew, while Timber swung his guns back and started to fire blindly as they weaved through the sky. Only one of his guns was working; the other three had frozen.

Freddie saw a Junkers 88 loom on their starboard quarter and called for more evasive action. But the intercom was dead, damaged by enemy fire, so they couldn't hear each other. He reached for the emergency call light.

In training, Cy and his crew had devised their own version of Morse code for this kind of situation. In the darkness of his cockpit, Cy saw the light flicker – the sign for a dive to starboard – and immediately threw the aircraft into a dive. Freddie's guns were out of action, so he concentrated on being a lookout, sending signals as quickly as he could, hoping Timber might still be able to squeeze off a round or two.

As the fighter disappeared, Timber pressed dot-dash-dot – or R – the signal to resume course. A few seconds later it reappeared on their port side; he punched out the instruction to corkscrew, starting with a dive to port. Cy responded as a Messerschmitt 210 joined the fight. Timber watched mutely as its tracer sprayed over their heads. As its shadow flitted to starboard he held his breath, scanning the night. Cy continued to run through his defensive dives and turns. When the fighters had gone, this time Freddie issued the order for his pilot to resume course. The two gunners and their pilot were working in perfect harmony. Cy brought the flailing Halifax level; in the course of the skirmish it had fallen to 9,000 feet.

Once again the Junkers popped into view on their starboard wing. Freddie reached for the call light. As he tapped out the code he could feel and hear rounds thudding into the side of the aircraft.

In Len Lambert's navigator's compartment 'there was a terrific clatter as cannon shells hit the nose of the aircraft' and he saw 'a brilliant display of blue flashes and then flames from the electrical circuits'. His table was riddled with cannon fire. As part of their usual drill, when the bomber had started its approach to the target, it was Len's job to fold up his chair, clip on his parachute and stand poised to open the hatch in case they needed to bale out.

As Cy threw the plane into a corkscrew to shake off the fighters, Len reached for his 'chute and inadvertently pulled the ripcord. He desperately tried to gather in the billowing folds of white silk as the parachute opened. 'However, I managed to clip the main pack on to my harness, holding the rest of the material in my arms. The main escape hatch was directly under the navigator's chart table and it had jammed. It may have been damaged in the attack.'

Because his hands were full, he had to try and prise the hatch open with his foot. What happened next is unclear. 'I don't know whether someone pushed me or whether it was the aircraft, but the next thing I knew I was in mid-air. I didn't jump as such ... But none of this would have happened if we'd had the intercom ... The rule was to count to 10 after leaving the aircraft before pulling the ripcord, to avoid the parachute fouling the tailplane. Clearly I had broken the rule. This is it, I thought, but, thankfully, the main 'chute deployed safely.'

For Len, the roar of the battle had ceased. The only sound was a piece of torn parachute flapping in the wind and the distant drone of aircraft somewhere above him. He gazed at the sinking moon, and the last of the vapour trails. The contrast between the cramped frenzy inside the bomber and the vast silent sky was stark and unnerving. But at least he was safely out. He wondered what had happened to the others on board, but his concern was brief. He needed to concentrate on landing safely; then he would need to cope with being on enemy soil.

In his remote rear turret Freddie Brice wondered what the hell had happened. He had seen the fighters come at them in waves; while sending a succession of messages to Cy he had counted at least four attacks. He knew the plane had been hit. The lights had stopped flashing. Sealed off from the rest of them, he could only guess the damage.

The aircraft started to vibrate and he could see sparks flying past his turret window. They were flying normally but he could see they were low. The silence troubled him. For a few anxious seconds he considered whether he should bale out. 'Not knowing what was happening up front I began to wonder if it was time I jumped, but at the same time I thought Cy would do everything possible to let us all know on the call light if he thought there was no hope of coming through, and if he didn't have time then it would be all over quickly.'

The night fighters had not finished with them yet. 'The mid-upper gunner saw him coming in on the port beam. He gave a series of dots on the call light and we took evasive action to port. Once again the fighter did not get in a burst, and as we weaved around the sky the sparks flying past my rear turret were even thicker. The aircraft was still vibrating badly, but we were still airborne.

'Another attack came from below and once again the fighter scored hits. How long were we going to hold out? We had resumed course once more, the sparks had stopped flying past my turret and the aircraft seemed to have stopped vibrating. Then I saw a fighter coming in above and almost dead astern.

I sent a series of dashes on the call light for evasive action to starboard and over we went.

'The fighter came down behind, down to our starboard quarter. Once again it didn't get a chance to open fire, and as he was breaking away the mid-upper got in a good burst. From the look of his tracer it seemed to head straight for the centre of the fighter's fuselage, but I did not see them actually hit. This was the only burst he fired from our aircraft, and the fighter never came back.'

They were through the worst, but needed to know how severe the damage was to the Halifax from the incessant skirmishing. Cy and his flight engineer Maurice Trousdale made a quick assessment. The starboard inner engine was badly damaged; its vibrations were causing the whole aircraft to tremble. As they flew on, its propeller loosened and flew out into the night 'like an enormous Catherine wheel'. The engine began to spark, but died before it could burst into flames.

Cy and Maurice quickly realised the engine was not their only loss: Len, Jack Kay the wireless operator and their bomb aimer Wally Crate had baled out in the chaos. Their situation was stark: they were an engine light; the plane was beaten up and ailing; they had no intercom, no one to guide them, no one to operate the radio or to release the bombs over the target. They had endured a relentless onslaught of night fighter attacks, and only came through it owing to the skill of their pilot and the reflexes, dedication and co-ordination of his remaining crew. The target area promised more of the same. Should they turn and head home or press on regardless and bomb the target?

Cy was not in doubt. He flew on to Nuremberg.

In their Halifax, Chris Panton and his maverick crew were preparing for their bombing run when cannon rounds streamed past the turret of rear gunner John McLaughlan, setting the starboard inner engine ablaze. A pilot flying second dickie reported the fire, but McLaughlan didn't need telling: the flames were already licking his turret.

Christian Nielsen did all he could; he dived and corkscrewed in the hope that the rushing air might quell the fire. But as he did so the plane lurched into an uncontrollable fall. Nielsen gave the order to abandon aircraft. 'The next thing I knew we were in a spin and heading down fast,' McLaughlan remembered. 'I reached for my parachute in between either being pinned down or thrown from side to side of my turret. I couldn't get the bloody pack clipped on to my harness. I was all thumbs and still being thrown about and burned. Rather than stay there and be roasted, I decided to bale out. I'd practised this many times before but never in a spin. I pulled the ripcord handle and was immediately plucked out of the aircraft. I had not pulled out the connections for my oxygen mask or the heater cords for my gloves and shoes and so smashed my head against the airframe. Down I went, though, covered in blood.'[62]

As he fell clear, an explosion blew Nielsen and Cooper, the wireless operator, out of the side of the fuselage at 15,000 feet. The rest of the crew, including Chris Panton and the second dickie, were still on board the Halifax as it plummeted towards the hills near Bamberg, approximately 20 miles north of their target.

On the ground, the air-raid sirens had sounded and Bamberg's residents scrambled from their beds. They gathered in their shelters, huddled together, wrapped in blankets. Those on fire-watch were the only ones out in the open. Among them was a young man who saw Nielsen's flaming Halifax streaking across the sky like a comet, then disappear from sight near the village where he and his family lived. He abandoned his post and ran all the way home to check whether his loved ones had been harmed. Another eyewitness said: 'I looked into the sky and saw nothing. Then I heard the engine noise of an aircraft.

Suddenly there was an explosion and a fireball spiralled down to earth. Then there was a further explosion as the aircraft hit the ground.'[63]

$\star$ $\star$ $\star$

At the family cottage in Old Bolingbroke, young Fred Panton slept on soundly, but in the small mining village of Ryhope, near Sunderland, the sirens were blaring. Twelve-year-old Alan Mitcheson was bundled out of his bed. Air-raids were nothing unusual; the area was home to shipyards and coal mines, prime targets for the Luftwaffe. Vast barrage balloons bobbed and drifted over their rooftops, and the RAF had installed anti-aircraft guns barely a football pitch away from his back door, and the sound when they fired was both thrilling and deafening.

Alan and his friends used to play war games around the nearby mine, in an area known as The Hope, a steep hill overlooking a ravine. Alan's bedroom window also gave him a view of the North Sea coast, and the chance to watch enemy aircraft approaching. But there was no way his parents would let him do it that night. He wrapped up warm and allowed himself to be shepherded across the damp garden to the Anderson shelter at the bottom of the garden by his mum, dad and sister to wait this one out.[64]

$\star$ $\star$ $\star$

At 12.53 a.m. Sam Harris and his crew reached the end of the long straight leg 120 seconds behind their flight plan. Sam ordered his skipper to alter their course to 177 degrees. The target should have been 19 minutes ahead of them.

'The target is off the starboard bow!' Mac yelled.

Bewildered, Sam started checking his charts. How could his calculations have been so inaccurate? He decided to get up and have a look. Perhaps Mac had been wrong. He looked out of the cockpit: approximately 20 miles to their right he could see bomb explosions on the ground. It didn't make sense. Someone had made a terrible mistake, and he knew it wasn't him. At least he hoped it wasn't.

'That's not the target! It's not the right place,' he told Ken. 'The Pathfinders don't start marking for another nine minutes. Someone has got it wrong. Keep on course.'

'OK, Sam,' Ken replied. 'No panic. We're keeping on 177 ...'

Even though he was confident he'd made the right call, Sam slipped back behind his curtain and pulled the lamp closer to his charts and reckonings. They still appeared to be correct. Why other crews were bombing so far from the target remained a mystery.

The first markers were illuminating the sky in front of them. This had to be Nuremberg. His calculations had been spot on. The bombing run was straight ahead and his job was done for now. Sam went out to see what was happening.

Lying flat out in the nose of the aircraft, Chalky started to pass on the information required to bring them dead on target; it was absolutely crucial that each aircraft dropped its bombs in the same line, and stayed on course to avoid colliding with one another. Chalky checked all the switches on the release panel and gauged the wind velocity before peering through the amber cross of the bombsight at the target indicators, now hanging in the sky below them. All was set.

Ken felt for the bomb jettison switch in case Mac had a problem. He scanned the temperature gauges. Full power might be needed at any time now. The gunners swung their turrets, eyes peeled for any night fighters that might be behind them or lurking beneath. Luff peered out of the navigator's astrodome. Everyone was on alert, looking for the approaching shadow which spelled death.

Chalky called, 'Open the bomb doors.'

Ken pressed the release button. 'Bomb doors open and checked open.'

'Bomb doors checked open visually,' Chalky replied.

They were now within range of the anti-aircraft guns. As they flew through the bursting shells, the air around them seethed with light and sound so loud they could hear it over the vast rumble of the engines. Everyone bar the bomb aimer and the pilot remained silent, holding their breath, willing the plane through the smoke-filled sky, waiting for that moment when their bombs were released and they could turn for home and safety.

'Left, left …' Chalky called. Then, 'R–r–right … Steady … Steady …'

Sam wanted this bit to be over, for them to drop the bombs and get the hell out of there. But he knew Chalky had things under control. 'Bombs away, hold it steady. Jettison bars across. All bombs gone. Close the bomb doors.'

Freed of thousands of pounds of explosive, the Lancaster became an infinitely lighter beast, leaping up and away.

'Bomb jettison buttons pushed. Bomb doors closing,' Ken replied.

'Bomb doors checked closed,' Chalky said. 'Flash bomb has operated; the camera has turned over.'

If the camera had operated successfully there would be photographic proof that they had attacked the target, and of the approximate position the cookie had detonated.

The fire and fury from below and the looming shadows of the night fighters had ramped up the tension in the aircraft during the bombing run to an almost unbearable pitch. Luff now slid round his desk and lifted up the left ear flap of Sam's helmet. 'Thank God that Chalky didn't do a dummy run. I would've shat myself.'

Sam smiled. Their mission had been accomplished. Now all they had to do was get home in one piece. But they knew they were far from safe. The Luftwaffe would still be on the prowl.

CHAPTER 12

The Bombing Run

Ron Butcher (back row, far left), Sutherland crew, 1944

The alarm clock beside Section Officer Patricia Bourne's bed at her quarters in Ludford Magna woke her at 1 a.m. She had a promise to keep. Her boyfriend, Jimmy Batten-Smith, had made a particular request earlier that evening as he handed her his writing case and papers. She now sat up and spent a few moments thinking of him, picturing his face and saying a silent prayer for his safety. Then she went back to sleep.

Over Thüringen Wald, Jimmy's mate Rusty Waughman had made the turn for the last leg of the journey. As they approached the target Rusty was punishingly aware that the endgame was not going to plan. He could see that a number of the markers dropped by the Pathfinders were over the target, but by no means all. 'Many others fell further to the east, in particular over the small town of Lauf ...'

Friedrich Ziegler's farmhouse was in the village of Kleinge-schaidt, not far from Lauf. He had been woken by the drone of hundreds of approaching engines. The farmhouse beds were reserved for the women, while the men and boys slept wherever was cosiest and most comfortable. But as soon as he heard the bombers in the sky Friedrich threw back his blanket alongside the still-warm oven and ran to the shelter in the basement. His heart hammered against the walls of his chest.

The night was bitterly cold, but the air inside the basement was thick with sweat and fear. It was so dark they were unable to see their hands in front of their faces. All 12 of them were crammed into this confined space: Friedrich's mother and father and grandparents alongside the farmhands and French PoWs who chattered away excitedly in a language the young German boy still found bewildering.

They were all wrapped in blankets, perched on suitcases, leaning back against the cold, bare sandstone walls. As the aircraft grew nearer, Lux, the family Rottweiler, started to whine at Friedrich's feet. When the boy heard the unmistakable whistle of falling bombs, a combination of fear and excitement coursed through him. He expected one to blast through the roof any second now and bury them beneath a heap of rubble. He could hear the older ones mumbling prayers in the darkness.

They often heard the British planes overhead and always had to take shelter until they had passed. The war had become a daily part of his and his friends' life – the weekly Hitler Youth meetings never allowed them to forget what the hated British and their bomb-laden planes were doing to their homeland – but Friedrich's village had not been hit before.

That night was different. He heard the Allied aircraft screaming from the sky, and felt the ground shake as they piled into it. If he got out of the cellar alive, Friedrich knew there would be a host of wrecks to explore in the morning. His father seemed to sense what he was thinking. 'Don't go anywhere near them!' he hissed. 'There may be men still alive near them and they might kill you!'

Right at that moment Friedrich had no intention of leaving the safety of the shelter. The bombs had started to fall – and they were not falling on distant Nuremberg; they were falling on his village.

★   ★   ★

Zero Hour had passed and only three aircraft at the front of the main stream had been able to drop their bombs on time. Over the next five minutes only another 33 managed to do so; far fewer than planned.

Rusty and his crew were bang on schedule. Norman, whose job it was to unleash their explosives, relished each second of this phase, but it was the most nerve-racking part of the operation for the rest of the crew. Rusty did what he could to try and keep the plane straight and level through the curtain of exploding flak. From the nose, Norman coaxed his pilot into position. The cloud beneath them formed an impenetrable shield over the city, but Norman's patience was rewarded. Once over the aiming point, he spotted what he believed to be Pathfinder target indicators through a small break in the cumulus and discharged their cargo.

'Bombs gone,' he said. It was exactly 1.17 a.m. As the 4,000-pound bomb left the bay, the aircraft surged upwards. Norman checked his control panel to make sure all the bombs were gone. In the distance, east of the target, a huge explosion lit up the sky. Another bomber had scored a direct hit on an ammunition wagon on a military train *en route* between Nuremberg and Lauf. Exhausted, thankful, and desperate to leave the carnage behind, Rusty turned *A Wing and a Prayer* for home.

Harry, stuck in his turret at the tail end of the bomber, was increasingly concerned. He hadn't yet informed his skipper, but his electrically heated suit had stopped working. The biting wind, accelerated by their own slipstream, was blasting straight through a gap in the Perspex canopy. Because it regularly frosted up or became smeared with dirt and oil, a protective section of the Perspex had been removed from all rear turrets. The gunners' visibility had been improved, but it meant they were exposed to temperatures of minus 30 or 40 degrees and the risk of severe frostbite. Harry didn't complain; it wasn't good form – and anyway, everybody else was too busy to listen to him moaning. He would just have to cope.

Navigator Harry Evans prepared for their bombing run, confident in his calculations; they were on schedule and on the right track. But dense cloud obscured the target indicators and any fires on the ground which might have offered them guidance, so his skipper decided to risk circling the target for a few minutes, searching for a gap.

Harry was feeling the pressure. Have I got this wrong? he kept thinking, even though his charts told him he hadn't. But where the bloody hell was the target? He wondered if the Pathfinders had been wiped out in the bloodbath on the long leg.

They continued to circle the area for 15 minutes, weaving between searchlights and constant bursts of flak, eyes fixed on the sky around them and the swirls of cloud below. They finally spotted a small fire through a break in the cloud and took the decision to bomb that. There was no question of returning home with a full load.

The perils of Nuremberg still lay ahead for Ron Butcher and his Canadian crew. As diminishing fuel forced the Tame Boar fighters to land, Ron felt safe enough to descend to the bombing height they were given at the briefing, but the fluctuating winds meant they were approaching the target more quickly than he had anticipated.

Ron stood up to stretch his legs. He had set their course; there was little else he could do until the return flight. As he made his way down the aircraft, he heard the staccato patter of shrapnel. He rushed back to his station. His seat cushion was nowhere to be seen. A gaping hole had been blasted where his backside had been only seconds before. The shredded cushion lay on the floor to one side. Ron picked up what was left of it, replaced it and tried to focus on his charts.

The numbers danced in front of him. His mind was reeling. Had the flak been fired a few seconds earlier, or had he not got out of his seat when he did ... It didn't bear thinking about. 'Here was the reality of death writ large. The roll of the dice in Bomber Command. A slightly different wind direction, a different choice of movement, a slightly different decision and I'd have been dead. Such were the chances we lived with. I was one of the lucky ones.'

He wasn't the only one with good reason to give thanks to the gods that night. Fred Stetson, a Lancaster rear gunner, was so superstitious that on each operation he draped his turret with more than a dozen St Christopher medals. They had protected him for 24 ops, and been sorely tested during the tumult of the long leg.

Their fuel tank was holed by flak at the beginning of their run over the target. They managed to drop their bombs, but the pilot couldn't prevent the plane weaving from side to side. Then a German night fighter swooped into the attack. 'I tried to swivel my guns. The turret would not work. I could turn it a little to port – not at all to starboard. Luckily the attack was from the port side and I was able to direct a stream of .303s in his general direction. I yelled to the wireless operator for help freeing the turret. The fighter turned away. Was I relieved! But the wireless operator couldn't get the turret working either. I fumbled on the floor, in case there was an obstruction. Guess what? One of those St Christopher medals I was so fond of had fallen during the weaving and jammed between the moving parts of the turret.'[65]

★　　★　　★

In Eschenau, 13-year-old Fritz Fink stood on the mound near his family's farmhouse and watched the sky above Nuremberg start to glow red. The rumble of aircraft above him was broken only by the howl of the bombs and their ear-splitting eruptions on contact. From their vantage point they had been able to watch the whole raid unfold.

First there had been the Pathfinders. They had dropped their skymarkers 'on little parachutes like enormous Christmas trees or multi-coloured cascades'. They burned with such intensity that the surrounding area was bathed in an unearthly yellow light.

Fritz realised something had gone seriously wrong. Nuremburg was on fire in the distance, but the markers were also landing near their village. Some had started to fall close to where they stood; the bombs would soon follow.

'Quick,' Fritz's father said. 'We need to get home.'

The boy felt his stomach turn to water as they stumbled back towards the house. The war had always been close, but never *this* close. They ran to their cellar. Why were the British bombs falling on the fields and villages and not on the distant city?

He and his family cowered in their dank cellar, usually reserved for storing potatoes, and listened to the bombs falling around them. When they hit the ground long cracks appeared in the cellar wall; windows were blown out above them and tiles shaken from the roof. Death was only metres away.

Had the Allied bombs fallen on Nuremberg they would have razed the city to the ground, but they rained down indiscriminately across the whole region, up to 30 kilometres north of their intended target. They were landing on open countryside, small hamlets, rural villages and towns of little strategic or symbolic importance.

★   ★   ★

As they completed their bombing run and swung westwards for the path back to England, Ron Butcher was still in shock.

But he was shaken out of his stupor when one of his crew pointed out a set of target indicators 30 miles to port. Ron felt his stomach lurch. Was the altimeter correct? Was the speed reading right? What else could be wrong? Had they bombed Nuremberg? Or somewhere else? Schweinfurt? He must have voiced his concerns, because a no-nonsense voice on the intercom told him his efforts would be better spent guiding them home, rather than trying to analyse what had already been and gone.

The headwind was almost gale force. The journey back stretched inexorably ahead of them, and the Luftwaffe would lie in wait, determined to pick off any stragglers. But Ron could only focus on the possibility that he had made an error. He reluctantly concluded that after being blown north of the track they had almost certainly bombed Schweinfurt.

They were not alone. Approximately 100 bombers, many of them manned by inexperienced crews, dropped their loads on the unfortunate town. Fifty miles north-west of Nuremberg, Schweinfurt was home to the German ball-bearing industry, but they had no orders to bomb it. Those that did so were at the mercy of the winds, and thankful for the sudden appearance of a large town beneath thinner cloud cover.

There were no Pathfinder markers, but the first crews assumed they had found the target because of the fires on the ground from other aircraft that had dropped their bombs, or were just a little too eager to get rid of their payload and head for home.

Ray Francis and his crew turned for the run on Nuremberg, and aimed for the optimum height from which to release their bombs. They managed to reach 25,000 feet; ahead of them were three distinct blazes. The question was: which should they choose? The bomb aimer elected to go for the middle one. All other voices fell silent as he coaxed the pilot over his chosen target.

Once their bombs had gone they turned for home, the searchlights and the flak behind them. But the drama was far from over.

'Are we diving?' The rear gunner felt the aircraft losing height.

'I've got the instruments in front of me and they don't show it,' the pilot replied. There was a brief pause as he checked again. The outside temperature was minus 40 degrees. The instruments weren't working. 'Hell, we've iced up! Where's the engineer? Where's Ray?'

In the tension of the bomb run Ray's absence had gone unnoticed. He was found lying unconscious and freezing cold on the floor of the fuselage, where he had collapsed earlier after helping the wireless operator. He was so focused on fixing the problem and rescuing his crew-mate that he hadn't noticed that his own oxygen bottle had run critically low.

They hooked him up to the main supply and he slowly regained consciousness. He had pains in his chest, but was otherwise unharmed. As soon as he was *compos mentis* he unhooked himself from the supply and went back to work. Rest would have to come later. They were in the middle of an op and his crew needed him.

George Prince, a flight engineer with 50 Squadron, had let himself relax. As they headed south towards the target, the worst, it seemed, was behind them. He could see flak ahead, but he had been through much worse, and the waves of night fighter attacks seemed to have diminished. Or so he thought. They were halfway between Schweinfurt and Frankfurt when there was a loud bang and the aircraft rolled to starboard.

He glanced out of a side window and saw tendrils of flame snaking from the starboard outer engine. They had soon consumed the whole wing, leaving a trail of smoke in its wake. The aircraft started to lose height and tilted into a gentle right-hand turn. George flicked on the Graviner extinguisher, propelling methyl bromide into the engines – one ounce of which could douse 10 ounces of flaming fuel. But the inferno was too far advanced. They were going down; they needed to bale out while they were still able. The pilot gave the order to abandon the aircraft.

George clipped on his parachute. A day before he had been expecting to go back home on leave. Right now he might have been tucked up in bed in New Malden, after a few pints and a dance with Jocelyn, instead of preparing to jump from a nose-diving bomber over enemy territory.

The bomb aimer battled with the escape hatch, trying to prise it open. George waited impatiently; every second they remained on board brought them closer to impact. He glanced across at the pilot's seat; it was empty. Had he baled out of the canopy escape hatch above it?

Cold air blasted through the cabin; the front escape hatch was open. The bomb aimer tumbled out and George followed, feet first, cutting his face and scraping his leg as he fell, but that hardly concerned him now. Once free of the aircraft he pulled on the ripcord and muttered a small invocation. The 'chute billowed above him. *Oh God, bloody hell!* In his panic he thought he saw a tear in the silk …

The rip was an imaginary one; he was floating down normally, or as normally as one could when one had baled out of a burning bomber at 20,000 feet. He made sure to inflate his Mae West lifejacket; he was a non-swimmer and petrified of landing in a river. The darkness swirled around him. He couldn't even see his plane.

Ron Auckland's Lancaster was north of the target when he first saw searchlight beams like giant fingers arcing across the sky ahead. The flak started to burst around him, pummelling the aircraft. He felt as if it was rolling over a thousand tiny marbles. The acrid stench of cordite was so overpowering that Ron opened the side window to let in some air.

Almost immediately he was caught in a dazzling blue light. The beam was radar-guided; unless he took drastic action it would stick to them like flypaper; it was only a question of time before the rest of the searchlights and the guns below were trained on them and they would be coned.

Eyes tight shut, he reached for the controls that lowered his seat, and he only opened them again once he was beneath the relative shelter of the cockpit coving. He blinked in the glare, but could see enough to throw the Lancaster into a dive. The nose went down and they started to plummet. The engine screamed as their fall gathered momentum. Freezing air from the open window rushed past his ears, making him gasp. Pinned to his seat, Ron did his best to wrench back the controls and bring the plane level, but it was falling too fast and he didn't have the strength.

In a final, desperate act, Ron decided to try the trim control. 'We came back up very nose high and at a low speed. I don't actually know whether we did a loop or a tail slide, or if the nose just flopped forward. All the gyro-operated instruments had toppled, and it was only because there was bright moonlight and because there were a number of searchlights on us that I could see a horizon. I could use that and get some sort of perspective and see which way up we were. I was able to bring the aircraft level. If the searchlights hadn't given me the light to see, then I'm certain we would have gone into a spin and crashed.'

They had managed to haul themselves out of the radar-guided searchlight cone. While the flak still erupted furiously around them, Ron was able to set them on course for the bombing run. He did not yet have the luxury of being able to dwell on the fact that he might have been the first pilot ever to have looped a Lancaster.

The sky over Nuremberg was ablaze with searchlights and flak, and some bombs were hitting the target – but it was a world away from the spectacle of earlier raids. 'There was usually a certain grandeur about the scene with the markers, the flak, the searchlights and the night fighters, even though there was always death and destruction,' as one flight engineer described it. 'But on the Nuremberg do it was eerie. It was as though we had no right to be there. I suppose we hadn't really.'

For the German night fighters, the riches of the previous hour had now become slim pickings. Fritz Lau's ground crew had forgotten to refuel his Me 110. When it was finally ready, he wondered if it was even worth taking off, but decided there was a chance he might intercept the bombers on their return trip. He had been a spectator as the night's action unfolded, watching the night sky turn red when bomber after bomber was struck by his comrades. Eventually he downed a rookie Australian crew with a burst of *Schräge Musik*, and only one man was able to parachute to safety.

Once the night's target had filtered through to the ground radio operators, Lau headed to Nuremberg. Most of his fellow pilots had been forced to land through lack of fuel. As he neared the city he could see the ground fires, but the stream had scattered completely.

'Luck was not with us. It was clear that the bombers, after unloading their bombs, were breaking out of their formation – each pilot taking his own course for England. In those circumstances, they could vary their headings and altitudes at will and this way better avoid us night fighters.'[66] Lau had no option but to return to Langediebach with only one kill to his name.

★   ★   ★

At 1.30 a.m., as Patricia Bourne fell back into a deep slumber at Ludford Magna, Jimmy Batten-Smith's Lancaster dropped its bomb load and headed away from the target area. Almost immediately a German night fighter raked its fuselage with a burst of cannon and machine-gun fire and sent it spinning out of control. It crashed beside the autobahn, six miles east of Nuremberg, killing everyone on board. Jimmy had entrusted the 'last letter' to his parents, to be opened in the event of his death, to Patricia before every mission as a matter of ritual. Now she would have the tragic task of sending it to them.

Adrian Marks's 101 Squadron Lancaster had developed a technical problem which prevented it from gaining altitude at the requisite speed. The crew decided to risk going it alone to and from the target rather than flying below – but at the same pace as – the rest of the stream and 'have the bombs of our own aircraft falling around us and possibly on us'.[67]

In the light of unfolding events, this may well have saved their lives. When they arrived over Nuremberg 25 minutes later than scheduled, 'the city appeared to be on fire in several areas' – but the absence of night fighters and flak allowed them to complete their mission untroubled. After what had appeared to them to have been a trouble-free and routine raid, they were the last crew to bomb the target.

★   ★   ★

Friedrich Ziegler's father emerged from their basement an hour after the last bomb had exploded and the sound of the aircraft engines had faded. An incendiary bomb had landed in the yard, but luckily it had only burnt two-thirds of the way down and had not fully detonated. When he was absolutely sure that the raid was over, he fetched the rest of the family.

Friedrich stumbled outside. The smoke in the air stung the back of his throat as he watched his father, the farmhands and the French PoWs tackle the blaze. Friends and neighbours ran to and fro, trying to help, to the sound of the bells of the approaching fire engines. 'People didn't know what had hit them – quite literally, as some had been splattered by the chemicals in the incendiary devices and showed their yellow wounds. Nobody had a clue what it was.' Fifteen people in Kleingeschaidt had been killed in the raid.

Fritz Fink wandered around in a daze when the all-clear was given. He climbed on to the roof of his house and collected the splinters of flak that had fallen like rain as the city's defences had tried to blow the bombers out of the sky. They would be souvenirs of a memorable night.

★   ★   ★

The bomber crews that had endured and survived the unrelenting danger of the long leg and had turned to brave the flak and searchlights over the target now faced a tortuous journey back to British shores.

CHAPTER 13

Homeward Bound

Cy Barton and what remained of his crew had managed to drop their bombs, though almost certainly on Schweinfurt, and turned their Halifax home. Now the gusting headwinds promised a protracted return journey – with no navigator to guide them, no wireless operator to call for help or obtain a radio fix, no intercom and only three working engines. Cy had no option but to use the North Star as his guide, in combination with his pilot's compass and a small captain's map that he taped to his knee to stop it sliding to the floor.

He increased their height to 13,000 feet and set a course he hoped would take them where they needed to go. In the distance he could see searchlights roaming the sky, but – as he had on the way out – he succeeded in weaving a path between their beams.

His flight engineer was at his side. Maurice Trousdale remained unruffled by the searchlights but troubled by the instruments which told him how their stricken aircraft was coping.

'What shall we do next?' Cy asked. 'Do you think we can make it, or should we head for Switzerland?' They might manage an emergency landing in neutral territory and get home to continue their war.

Maurice said nothing. They had two ruptured fuel tanks and had lost 400 gallons of petrol. There was no way of telling exactly how much fuel remained in the tanks, but he made some hasty calculations. 'We can make it back to England,' he replied. 'But we'll be running on fumes.'

'I think we should go for it,' Cy said. 'But it's only right that we ask Freddie and Timber what they think.'

Their guns were no longer functioning but both men had stayed at their posts, on watch for night fighters. Maurice found Timber, outlined the situation and explained they were three crew short.

'Have we got enough fuel to get back?'

'I think so. We either go back or make a course for Switzerland.'

'What do you think?'

'Cy and I want to carry on for England.'

'Then so do I,' Timber replied.

Freddie Brice stared into the infinite darkness from his immobile rear turret. The call light had stopped flashing, and there was no noise save for the drone of the Halifax's three working engines. 'I now had time to wonder how far we were from home, and how they all were up front. Not being able to speak to anyone was leading me to think all sorts of things about what could have happened. It all seemed so quiet now as we made tracks for home. No one was bothering us; no flak, no searchlights. We were now so low that I remember flying over a wide river and the moon was shining on the mud flats and I could see little huts built on the banks.'

Freddie began to wonder if everyone else had baled out. He was tempted to leave his turret to look, but he resisted the urge. Unless otherwise ordered by his pilot, he needed to stay at his post and keep a lookout for enemy fighters. If they needed to make an exit, he had absolute faith that Cy would find a way to let him know.

There was a knock on his turret doors. He twisted around to open them, and was mightily relieved to see Maurice. 'I asked how they all were up front and he told me that Jack, Len and

Wally were gone. By this I thought he meant they had been killed, so asked no more. He also told me that on the way back Cy had asked him if he would like to try to head home or head for Switzerland, and to go back and ask Harry the mid-upper what he would like to do. They had both decided to try for home, and here we were.'

The moon had now set and the sky was dark – and apparently free of danger. Freddie left his post and clambered gratefully over the main spar. When he reached the cockpit, he tapped Cy on the shoulder, and he was greeted by the familiar boyish smile and a thumbs-up.

'We'll soon be near the English coast,' Cy said. 'With a bit of luck.'

Freddie felt immediately reassured. Cy had that effect on everybody. If Cy thought it was going to be OK, then who was Freddie to doubt him?

Maurice said he was going into the nose to look around, and Freddie went with him. The open escape hatch told its own story. There were no patches of blood to suggest that any of his three crew-mates had been wounded before they baled out.

The wind gusting through the hatch had scattered maps and notepaper across the front section of the aircraft. There was nothing they could do in the nose to alleviate their plight. Nor anywhere else, for that matter – at least as far as Freddie was concerned. They were at the mercy of fate and reliant as ever on the skill of their pilot. On that basis Freddie still fancied their chances. Timber went aft to the navigator's position; Len's desk was peppered with holes, and his maps had been shredded by cannon fire.

Cy had always insisted that his crew should have a working knowledge of each other's roles. Timber had enjoyed some success when playing with the GEE navigation system on the ground, and had a basic understanding of its subtleties, but Len's set, like the radio, had been shattered by incoming fire.

He did all he could to try and get it up and running, but without success. The charts were useless too; they had been damaged beyond all recognition. Timber reported the bad news to Cy.

By now the North Star had disappeared and it was too dark to navigate by sight. Cy started to send Mayday calls in case they were able to transmit but not receive, but there was no hint of a response. Cy took the decision to continue flying; if the engines started to fail, he would ask Maurice if he could change over the tanks, and hope for the best.

But there was no escaping the grim reality of their situation: they were lost, alone and badly damaged.

★　　★　　★

As they flew south of Stuttgart, Sam Harris watched as the other bombers flew directly over the heavily defended city, and offered thanks that he wasn't in one of them. He had tried to avoid the strong headwind by descending to 19,000 feet. It was less gusty at that height. He reckoned it would be around 80 minutes' flying time from the French border to the Channel; plenty long enough for the night fighters to hunt them down.

Mac, the flight engineer, sat up front, watching the instrument panel. Ken had taken a 'wakey-wakey' tablet an hour before the target, as usual, to make sure he was as alert as possible for the 'business end' of the flight. The snag was that when it wore off during the return he had a tendency to fall asleep with the plane on auto-pilot. Mac was there to keep an eye on things and wake him up if they got into difficulties.

At his desk, Sam had his work cut out. Before take-off they had hatched a plan to make their own way back, steering clear of the most heavily defended areas, and away from the bomber stream. They were banking on the German night fighters being more likely to follow the crowd. The problem was that his Squadron Navigation Officer was an irascible martinet – not the sort to look kindly on an underling stepping outside well-defined orders and acting on his own initiative. Whenever they returned from an op, he went through their logs with a brutal, uncompromising eye, writing caustic comments in red pencil whenever he spotted sloppy calculations or errors. Sam needed to 'fiddle' his log so it appeared to show they took the route they were given at briefing, while simultaneously making sure their aircraft followed the alternative course he and his crew had agreed.

It was now 3.30 a.m. Sam had been awake for the best part of 22 hours; this was a real test of his skill and concentration. He had hoped the GEE box might give him a fix, but he wasn't able to make sense of the signals. 'It was like looking in knee-high grass for three-inch blades.' Finally, he found what he was searching for, and was able to fix their position with the necessary accuracy. They were on the right track; there was no need to change course.

★   ★   ★

Luftwaffe pilot Martin Becker had landed near Mainz to refuel and take on fresh ammunition. While he was there, he learned that there were Allied bombers returning to England on a route between Stuttgart and Mannheim. Once in the air, a ground control operator directed him to the nearest available target. 'You should see him now!' the officer yelled, and gave him the order to attack. *'Pauke machen! Pauke machen!'*

Becker was less excitable than his earthbound guide. He picked up the bomber – a Halifax from 429 Squadron – and eased calmly into position beneath it.

The first hint of Becker's presence to anyone on board came when their plane was ignited by cannon fire. The bomb aimer saw the twin-engine fighter passing their wing tip. 'It was so near that I almost could have reached out and shaken hands with its pilot.'[68]

The pilot managed to keep the flaming Halifax level long

While still lying down, he could feel that his neck and back had been injured on impact. He tried to stand up, but his right leg collapsed. He felt a searing pain, so strong it almost made him pass out. Looking down, he could see from the awful way his leg kinked above the ankle that it was definitely broken. The shock and the pain caused him to lose consciousness once more.

★   ★   ★

Len Lambert's landing, after he baled from Cy Barton's damaged Halifax, was softer than Dick Starkey's, even though he hit the ground at a 'terrific' rate. He was winded, but no more than that. He took off his parachute and Mae West and buried them beneath a bush.

Len tried to work out what his next move should be. He needed to get rid of any clothing that might identify him as an RAF airman. Off went his heated flying suit, then he used his penknife to slice off the tops of his flying boots so they would look more like normal shoes. He would be much colder, but less recognisable.

His best option, he decided, was to head for the Swiss border. He set off, armed only with a silk handkerchief escape map, sorely lacking in detail, and a miniature compass from his survival kit, which also contained chocolate, Horlicks tablets, a tube of condensed milk, a rubber water bag and water purifying tablets.

Initially he made good progress. He found a main road to follow. When a motorbike passed he ducked for cover behind a hedge. The distant bark of a dog and the faint chimes of a church clock indicated life nearby. He reached the outskirts of a small village and decided to skirt around it.

He soon found himself in thick woods, split by streams and difficult to pass. Finally he came across a rough track that led him though more woodland. As he forced his way through high grass and thickets which tugged at his clothing, then staggered up a steep hill, the Swiss border seemed impossibly far away.

At the first watery signs of dawn, he knew he needed to hide and rest.

★　　★　　★

Roger Coverley had jumped from his flaming Halifax and floated serenely down to the earth – until he collided with a tree-top. Thick branches scratched his face and bruised and battered his body as he tumbled through them. Then he came to a sudden stop, and was left dangling in the darkness. He couldn't see how far he was from the ground. What should he do? He could be 20 or 30 feet up; far enough to do himself some serious damage. But he could hardly just hang there until the Germans found him. He took a deep breath, reached for the release harness and braced himself for the fall.

He fell 10 inches on to German soil.

Roger looked up. The parachute was spread out above him, a beacon in the darkness 'like a bloody great umbrella giving a big signal where I was'. He needed to get as far away from it as he could, and as quickly as possible. He was no longer Roger Coverley, veteran pilot, carving his way through the air towards prime German targets; he had no crew, and he had no plane. He was on his own, deep in enemy territory, and it was his duty to try and find his way back to safety.

Every crew had been sent on escape and evasion courses as part of their training, but not everyone paid close attention. Some airmen didn't want to contemplate worst-case scenarios, in the same way that some didn't want to know their identity tag was made of asbestos so it wouldn't perish if they burned to death. Roger was one of the ones who had listened, and he was determined to put his training to good use.

They had been instructed to travel at night and hide by day, so he knew he had to start walking immediately. He found his way to a railway track and followed it to the mouth of a tunnel. Depending on its length, its cover would allow him to make valuable progress by day. Before stepping inside, he looked back. Strips of silver Window decorated the trees like tinsel, and the earth around them was littered with Allied propaganda leaflets. I won't have a problem finding something to read, he thought to himself.

★ ★ ★

As those on the ground adjusted to life on the run, in the skies above them, from Stuttgart to Strasbourg, on to Metz and north of Paris, the surviving bombers crawled back towards the Channel. The weather had worsened; the clear skies had given way to sleet and rainstorms. Australian Pilot Officer J.A. Forrest was keeping his Lancaster steady at 4,000 feet when the adverse conditions forced him to shift his track eastwards and climb to avoid the turbulence. A bolt of lightning hit the nose of the aircraft and danced along the fuselage.

Momentarily blinded, Forrest was unable to see his instruments. In a sudden fit of panic he believed his aircraft was mortally damaged and going down. He bellowed over the intercom for his crew to bale out. The mid-upper gunner and wireless operator were unaffected by the lightning strike and complied immediately. The rest of them were too stunned to respond and remained at their posts. Forrest regained his vision in time to bring the diving plane level. He checked their altitude and the state of their engines: they were fine. They would be able to make an emergency landing in England.

Only then did Forrest realise that, in the confusion following the lightning strike, they had been flying over the Channel. His two crew-mates must have landed in the water; given its temperature, they would have had no chance of survival. Both men were never found.[70]

★   ★   ★

Sam Harris and his crew had managed to edge their way to the French coast without incident, and at 4.12 a.m. they were over English soil. They skirted the anti-aircraft guns that ringed London, in case any of their crews were feeling trigger-happy. Three minutes later they started the slow descent to their base at Elsham Wolds. In the distance they saw the beacon which flashed their airfield's code signal to the returning aircraft.

At 5.05 a.m., an hour ahead of schedule, Ken asked for permission to land. There was no sign of life in the darkness below them. Nothing stirred. There was a brief delay as they circled the airfield; he had to convince the startled air control officer that this was one of their planes returning. The flurry of familiar voices failed to dispel the tension; it was not uncommon for opportunistic German night fighters to shoot down bombers as they flew in to land.

The runway lights were switched on, the paraffin flares ignited.

Ken started his approach. 'Undercarriage down ...'

'Undercarriage selected down. Two red lights. Lights out,' Mac replied. 'Undercarriage down and locked down.'

The tyres squealed as they kissed the tarmac. There was a bump and a bounce and a roar of brakes as the bomber staggered to a halt. They were back; exhausted, but still alive.

As they climbed unsteadily from G-George, their delighted ground crew were there to greet them. Ken asked if anyone else had returned.

'No, you're the first ones back,' they were told.

Sam didn't know what to think. Where were the others?

They lit cigarettes, hands cupped around the flame to protect it from the wind, inhaling the sweet smoke in the misty pre-dawn light. Ken gave his thanks to the ground crew. It had been a terrible raid; the old plane had been the only reliable part of it. She had seen them through yet another mission, their toughest yet, and brought them safely home.

Across eastern England weary crews and wounded aircraft prepared for their descent. Squadron Leader 'Turkey' Laird of 427 Squadron was warned by his navigator that they were off course and asked for a turn to port. The alteration was a minor one, but enough to bring them into the path of another Lancaster.

'What the hell!' Laird's cry echoed in rear gunner John Moffat's intercom, but it was too late. The other incoming aircraft struck the top of theirs with a world-shaking crash. Everyone apart from John was killed instantly. He was able to parachute to safety because he was facing away from the impact and had been protected by his turret. 'I saw the Lancaster off to my left; he just seemed to nose down. There was no fire.'

The navigators of both aircraft were from the same town in Canada, Saskatoon. After everything that had been thrown at them in the last few hours, there can have been few men more unfortunate than these. Collisions took place in crowded skies, during take-off and landing, or during a bombing run. Rarely did they happen in open skies.

But this was the night when everything had conspired against the men of the Bomber Command.

★   ★   ★

Dick Starkey came to once more; the moon was lower, a fading orb on the horizon. He lay there wondering what to do next. He couldn't walk, and couldn't bear to just lie and wait until he was found.

Racked with pain, with little idea of his precise location, his mind churned with a host of conflicting emotions. Only a few hours before he had been laughing and joking with his friends on base; now many of them were heading home from

Nuremberg whilst he was marooned behind enemy lines, unable to move and in real danger of freezing to death. 'I was in shock. I was in enemy territory and I was scared and unsure of what was going to happen. I didn't know if I was going to survive or not. This made me sad and frightened. But I was also relieved that my war in the skies was now over.'

He heard German voices on the wind and, given the state of his leg, he resigned himself to capture. As they drew nearer, he saw the sweep and flicker of torchlight. He cried out; the beam swung in his direction. A group of men converged on him and the light was shone directly in his face.

One of the younger Germans started to shout and pulled back his rifle butt, as if poised to smash Dick in the head, but he was stopped by one of the older ones. They wrapped the injured airman in his parachute, lifted him on to a stretcher and carried him to a horse-drawn cart.

The cart was driven with agonising slowness along a dirt track. Every protrusion and pothole reverberated along his broken leg. Above him the skies had fallen silent; the bombers would be almost home, a place that seemed impossibly distant now. He was increasingly haunted by the lesson of his escape and evasion course: more important than the skills they might use to avoid capture was their conduct if they were captured. The message was drummed into them: don't let the side down and blurt out everything you know. Instead, give only name, rank and number; nothing else.

They finally pulled up outside a small brick building – the office of the *Bürgermeister*, the local mayor. Dick was carried up the stone steps and his stretcher was laid none too carefully on the floor.

A policeman asked for a volunteer to keep watch on their prisoner. The man chosen was a veteran who had been invalided out of the German army after losing an arm on the Eastern Front.

Those early-morning hours were as long as any Dick had lived through. The pain from his neck, back and smashed, misshapen ankle was relentless. He hoped a doctor might come with medication to help ease his misery, but the only visitors were a stream of curious and excited locals, sometimes whole families with children, who had come to see the exotic enemy flier who had dropped so suddenly from the skies.

The women clucked their tongues and gave him sympathetic glances as he lay wincing on the floor. Dick wondered what was going through their minds. 'It's almost as though you're an alien, or in a zoo or something like that. They came from miles around to have a look at this guy who'd landed in their midst. They'd been told all their propaganda: we were *Terror Flieger*, terror fliers, who were getting paid bonuses to kill them; and here was the reality: me – a frightened young lad.'

One man came in brandishing a bloody flying boot, inscribed with the name of one of Dick's crew. He tried to ask if they had found the man to whom it belonged. Eventually he made himself understood.

'*Kaput*,' came the reply.

In his discomfort, he had only been able to worry about himself. Now he wondered how many of the others had made it out alive. And perhaps the most agonising thought of all: we were all meant to miss this op and were only put on the battle order because we insisted on it.

CHAPTER 14

A Terrible Dawn

Harry Evans

After watching his crews depart, Eric Howell had slept fitfully in the back of the dispersal hut. 31 March 1944 was his 23rd birthday, but all he asked for was the safe arrival of the 15 aircraft that had left Dunholme Lodge the night before.

At 5.30 a.m. he was woken by the duty NCO; the returning bombers were flying a circuit above the airfield. He rubbed the sleep from his eyes and waited for the call confirming that his new Lancaster, C-Charlie, flown by Pilot Officer Charlesworth, was on its way in.

For the ground crews the vigil was over. When the phone rang in their hut to let them know their aircraft was on its way in, they grabbed their torches and headed out into the dawn gloom. Red, green and white navigation lights did battle with flashes of torchlight, and the air was filled with the roar of idling engines as the bombers taxied to a halt. Once the chocks had been put in place and the weary crews had disembarked, there was a chance to ask them if there had been any snags. That morning they knew it had been a bad one; the fatigue was etched on their faces.

In his hut Eric Howell watched an hour crawl by. There was still no news of C-Charlie. Eric went outside, hoping to see a dot in the grey sky and the blink of navigation lights, or to hear the sound of distant engines. One by one, 10 other Lancasters landed, taxied on to the hard standing and shut down their engines. The silence that followed seemed like a reproach.

He knew then that his aircraft was not coming home; neither were four others from the squadron. Eric was beside himself. 'My stomach was knotted. It wasn't just the loss of a single aircraft; it was the loss of so many of them! When a ground crew lost an aircraft, a little niggle of conscience invaded the mind and made you all the more determined to do a better job of servicing.'[71]

Eric trudged disconsolately across to the mess with the other ground crew whose planes were missing. C-Charlie was the fourth of his bombers to go down in the past three months; he knew the guilt and sadness would burden him for months to come.

Sam Harris and his crew had been amongst the first to return. They climbed aboard the truck which would take them to the debriefing room. This was normally a time of relief and laughter, a time to enjoy a coffee laced with rum as other crews arrived and the intelligence officers and flight commanders made a note of all that they had seen and done; a time to swap stories and jokes and pats on the back.

That morning was different. There was no light relief. Few of them spoke; each dwelt on his own thoughts; each tried to absorb and process what they had experienced that night.

Ken, Sam's pilot, leaned back in his seat and lit a cigarette. The Station Commander asked if he had seen many losses. Ken tilted his head back and exhaled. The smoke hung over them like a pall. It was a few seconds before he spoke.

'I think there were tremendous losses tonight.'

Sam raised an eyebrow. To maintain their morale whilst they were still in the air Ken had blamed the carnage on 'Scarecrows', the mythical shells the Germans fired that were rumoured to mimic the appearance of exploding aircraft. But here on the ground he was not going to varnish the truth.

★ ★ ★

As their Lancaster stuttered across Europe, Andy Wiseman clutched the lucky doll given to him by his girlfriend Jean. They managed to clear enemy territory without incident, but as they crossed the Channel the bomber started to falter. His pilot knew they wouldn't be able to make it back to Leconfield. They needed somewhere else to land, and quickly.

The wireless operator broadcast their distress, and a searchlight beam appeared to indicate the path to their nearest airfield, a US base in the south of England. 'That beam was a lovely sight. It was almost like a saviour – there's somebody down there who knows we're up here and in trouble.'

As they came down through the thick cloud, Andy could see the distant flicker of the paraffin lamps marking the runway. It was not home, but it was a very welcome sight.

Their pilot brought them in slowly and steadily. As they neared the ground, Andy could see fire engines and ambulances gathering beside the runway. He braced himself. There was a small bump as they touched down, but that was all. The landing was perfect. Andy uncurled his fingers from around the doll. They had needed every ounce of her help that night.

The emergency vehicles swarmed around them as they came to a halt. Even though none of them was injured, they were helped off the aircraft and taken to the mess for a much-needed beer and breakfast. But the hospitality ended there. Looking like zombies, still in their helmets and flying suits and clutching their parachutes, they were issued with railway vouchers for the journey back to their base – third class.

★　★　★

On board B-Beer, heading for 622 Squadron in Mildenhall, Ray Francis had every excuse to rest after passing out earlier. But the aircraft had developed a fault in the pneumatic line that served the brakes, and only he was capable of fixing it; without his expertise they would have had to head for the emergency airfield at Woodbridge.

Only 40 miles from Mildenhall, Woodbridge boasted specialist rescue and medical teams and a three-mile runway to give damaged aircraft room to stop, but it was known as 'the graveyard of many bombers who had crash-landed there' – and every man on board was desperate to sleep in his own bed after the debrief.

Ray made his way woozily back up front. He had lost his pliers when they were corkscrewing to escape the swarms of night fighters, but he was determined to do what he could. The ruptured line was under the pilot's seat. As Ray crouched beneath his skipper, his pullover started to feel warmer than usual – then damp and cold. He looked up, wondering what the hell was happening, but only for a moment. This has not been my night, he thought. The pilot had decided to relieve himself into a contraption they called the Pissophone, and the bottom end of the hose had come loose.

★　★　★

Rusty Waughman and his crew, lightened of their bomb load, made good progress back to the UK. The night fighters were still patrolling the sky, but Ted could tell from the

German controllers' broadcasts that the frequency of their attacks was diminishing.

As they approached the English coast, Rusty fired up the VHF radio to let their ack-ack batteries know they were coming in. Despite their relief, no one felt like giving voice to their usual homecoming rendition of 'Coming Home on a Wing and a Prayer'. The op had been too traumatic to allow the luxury of celebration.

Despite Rusty's broadcast, they were misidentified as they flew closer to London and flak shells started to erupt around their aircraft. They were plunged back into the kind of nightmare they had somehow survived four hours earlier. But no damage was done and they started their descent towards Ludford Magna.

They circled the airfield with four other bombers before coming in to land. Rusty eased back on the throttle as they touched down and then guided *A Wing and a Prayer* to dispersal. The crew climbed out and lit their cigarettes. Only then did they realise that Harry the rear gunner was missing. A flicker of alarm swept through them as they ran to his turret.

Harry was still in position, but unable to move or speak. He was frozen in place. Literally. His face was badly frostbitten. Where the spittle had drained from his mouth, an icicle as thick as a wrist hung below his mask, from his lip to his lap. Two of the crew helped him out of the plane. There would be no ops for him for a while.

The crew bus appeared. While Harry went away to thaw out, the discussion in the debriefing room focused on the night's losses; Rusty and his crew spoke of the massacre, of the scores of planes they had watched being blasted from the sky. When asked how many, they estimated as many as 100. The intelligence officers snorted in disbelief.

Though the intelligence officers continued to dismiss their 'wild' guesses, Rusty and his crew refused to back down. Rusty felt increasingly exasperated; while these men had been warm and safe back in England, he and his companions had been in the thick of it. They were adamant that there had been terrible losses; the intelligence team remained adamant that the airmen were mistaken.

The atmosphere grew sour and antagonistic. Rusty had never experienced this before. He was relieved when the debrief was over.

★   ★   ★

For Ron Butcher's crew and the other stragglers, the stiff head-wind made the journey back to England feel interminable. At times the coast appeared to be getting further away rather than closer. The leg from the target area to Dieppe took more than four hours.

They reached the English coast shortly after dawn. As they came in to land, Ron wondered which other crews from his squadron had made it back. He knew their losses had been catastrophic.

Habitually as thorough as possible in debriefing, he was less forthcoming that morning. He was still uncertain about the precise location of their bombing run, and wanted to revisit his charts and logs before deciding exactly where they had ended up, what had happened, and why.

As it turned out, his questioners didn't notice his reticence. 'Goodness knows, there were lots of other activities to describe – such as aircraft taking a direct hit in the bomb bay, exploding into balls of white and orange, falling quickly to earth without the appearance of parachutes.'

★   ★   ★

Phew, thank God we're home, Chick Chandler thought as his Lancaster touched down at Mildenhall. We got away with another one ...

His 14th operation was done and dusted; only 16 more to go. In the briefing, he was glad of the shot of rum in his cocoa.

'How many were lost?' he was asked.

'Forty. Possibly fifty.'

A conservative estimate, but the officers present still exchanged anxious looks. 'Are you sure?'

Chick nodded. He could see they didn't believe him, but he wasn't going to worry too much. It wouldn't change anything. There would still be another operation just around the corner. All he wanted to do right now was get into bed and go to sleep.

Les Cromarty, a rear gunner with 61 Squadron, was back half an hour later than they had envisaged because of the headwinds. As they approached their base in Coningsby, they identified themselves to those on the ground and waited to be given a landing number. 'We expected to get at least 15 or 16 and be stacked, but instead we got Number One ... We just couldn't believe it, so we called again, but got the same reply. We were in fact the first to land, shortly after an aircraft from 619 Squadron crashed off the end of the runway. One or two more aircraft landed, but I think most of the others landed at other airfields.'

Three of the 12 crews that set out from Coningsby the previous night had been lost. Among them was an Australian friend of Les's, a mid-upper named Harold Pronger. Some of his crew had baled out over the North Sea and Les wanted to go straight out on a search. He was told firmly that it would not be worth it; the water temperature was so low that no one could have survived in it for more than an hour. The men would be dead. 'I think the worst thing about those raids was losing one's friends. After a while you just became hardened to it, but eventually you stopped making close friends with anyone outside your own crew.'[72]

Harry Evans, a navigator with 550 Squadron, sat with his crew in their debriefing room, unable to banish the horrific images of the raid from his mind. Bled of all colour, the skin on their faces was still etched by the outline of their oxygen masks. When they had lost crews during previous raids the cloud cover had often shrouded the course of events. This time it had played out in vivid detail before their very eyes. The debriefing officers offered them cigarettes, hot sweet tea, even a tot of rum, but Harry and the lads were not in the mood.

'We saw a lot of aircraft go down,' his pilot said.

'How many?'

'No idea. A lot.'

'How would you describe the trip?'

'A shaky do!'

It was a brief moment of levity.

'Do you know how many we lost in total last night?' someone asked.

'Too early to say,' came the reply, but everyone knew it had been a bad one.

That message was already seeping through to the upper echelons of Bomber Command. The Pathfinder chief, Air Vice Marshal Donald Bennett, had voiced opposition to the route the day before. Now he was waiting in the debriefing room at Graveley for the first of his crews to return.

The first through the door was Wing Commander Pat Daniels, a skilled pilot who had accompanied one of the new Pathfinder crews. His experience had saved them; he had taken their aircraft higher, way above their usual height, using every inch of sky to avoid the worst of the night fighter activity. When he saw Bennett, his customarily affable demeanour melted away. 'Bloody hell!' he bellowed. 'Why did we have to go *that* way?'[73]

Bennett knew Daniels well and calmly asked why he was so animated. Daniels refused to be pacified. He told Bennett that in 76 previous operations he had never seen losses on this scale.

The chief's initial assumption was that Daniels must be exaggerating. But he knew he was not prone to hyperbole.

He began to worry that his fears of the previous morning had been realised.

Daniels gave him the headlines: the moonlight, the condensation trails, the sparse cloud on the way out, the thick cloud over the target, and the swarm of night fighters which had wreaked havoc on the stream.

His normally brisk and resolute superior said little, but he was clearly shaken by Daniels's account.

★   ★   ★

As the last few bombers landed at their bases that morning, Cy Barton's crew was one of the many still unaccounted for. His Halifax had become lost somewhere over mainland Europe. As they flew on through the darkness, unable to see any landmarks below, those left on board tried frantically to calculate their position.

The searchlights they had evaded earlier had been near Frankfurt; since then they had travelled due west. Someone suggested there was a chance they would fly over the English Channel and out into the Atlantic unless they altered course. Unaware that the safety of the emergency airfield at Woodbridge lay only 20 minutes ahead of them, Cy decided to follow a more northerly route to make sure they crossed British soil.

Timber saw a faint glimmer of blue below. If they were convoy lights attached to a ship's stern, it meant they were flying over water. But where? The Atlantic, the English Channel or the North Sea?

Cy turned back on to a westerly heading. A watery grey dawn started to break, much to their relief; they would soon be able to see more. Through the gloaming they saw a Beaufighter flying past. They flashed an SOS signal with a torch, but it showed no sign of acknowledgement. The flicker of hope faded and they were alone in the darkness once more.

Freddie Brice, the rear gunner, mouthed a silent prayer for their safe return. He turned to look at Cy. Once again he got the thumbs-up and a broad grin. His anxiety eased.

Eyes straining through the Perspex canopy, they were finally able to make out the vast silhouettes of barrage balloons outlined against the dawn sky. Though they now had no working wireless or intercom, they began to hear the distinctive 'squeaker' radio noise the balloons emitted to warn Allied aircraft of their presence.

As Cy skirted around them, they heard the familiar boom of anti-aircraft fire resounding through the sky. Shells started to explode around them. *We're being fired at by our own defences!* Freddie could not believe it. They had been chased and harried by enemy fighters, avoided the glare of enemy searchlights, been targeted by enemy flak and managed to navigate their way across Europe by their wits – only to be fired at by their own side.

Cy immediately banked the bomber and flew back out to sea. Timber crawled into the nose, wired up the Aldis lamp and started sending out frantic SOS signals to those firing at them from the ground. The guns fell silent. Freddie again looked to his skipper for reassurance. 'We cruised in over the coastline. I was standing beside Cy and he was grinning all over his face and giving the thumbs-up. Then he shouted to me to go back and tell the engineer to change tanks. He must have noticed a failing in the engines.'

Maurice was at the main spar, standing over the tank selector cocks. He knew he had to work swiftly. He switched the tanks. The air was filled with the pungent odour of aviation fuel. The damage they had suffered during the endless night fighter attacks had caused the fuel to run out of the engine rather than into it. The tanks were empty. The aircraft was running dry.

Freddie was clambering back to the cockpit when he met Timber heading the other way. 'Crash positions!' he shouted.

Cyril had decided to put his faith in luck and the Lord, and try to land the plane wherever he could.

★   ★   ★

Twelve-year-old Alan Mitcheson was tucked up in his bed in Ryhope, on the Durham coast, after leaving the family's Anderson shelter at 5.30 a.m. He had turned down the offer of a cup of tea from his mum because he needed to be up for school in only a few hours. As he drifted off, he was jolted awake once more by the sound of a bomber in the sky.

Like many of his contemporaries, he had learned to distinguish between the sounds of the RAF and enemy bombers. This is definitely one of ours, he thought. But that didn't stop the anti-aircraft guns firing off a deafening burst. That's strange; guns firing *after* the all-clear had gone. He went to his bedroom window in time to see the roundels of a four-engine British bomber overhead. He watched it bank and disappear into the distance.

Les Lawther usually finished his night shift at the colliery at five, but that morning it was his turn to check the water pump in the yard. To reach it, he needed to be lowered by the engine operator, who didn't start work until seven, so he ambled down to the spotter's shed, a cabin built for watching aircraft, which was manned 24 hours a day.

Jack Coxon was on duty. He and Les chatted for a while, then he wrapped himself up against the nagging east wind and went out for a smoke. That was when he first saw the crippled bomber coming in over the sea.

Jack raised his binoculars. 'She's one of ours,' he called.

Les could tell that the Halifax's propellers were only working on one side, which must have been why the pilot was flying low. Someone on board was flashing a light – some kind of signal, he assumed. Then just before it reached land, the bomber turned and headed away from them.[74]

Alan Mitcheson had climbed back into bed when he heard the bomber return. Except now it sounded different, wounded, as if the engines were failing. He dashed back to the window. He knew it was the same aircraft, a Halifax, and that it was struggling to stay airborne. It was flying directly towards him, its lights piercing the early-morning gloom. The engines were starting to splutter, like the sound of a car misfiring. With every second it was getting lower and lower. There was no way it would be able to stay in the sky much longer.

On board, Cy remained at the helm. Maurice, Fred and Timber sat with their backs to the cold, vibrating metal of the rear spar, hands behind their heads, leaning forward, bracing themselves for the impact.

Alan Mitcheson watched as the Halifax flew in, no more than 100 feet above his house. He hurtled to his parents' bedroom as the plane flew directly overhead and watched from their window as it appeared to bank to its left, trying to avoid the houses across the street. And then there was 'a noise like thunder'.

Les Lawther hadn't been able to move a muscle as the bomber strained to remain clear of the pewter-grey swirl of the sea. He watched, open-mouthed, as it stumbled towards the hulking gantry at the pithead. He could see the pilot fighting every inch of the way, nursing the starving engine as it went through its death throes. 'I contend he saw the headgear, because he was very low, and naturally he tried to avoid it. But he was too near to get round and his wing just caught the end house on West Terrace and the plane just tumbled ... If he went the other way, he would have hit the house on Hollycarr Terrace.'

Seventeen-year-old Arthur Milburn was out in his back yard when he heard the whine of the dying aircraft. As soon as he saw it heading his way he fled towards the cover of the doorway, fearing it was an enemy bomber. 'I saw it going down between the houses of Hollycarr Terrace and Powell Terrace, catching the houses on each side with its wings, then eventually hitting the end house of West Terrace ... I heard an almighty crash; there was no fire or explosions, just the crash and rumble of buildings being demolished.'

Tom Richardson lived in the end-of-terrace house on West Terrace with his mum, dad and younger brother. He was on the front step when he heard the sound of rushing wind. As it grew louder, he dived instinctively for cover. Seconds later there was an almighty crash, the agonising shriek of tortured metal and stone, and the air filled with dust.

His younger brother Ken had gone inside with their mother. She was putting the kettle on the fire when the plane hit; he had been standing next to the fireplace. The impact tossed them both into the corner next to the window. Rubble cascaded down around them. The next few seconds seemed to last an eternity.

Coughing and choking, Ken hauled himself to his feet. His mum cried out from somewhere beside him. His scrabbling hand found hers. As the dust started to clear, he began to realise that the only wall of their house still standing was the one they had been thrown against. His mother thrust him through the smashed window into the arms of a group of men who had sprinted to the crash site. 'Then two of them walked round and had to prise her fingers off the windowsill. She wouldn't leave go.'

Tom got up, brushed the debris off his neck and shoulders, and squinted through the dust cloud. The door he had been standing by, the step he had been standing on, were no longer there; in fact the whole front of his home had disappeared. Two bedrooms had been demolished; iron bedsteads hung out of the side of the building.

The wreckage seemed to be strewn as far as the eye could see. An engine steamed gently in the Richardsons' garden;

the wings were nearby, cast aside like driftwood. Much of the body of the plane had careered into the colliery yard; some had settled on the hillside leading up to the chalk-faced ravine above the railway track.

Men from all around the village converged on the ruined Halifax. Alan Mitcheson prepared to follow them, desperate to see what had happened, but he was ordered back to bed. He lay there, wide awake, vibrating with tension, hearing the sound of excited voices in the gardens below, wondering what had happened to the men on board the bomber.

Les Lawther sprinted from the spotter's shed as soon as he saw the crash. He found the rear fuselage lying almost upright, across a gangway and a mud heap. The wings had been severed; there were only a series of gaping holes where they and the rest of the plane should have been. The bomber's signature code, LK 797, and mark, LK-E, were clearly visible alongside its distinctive roundel. The shell was remarkably intact. He looked through the nearest hole and saw three prone figures.

As the plane had come down, Freddie Brice felt a bump, a lurch to starboard and port and a blue flash. Then silence.

He sensed a pathway opening up before him. Where was he? He felt as if someone was coming to lead him along the path. Then, in the distance, he heard a voice calling for help. The path vanished. There was another voice too. It all came back to him then: Cy up front; he, Timber and Maurice assuming crash positions, and then the bang and the lurch and the mind-numbing force of the crash. He started to cry out too. He became conscious of grimy faces looking down at him. He raised his hands and felt the firm grip of his rescuers.

'How many were in the aircraft?' a gruff voice asked as soon as he was eased out of the wreckage.

'Four …' He turned to point to the aircraft's nose, where Cy would be. It wasn't there. Nor were the wings or the engines.

There was only one half of the fuselage, where the three of them had miraculously survived.

Les helped the other two out, one by one, and then told the driver to get the colliery ambulance out of its shed. 'The crew were in shock. All they said to me was "Get the pilot ..." I got back in again. I knew where the pilot would sit, but the front end was missing. There were some men on the gangway then and I said, "Will you have a look in the gardens to see if you can see the pilot?"'

The men reported back. The nose was at the top of the ravine, above the railway track, an area of land the local kids called The Hope. Someone said the pilot might have fallen down it. Les rounded up a group and headed to the scene.

CHAPTER 15

Disaster

The wreckage of Cyril Barton's Halifax

Through the soft grey light of dawn, Fritz Fink, his family and their neighbours surveyed the damage to their house, their village and those nearby. Pettensiedel had been hit hardest. A bomb had landed at its centre, obliterating four residential houses and damaging several others. The villagers started digging through the rubble. They found six bodies.

In Nuremberg itself 75 civilians had been killed, most of them in an apartment building that suffered a direct hit, and a further 100 or so had been injured. The archives record that 256 buildings were destroyed and 11,000 people had been bombed out of their houses, though many were able to return after only a few repairs. When they compared this figure to the thousands killed by each raid on Hamburg in 1943, they may have thought themselves lucky.

Albert Speer's imposing Nazi monoliths remained mostly intact, and the industrial centre to the south of the city was barely touched. The only factories destroyed in the raid manufactured cables and margarine. There were direct hits on a fire station and one near the telephone exchange; both would have impeded rescue attempts if the raid had been successful, but meant little in isolation. Not a single person was killed in the old city centre, and the historic buildings of Nuremberg had survived.

There was anger and grief amongst its residents, but little damage to their morale. Given the scale of the raid, when the people of Nuremberg emerged from their shelters to assess the damage they knew they had escaped lightly.

★　　★　　★

In England, it was also time for taking stock.

Their acrimonious debriefing over, Rusty Waughman and his crew headed for the mess. Norman, irrepressible as ever, was looking forward to his eggs and bacon, but few of the others could summon up an appetite. The atmosphere at Ludford Magna felt different that morning; it was as if something had changed, irreparably. Rusty and the boys were accustomed to seeing the friendly, smiling faces of the WAAF girls serving breakfast; it provided much-needed comfort after the ordeal of an op. Today the food counter was laden with fried eggs, fried bread and bacon, but there was no one to dish them out. A notice pinned to the wall asked people to help themselves.

They eventually found the WAAFs crying in the rest room. The squadron had lost seven crews: 56 men whose familiar faces wouldn't be around any more; men with whom they had joked and flirted. The prospect of empty tables and chairs that morning, and of discovering, as the hours passed, which men were missing and which had returned, was simply too traumatic for them to handle.

Norman offered to go in and console them, but Rusty said they were better left alone. A few minutes later one or two emerged, hollow-eyed, their cheeks wet with tears. Rusty would never forget the pain etched on their faces. Nor would he forget the 'unsavoury' atmosphere that hung over the base that day. 'We walked around in silence, like we were zombies. The after-effects of that op hit me more than any other. The empty bed spaces, the friends who had gone; it affected everybody on the station, and not only the aircrew. We all had this sense it was a disaster.'

The strain was perhaps felt most heavily by the senior officers on the base, the station commander Group Captain King and Wing Commander Alexander. To them fell the grave task of notifying the relatives of their missing husbands and sons. Rusty was to get to know Bob Alexander well. 'He told me about the incredible burden of having to write hundreds of letters to the relatives of those who'd died.'

Back in their hut after breakfast, Rusty opened his diary and started to write.

'Ops NURENBURG [*sic*] Wholesale slaughter – must have seen at least 16 a/c shot down ... Navigation was bang on!! Nearly all sightings on the way in south of the Ruhr & home much quieter!! (Moon well up – almost daylight) ... We lost 7, quite a blow. All pretty tired and shaken! Never the less we must "press on" regardless.'

★ ★ ★

Sam Harris finally climbed into his bed at Elsham Wolds at 9.00 a.m., but he didn't feel much like sleeping. He lay there for a while, smoking a cigarette. The hut wasn't any warmer than it had been the previous morning. The icicles still hung from the roof, though the heat from the stove would soon melt them, he hoped. But all that mattered was that he was alive. He wondered how many others would not be returning to their beds that morning. For him, after some shut-eye, it would be another day in Bomber Command.

Harry Evans was so troubled by his experiences over Nuremberg that he did something he had never done before and would never do again. He realised that news of the raid and its losses would start to trickle out as the day wore on, when it was released to the press and radio, and the public would learn that Bomber Command had suffered a serious setback. Telegram couriers would soon be delivering their heartbreaking news to unsuspecting families across the land, and he was concerned that his parents might worry. More than 65 years later his eyes brim with tears as, sitting in the comfort of his spacious home, he recalls making that phone call. 'I rang them to say, "I'm still about." That was the only time that I ever rang them to tell them I'd made it home from an op.'

After the debrief and breakfast, Ron Butcher and his crew went back to dispersal to check the damage to their aircraft. The ground crew was hard at work fixing her up. They had been hit five times by flak, twice through the left bomb bay door and three times in the fuselage next to the bomb bay. Two pieces of flak had travelled back with them: one large one embedded in the wireless set, and another smaller splinter near the navigation desk. The other shrapnel had probably fallen from the bay when the doors were opened and the bombs released. They had been extraordinarily lucky. The hits to the door had been inches from detonating thousands of pounds of explosives and killing them all.

Their good fortune was felt more profoundly when Ron learned that his roommate and friend, Gord Schacter, was among the missing. In some respects, it was no surprise; Ron had flown with that crew when Gord was unwell and he knew how uncoordinated they were. But it did not ease the shock. He was asked to help the Service Police identify and catalogue Gord's belongings, bag them up, and then prepare a casualty telegram for the adjutant. It was a sobering task, especially as Ron reflected on the fact that Gord could have been doing the same for him if the cards had fallen in a different order.

Gord was not the only friend that Ron lost that night. Bill Dixon, another navigator with 578 Squadron, born in a village very near Ron's family home, was also killed. 'Every crew became hardened to seeing others go down,' he said, 'and felt that surge of guilty gratitude that it was someone else's turn.' Nonetheless he was gravely affected by the loss of two close friends.

Others were even less able to shrug off the constant spectre of death. Another roommate of Ron's, Captain Charlie Duke, was a Canadian dentist who had arrived on base only a few days before Nuremberg, and was so traumatised by the extent of the losses that he requested an immediate move away from the base to a training station. He left that day and they never saw him again.

Alan Payne landed back at East Kirkby to be met with the disbelief others had reported when he described the legions of losses he had witnessed. After a sleep, he went into Boston and sank a few beers before heading for the Regal cinema with his girlfriend Pat to see *DuBarry Was a Lady*, an escapist musical about a washroom attendant who strikes it rich. It was a chance to take his mind off the events of the last 24 hours. 'Pat and I didn't discuss the op in any great detail; she asked how we'd got on but I brushed it aside. My time with her was when I tried to forget the reality of the war: I just wanted to enjoy the moment.'

He doesn't remember being more shaken on this occasion than he had been previously. 'We knew it was a heavy chop rate that night, but a few days before there'd been a heavy chop rate on a Berlin raid, with about 70 or 80 aircraft going down.'

★   ★   ★

The pain from Dick Starkey's fractured ankle grew worse with each passing minute. Were his captors simply going to leave him here in this small office to die? Finally, that afternoon, he heard a motorcycle pull up outside. The local doctor had arrived. Dick almost wept with gratitude.

The doctor walked in and stared at him. There was no compassion or concern in his expression, only anger. Dick tried to smile, but the doctor began to yell words he couldn't understand. What was wrong? He grabbed hold of Dick's legs and started to shake them. The agony from his shattered ankle coursed through him like wildfire and he was unable to stop himself screaming. He started to gasp for air. Once the pain lessened enough for him to be able to open his eyes again, he looked around the room. The veteran designated to guard him was still there, his face taut with concern. The doctor had gone.

He resolved not to put his trust in the local medical profession but in the enemy soldiers, who would at least escort him to a camp or a military hospital where he might receive some treatment.

His next visitor was a boy who looked no older than 10. In broken English he told Dick, 'Me … English … tutor …'

Dick, his mind fogged by pain, thought the child was telling him he was an English tutor, which seemed highly improbable. Then he understood: the boy was telling him he had an English tutor. Thank Heavens, he thought, and asked the boy to bring him over as fast as he could. Half an hour later an elderly man arrived and explained in English who he was.

'I saw your plane crash,' he said.

Dick was amazed.

'I saw it explode,' he continued. 'It was a terrible sight.'

The old man would not stop talking about what he had seen. It had clearly affected him, but Dick was becoming increasingly impatient, more concerned about the present than the past. 'I am in terrible pain,' he gasped. 'Can you ask the police officer if I can be taken to the hospital?'

'You will be taken later in the day,' the old man replied.

★   ★   ★

News of the night's losses started to spread. Ron Butcher and his crew were eating in the mess to the sound of Alvar Lidell's radio news bulletin. The grim announcements Lidell often found himself having to make in his 'stentorian but nicely modulated' tones had earned him the nickname The Voice of Doom. He certainly lived up to it that day.

'Last night our bombers attacked Nuremberg. Ninety-six of our aircraft failed to return ...'

The silence that followed seemed endless. There wasn't even the scrape of a knife or fork on a plate. No one spoke. Lidell's words seem to hang in the rafters before they settled on those present. Ron knew the losses would be heavy, but no one suspected they would be that high. It had been Bomber Command's worst night of the war. 'I'd never heard the mess so deathly quiet. It seemed as if everyone had died or gone elsewhere.'

When the conversation started once more, its tone was bleak; everyone agreed that unless the choice of targets and the tactics of Bomber Command were altered, then the chances of them surviving their tours were non-existent.

After the meal they made their way back to their quarters. Just as they had on that cold February night a few weeks before, Ron and his crew spoke of their fears and doubts about whether they would see their homes, friends and families again. It appeared inconceivable that they would survive if asked to go on more raids like Nuremberg. Death had never seemed more imminent or inevitable.

Ron Auckland's wife, Sheila, was in their kitchen preparing lunch when she heard the news. Sheila froze, and was then overcome by a wave of nausea. She couldn't believe it. *Ninety-six aircraft?* That was more than 500 men ... Ron might be among them ... Her hands started to tremble. Her sister asked what was wrong. She told her about the radio broadcast.

'I really think I've lost Ron,' she whispered.

Her sister tried to reassure her. 'You don't even know if he was on that raid ...'

Sheila would not calm down, so her sister tried a different tack. 'Let's just stop what we're doing and go shopping to take your mind off it.'

They went into Portsmouth. People brushed past them, going about their daily business, but to Sheila they were as distant as ghosts. As they trudged from shop to shop, Sheila could not shake the belief – 'in my heart' – that Ron was dead. 'Something seemed to click. I just felt certain he was gone.' They returned home later that afternoon, with Sheila wondering how she was going to cope as a widow. She turned the key in the door and walked into the house, aiming for a quiet corner to sit and cry.

There, standing at the bottom of the stairs, was Ron.

'Hello, love,' he said.

He had been so desperate to get home and see his wife that he had only slept for an hour and then hitched a ride on an Oxford aircraft – which the RAF used to ferry crews between bases – taking a group to Tangmere, near Chichester. From there it was a short train ride to Portsmouth.

Sheila flung herself into his arms.

★   ★   ★

The aftershock from the operation rippled through every base across the land. Messes fell quiet; in their quarters and billets airmen spoke in hushed whispers; in parlours and kitchens civilians offered up prayers for brave men lost, and for the protection of those still serving.

The shock was even greater for those airmen who had made it through the raid unscathed, like Tony Hiscock, a Pathfinder pilot who had been at the front of the stream, oblivious to the slaughter. Their only problem had been landing in their fog-bound base at Upwood. They were re-routed to RAF Marham, where they had a hearty breakfast while waiting for the sky to clear, and it was only as they climbed back on board their Lancaster and the wireless operator switched on the radio that they heard the appalling news. 'Good grief; that was a real shock for all of us. The number stood out so much. We wondered how it had happened, because we hadn't noticed anything at all unusual. We were utterly astounded that so many aircraft had gone down.'

★   ★   ★

Thomas Maxwell had baled out of his rear turret in dramatic fashion during the Stuttgart raid on 15 March. In the fortnight since, he had managed to avoid being captured, even though he had landed only 500 metres away from a German army base. Now he was working his way through France towards the Pyrenees, hiding by day and travelling only at night, relying on the Resistance and the friendliness of the locals to keep him out of the hands of the enemy.

The day after the Nuremberg raid he was concealed in the loft space of a French farmhouse. It was so cold he could barely feel his fingers, but he still managed to turn the dials on an old wireless he had been given so he could listen to news from home. Through the crackle and hiss, he heard about the losses via the BBC World Service. His first response was relief; yes, he had been shot down, and he was shivering in the roof of a house in the middle of France, but there were reasons to be cheerful: he was still alive, and he had not been in the battle order for the night of 30 March.

Then he contemplated the mood back in the UK, the gloom that must have settled on Bomber Command bases across the country. He thought of the families of the missing colleagues who, like his, would be wild with worry about their loved ones. At least his family wouldn't be getting a telegram telling them he was dead. Not yet at least. It made his determination to get back safely to England all the greater.

★   ★   ★

Later that afternoon Dick Starkey was loaded on to another horse-drawn cart. He had been brought to the mayor's office in the dark, so this was his first chance to take a look at his surroundings. The village was built on top of a steep hill. In the distance, perhaps a quarter of a mile away, he could see plumes of black smoke curling up from a densely planted wood. They had to be coming from the smouldering wreckage of his Lancaster.

The cart moved slowly, its wheels crunching on the rough, dirt road. Dick was cold and in great pain but he still managed to savour the scenery. His brush with death had changed his perspective. As they made their way between tree-fringed hills and past undulating fields, he realised he was seeing the world anew.

After about three miles the cart descended into a valley, where it continued its slow journey. Eventually he started to see houses. They were nearing Wetzlar, a city in the state of Hesse, an industrial stronghold that had been heavily bombed. The historic old town had survived, and it was here that Dick was brought to a makeshift hospital used to treat German soldiers wounded on the Russian Front.

Dick was stretchered in and given his own room. The veteran who had guarded him all day wished him luck and Dick offered his thanks – two combatants, on opposing sides, each wounded while fighting for their country, who bore each other no ill will. Inside the hospital Dick was lifted off his stretcher and laid on a bed. Three doctors arrived and examined his injuries. They told him he needed an operation. Dick nodded his understanding. Then one of the doctors hesitated, as if he was about to ask a question. Finally he asked: 'What sort of man is Winston Churchill?'

Dick was not sure what to say. This was the fifth year of the war. Surely they would know all about him by now? Perhaps they believed the war might end soon, that they would be on the losing side and were looking for a sign that Churchill would not seek to punish the German people. He mumbled a reply, hoping it did not sound too inadequate. Their friendly, inquisitive demeanour could not have contrasted more dramatically with that of the hate-filled medic who had ranted and raved and twisted his splintered ankle.

When he came around from the operation, a small piece of metal had been removed from his right foot, which had been set and plastered. His left leg and foot had also been bandaged. His neck had been X-rayed; it was badly jarred but not broken. Then he was put on a ward with a group of German soldiers no older than he was.

They brought him books, or simply came to gawp at him. Lying there in their pyjamas, they could all have been on the same side. They were certainly no strangers to the conflict and its horrors. 'These young soldiers were from the Eastern Front, and they must have seen terrible battles between Russian and German forces. Most of them would have made up their minds that Germany had already lost the war, because they were taking severe punishment on the Russian Front. Many of them would be sent back there once their wounds had healed.'

★　　★　　★

Len Lambert, who had baled out of Cy Barton's Halifax, lay hidden all day in the woods. In the valley below he could see a village studded with timber houses, surrounded by fields and farmland. He pored over his map, desperately trying to work out where he might be, but without a more obvious landmark it was impossible. He grew colder and colder, until dusk fell. Then he emerged from his refuge and decided to head south.

Aided by the same brilliant moon which had been the downfall of so many the previous night, he was able to cover a considerable distance. As the cold seeped into his bones he started to suffer terrible cramp, but he remained determined to preserve his rations, even using melted snow for water. He managed to find and follow a network of dirt tracks through the trees to speed his progress, but was all too aware that hunger and the pervasive cold were starting to sap his strength.

He began to regret slicing the tops off his boots.

★   ★   ★

At seven o'clock in the evening of Friday 31 March there was a knock at the door of the Bartons' home in New Malden. A solemn young man stood on the step clutching a telegram. 'I hope you've not brought bad news,' Mrs Barton said, as she took it from him.

It was addressed to Cy's father, but, hands trembling, she opened it.

All she saw were the first few lines ... 'regret to inform you' ... and then the word 'FUNERAL'.

She stood motionless for a few seconds, unable to speak. Finally she managed to murmur a few words to Roy, Cy's younger brother, who had walked in a few moments earlier. 'Go and get your Auntie Dot and Uncle Reg.'

Then she burst into tears.

The telegram was brutal in its finality, and could only have added to Mrs Barton's distress in its staggering bluntness:

DEEPLY REGRET TO INFORM YOU THAT YOUR
SON PILOT OFFICER C.J. BARTON WAS KILLED
THIS MORNING AS THE RESULT OF AN AIRCRAFT
CRASH. DESIRE TO EXPRESS DEEPEST SYMPATHY
IN YOUR LOSS. YOUR SON CAN BE BURIED AT
THE ROYAL AIR FORCE REGIONAL CEMETERY

AT HARROGATE WITH SERVICE HONOURS AND
THE COST OF BURIAL WOULD BE BORNE BY
THE GOVERNMENT. IF YOU WISH TO ATTEND
THE FUNERAL A FREE THIRD CLASS RAILWAY
WARRANT FOR TWO PERSONS ONE OF WHOM
MUST BE A RELATIVE WOULD BE ISSUED ON
PRODUCTION OF THIS TELEGRAM AT THE NEAREST
POLICE STATION. IF YOU DESIRE A PRIVATE
FUNERAL THE BODY WILL BE SENT HOME AT
GOVERNMENT EXPENSE AND THE COST OF THE
COFFIN WOULD BE MET FROM GOVERNMENT FUNDS.
IN ADDITION YOU WILL BE ALLOWED A GRANT
OF FIVE POUNDS TOWARDS FUNERAL EXPENSE BUT
NO OTHER EXPENSES WILL BE ALLOWED. PLEASE
TELEGRAPH YOUR DECISION AS SOON AS POSSIBLE
TO RAF STATION USWORTH. HIS BODY IS AT
CHERRY KNOWLE HOSPITAL SUNDERLAND.

Even without reading its abrupt text, Cyril's sisters Cynthia and Joyce knew all too well what the telegram meant, and why their mother was crying. Joyce put her hand on her mother's shoulder. 'It's all right, Mum,' she said. 'He's only gone to live with Jesus.'

When Cy's father returned home, she showed him the telegram. He too was devastated. All his most deeply held fears, expressed in his letter of grudging acceptance of his son joining the RAF, had come to pass. Both of them were in tears. Their beloved boy would never fill the house with laughter again.

Cy had been in the nose of the plane, which had come to rest at the top of the ravine beyond the colliery yard. John Douglas, an off-duty Royal Marine, had dragged Cy from the wreckage. A local GP had been next on the scene. Cy had suffered head injuries and lost a great deal of blood. He was still alive but unconscious, and the doctor knew he needed an immediate transfusion if he were to have any chance of survival. The ambulance arrived to take him to Cherry Knowle Hospital, but he was pronounced dead on arrival.

Cy was not the only fatality in Ryhope that morning; George Heads, a miner, had been hit by the wreckage of the plane on his way to work, and died instantly.

CHAPTER 16

The Reckoning

Freddie Brice, Maurice Trousdale and Timber Wood were told the devastating news in the emergency ward of Cherry Knowle hospital, early on the morning of 1 April. Freddie burst into tears. 'Words cannot explain our feelings at this time, one could not stop the tears that were shed; he had given his life for ours and with only one engine remaining had made a gallant attempt to miss houses over which we were flying. How can words portray a true picture of a man like Cy?'

That same morning, Cy's sister Joyce was sent to the post office to collect a stack of blank telegram forms so her mum and dad could start writing to other relatives. To Cyril's younger brother, they wrote simply: 'Ken, come home, Cyril's killed.'

Later that morning, a letter of sympathy arrived at the Barton house from Wing Commander Williamson, Cy's Commanding Officer. 'He was one of my most experienced captains,' the tribute went, 'and led one of my finest crews. His loss leaves a gap in our ranks which it will be impossible to fill ... He always showed a devotion to duty and a keenness which was an example to us all, and you may be proud of the fact that he died doing a magnificent job of work ...'

⋆   ⋆   ⋆

The evening newspapers of 31 March were the first to carry reports of the raid. '2,000 TONS ON NUREMBERG,' screamed *The Star of London* from its front page. 'A raid that seems to have been on the 2,000 to 2,500-ton scale was made on Nuremberg, home of the great Siemens electrical and engineering works, and an important rail centre, during the night ...' it began. It wasn't until six paragraphs later that it quoted from an official press release announcing the number of missing aircraft. 'The loss of 96 aircraft is the heaviest the RAF have yet experienced in a single night's operations,' the article went on, before trying to reassure its readers with an explanation: 'And it has been frequently stressed that we must expect our losses to vary according to the weather conditions prevailing at the time, the distance to be flown over hostile territory, or other obstacles that may be encountered.'

The Star did not make any mention of bright moonlight and veering winds, though the next morning's editions did. The *Daily Express* headline trumpeted: 'Why RAF Lost 94 Bombers' (claiming that initial reports of 96 having been lost were incorrect), before listing why the raid had been so costly. The Germans had mustered their 'biggest effort' of the war; the moonlight was uninterrupted by cloud; the Germans were using a new kind of flare. The *Yorkshire Post* quoted an unnamed Lancaster pilot talking of how the vapour trails had given them away to the enemy, and went on to say, less accurately, that so many bombers hit Nuremberg that the city had been 'saturated' with explosives.

The Air Ministry's internal communications were less bull-ish. They knew that many had lost their lives for little gain, made no reference to new German flares or the use of 'Scare-crows', and admitted that Nuremberg was not successfully bombed. The only similarity the official communiqués shared with the newspaper reports was the need to downplay how disastrous that night had been.

The initial German reaction was understandably ecstatic. The High Command communiqué issued the following morn-ing read: 'Last night our air defences achieved their greatest success while warding off British terror raids on Nürnberg. They prevented concentrated attacks from being carried out and destroyed 132 4-engined bombers. Damage was caused and the population had losses in the Nürnberg built-up area and in several other German localities.'

★   ★   ★

On the German bases, there was widespread satisfaction. For the most successful aviators, there would be awards, medals and leave. The 'Night Ghost of St Trond' was one of the few who didn't share in his colleagues' delight. Heinz-Wolfgang Schnauffer had tried to intercept the main stream as early as possible, as it crossed the coast, but he was too late, and by the time he returned the battle was over. A pilot of his skill, work-ing under a bright moon, would have inflicted even greater destruction on the main stream if he had caught up with them, but he had been too eager.

Despite the failure of their ace, the German top brass were jubilant. Reichsmarschall Hermann Goering sent a telegram of stirring congratulation to the command of 1 Fighter Corps: 'The enemy suffered its worst defeat by night so far during its criminal attacks on our beloved Homeland and the German people were given their first revenge through the merciless spirit of the night fighters.'[75]

★   ★   ★

Jocelyn Norfolk had browsed the account of the Nuremberg raid in her morning newspaper, but never imagined that her friend George might have been involved. She wasn't to know that he had fallen behind enemy lines and been spotted as he emerged from hiding that morning by a young boy, who raised the alarm. The police duly arrived and he was marched to the nearest station.

George had been told stories of airmen being beaten and even killed by civilians in their fury at the invaders who had flattened their cities, towns and villages, and killed their women and children. Much to his surprise, he encountered no hostility whatsoever. He was taken from the police station to a nearby Luftwaffe base, where he was invited to share the mess like any other airman. 'There I was, sitting with these men, sharing their food. Only a few hours before, they were trying to kill me. It struck me as more than a little curious.'

The same morning Dick Starkey and the other captured airmen were taken by train to the Dulag Luft Interrogation Centre at Oberhausel, near Frankfurt. The railway station was a hive of activity, with SS officers mingling with Wehrmacht. There the mood was hostile. One Nazi storm-trooper stared at the group of PoWs with 'hate and murder in his eyes'. He picked arbitrarily on an Australian, smashing him to the floor with his fist. The Aussie jumped to his feet, as if to retaliate, then stopped, aware that if he did so he risked getting them all shot.

They were herded into cattle trucks, their coaches for the journey, and crammed in like beasts. The only concession to decency, as they travelled through the German countryside, was a few open doors to allow fresh air to get in – and Dick and his companions to see the smoking hulks of burnt-out bombers strewn across the fields and hills around them.

Those, thought Dick, are the funeral pyres of fallen friends and comrades.

★ ★ ★

When Len Lambert, the navigator who had baled from Cy Barton's Halifax, woke from a night of broken sleep on 1 April, the mist which had enveloped the valley had cleared. His makeshift bed had been a pile of fir branches in a small cave, but that meagre shelter had not been enough to prevent the chill leeching into his marrow.

From his vantage point he could see, through the morning haze, three small towns joined by a railway. He was nearer an accurate fix of his position. By his calculations he had walked approximately 30 miles, which meant he was somewhere between Bamberg and Schweinfurt, and still had a vast distance to go to the Swiss border.

Despite the penetrating cold, he decided there was no point feeling sorry for himself. Len set off. At midday it started to snow. He grew damper and more downhearted. Maybe he could cope with the temperature if he could find more food? The chocolate and condensed milk had gone, and his milk tablets did not provide enough sustenance for walking 10 miles a day in this weather. He passed a farm and saw a vegetable patch. This was his chance. Checking there was no one in sight, he crept out into the open and started to uproot some vegetables.

But the farmer had spotted him, and there was no point trying to run in his weakened state. He was taken to the farmhouse. A young Panzer trooper was there on leave from France and his English was good. Len was given cider to drink, some bread which he wolfed down, then coffee. Word of his capture spread, and the locals came from miles around to have a look at this mysterious stranger.

Len was then escorted to the nearest police station, a few miles down the valley. They tried to interrogate him, but no one spoke English, and Len was unwilling to divulge more than name, rank and number in two hours of questioning. Later that afternoon he was taken on a civilian train to a larger police station, and eventually to Schweinfurt, where he met other captured airmen at a Luftwaffe base. Among them were the two others who had baled out of Cy Barton's Halifax: bomb aimer Wally Crate and wireless operator Jack Kay. They enjoyed a brief reunion, tempered by their concern about what might have happened to the rest of their crew. 'I feared the worst,' Len said. From there, it was a train ride to Dulag Luft. Their war had come to an end.

★   ★   ★

For their fellow airmen in England, the end of the war seemed further away than ever. A little more than 24 hours after landing, Sam Harris and his crew were back inside G-George on an affiliation exercise: being 'attacked' by fighters from a neighbouring airfield so their pilot could practise his evasive drills. They spent the morning being tossed around their aircraft in a grim parody of their most recent raid.

Back in his billet, Sam reviewed his logs and charts. After debrief he had submitted them to his nit-picking Squadron Navigation Officer, which always felt like handing in his homework. Because of the tribulations of the Nuremberg raid his log was incomplete, so he expected a few critical comments – but not the torrent of disapproval that spilled across each page. Next to Sam's observation that he had discovered the wrong ETA, the red pencil scrawl read 'A good job too!!' When the log stopped abruptly on the second sheet, the criticism became even more caustic: 'Don't be lazy. You are supposed to be a navigator, so navigate! Poor effort. You must do better than this.'

At Ludford Magna the atmosphere remained funereal. For those crews still coming to terms with 101 Squadron's losses, the only small consolation was the news there would be no ops for the next few days. Seven aircraft had been lost over Nuremberg, and there were simply not enough crews available.

Rusty watched as replacements arrived by bus from their training units. Within a few hours, both the officers' and sergeants' messes were filled with unfamiliar faces. Soon the faces of those who had died would fade from their memory, even if their deeds would not.

There was better news for Andy Wiseman. When he and his crew arrived by train at Leconfield, after being forced to land at another airfield, they were told they would be going on immediate leave. For the Aussies in his crew, that meant a few nights carousing in London. For Andy it meant a trip to see his beloved Jean.

From the moment he walked through the door, to be met with an enormous hug, until the moment he left a week later, Andy was unable to talk about anything other than his experiences on the Nuremberg operation. In Jean he had someone to counsel him and console him; to hold his hand, comfort him and allow him to unburden himself before his return to base.

Andy was blessed; few others had the opportunity to contemplate and discuss the events of that night in such convivial surroundings.

CHAPTER 17

'I'm Quite Prepared to Die ...'

Roger Coverley's POW card

Fred Panton immediately recognised the boy who had cycled up the hill towards his family's cottage at dusk on 3 April. He and Maurice Fenwick, the son of the local postmaster, had shared a desk at school.

'Is your mother or father in?' Maurice asked, a serious look on his face.

'Yes they are, Maurice,' Fred replied, glancing down at the envelope in his hand. I bet that's a telegram telling them about Chris, he thought.

It had been four days since news of the disastrous raid on Nuremberg had broken. They had known before the radio broadcasts that it had been a bad one. His dad's diary of the comings and goings of the crews at the nearby bases, and the disparity between the number of bombers he counted out and those he counted back, had told their own sorry story.

At first they had been worried, but as March became April and they still heard nothing they dared to persuade themselves that no news was good news; that Chris had come through unscathed and life was carrying on as normal at RAF Skipton-on-Swale. But now the telegram in Maurice's hand told Fred otherwise.

It also told him it would not be a good idea to accompany Maurice to the front door, so he ran across the paddock to the crew yard of the farm where his father worked as gamekeeper. There he sat on a ledge and watched his school friend walk up to the front door of his house and knock. His mother answered. His father had been in bed for the past day or two, suffering from a bout of the flu. He saw her take the envelope and then disappear upstairs.

Fred sat there until nine that night, swinging his legs, watching the sky darken, feeling the air become colder and colder. Shivering in the yard still seemed a whole lot better than going home and finding out what was in that envelope. He knew it was bad news, and the longer he sat there, the longer he could pretend it had not happened. He knew that as soon as he walked back into the house everything would change.

Eventually tiredness, the cold and a sense of duty made him return. The awful truth was confirmed: Chris was missing. That was all they knew. His father was up and about, pacing the floor like a caged lion. The flu had gone, vanquished by the shock of the news about his son.

★   ★   ★

A few days after his death, Cy Barton's personal effects arrived at the family home in New Malden. Among them was the birthday card he had written for Joyce on the day of the Nuremberg raid. Ken also gave his mother the letter Cy had prepared before his first op.

Dear Mum

I hope you never receive this, but I quite expect you will. I'm expecting to do my first operation trip in a few days. I know what 'Ops' over Germany means and I have no illusions about it. By my own calculations the average life of a crew is twenty 'Ops' and we have thirty to do in our first 'tour'.

I'm writing this for two reasons. One to tell you how I would like my money spent that I have left behind; two to tell you about how I feel meeting my Maker.

1. I intended, as you know, taking a University Course with my savings. Well, I would like them to be spent on the education of my brothers and sisters. Ken is a bit old to start part time study now and I would like him to have as much of it as he needs for full time study. All of it, if he can use it. Roy is still young and has his teens before him. It's up to him to help himself. The girls likewise. I'll leave it to you to decide what to do with my belongings.

2. All I can say about this is that I'm quite prepared to die. It holds no terror for me. I know I shall survive the Judgement because I have trusted in Christ as my own Saviour. I've done nothing to merit glory, but because He died for me it's God's free gift. At times I've wondered whether I've been right in believing what I do. Just recently I've doubted the veracity of the Bible, but in the little time I've had to sort out intellectual problems, I've been left with a bias in favour of the Bible.

Apart from this I have the inner conviction, as I write, of a force outside myself and my brain, that I have not trusted in vain. All I am anxious about is that you and the rest of the family come to know Him. Ken, I know, already does. I commend my Saviour to you …

Well, that's covered everything now I guess, so Love to Dad and all,

Your loving son, Cyril.

A funeral date was set. Cy's body was returned to New Malden, later than planned. In her grief, his mother was determined to know what had killed him and see his injuries for herself, but when the coffin finally arrived there was a notice on it: 'Not to be opened under any circumstances.'

The funeral took place on Maundy Thursday, 6 April 1944. The spring flowers were out, and a long, cold winter was behind them, but all that lay ahead for the Barton family was grief and misery. Mr Barton was especially devastated. 'He was in an awful state,' Cynthia says. 'If Mum hadn't been there I don't know how he'd have coped at all. Mum had to hold him up.' Of the girls, only Cynthia was allowed to attend. Joyce and Pamela peered through a window as the funeral party left; they remember the Union Jack draped over their brother's coffin all too vividly.

Cy's friend Frank Colquhon, a curate of the local church, gave the eulogy. He spoke of Cy's 'radiant Christian character' and his faith in God. He also reminded the gathering that Cy's last flight was not one in which his aircraft had crashed and he was killed, but one in which his spirit had flown upward into the arms of God. They sang 'When I Survey the Wondrous Cross' and 'Abide with Me', and then Cy's body was buried at Kingston cemetery among the sprouting daffodils.

An excerpt from Romans 8.28 was carved on to his tombstone: 'And we know that all things work together for good to them that love God, to them who are the called according to His purpose.'

★   ★   ★

Roger Coverley had spent four days on the run in the heart of Germany. The railway tunnel he walked into a few minutes after parachuting to the ground had given him cover, and then, hiding by day and travelling by night, he managed to make good progress to the west, eking out his meagre escape rations. The cold was not unbearable, but after four days the hunger became so. At one stage he stole into a vegetable patch, dug up some leeks and ate them raw. They were disgusting. 'It put me off that vegetable for a very long time,' he says.

He estimated he had covered 30 miles in four days by the time he reached the River Rhine. Given the current, and the cold, there was no way he could swim across; he needed a bridge. He found one, near Bonn, but he was captured as he walked across it. Imprisoned with fellow captured airmen and taken to Dulag Luft, he discovered that his determination to stay at the helm of his plane for as long as possible had not been in vain. All but one of his crew had managed to parachute to safety.

The only casualty had been Sergeant Motts, the flight engineer. He managed to escape the burning aircraft, but as he jumped his parachute had caught fire and his body was found hanging in a tree, the remains of his canopy draped around him. The wreckage of their Halifax was scattered over an area one mile wide.

★   ★   ★

Three days into his incarceration at the interrogation centre at Dulag Luft, in a tiny cell with the heat turned up to maximum at night to make him as uncomfortable as possible, Dick Starkey noticed a black discharge seeping from the plaster cast on his leg.

He knew immediately it was frostbite, caused by parachuting to the ground through sub-zero temperatures, without boots, then lying in the snow for several hours. The camp medical orderly checked on him each day, but ignored Dick's concerns. He was taken to another building in the camp and interrogated, still in shock and racked with pain. Despite being questioned twice and threatened with a visit by the Gestapo, he still did not crumble.

During his second interrogation, an 'immaculately dressed and perfumed' Luftwaffe officer told him that 97 Allied bombers had been shot down. 'It was a hell of a shock,' Dick says, but he did not doubt what he was being told or dismiss it as propaganda. The evidence of his own eyes told him it was 'near the mark'. He couldn't help but add those losses to the ones racked up in the week before Nuremberg, during raids on Berlin and Essen. He estimated that Bomber Command had lost 204 aircraft, which meant 1,440 men killed or missing, in the space of a single week. That's the equivalent of 10 squadrons, he thought.

Of the men who were shot down over enemy territory on the night of the Nuremberg raid, all but one were apprehended and sent to Dulag Luft. Don Brinkhurst, a mid-upper gunner in 101 Squadron, was the only airman to escape. His Lancaster had been brought down, probably the result of friendly fire when a nervous gunner on a Halifax just 300 feet away mistook them for a German fighter. Brinkhurst was one of three who parachuted to safety; the other five all perished. They were only two ops short of completing their tour.

On the ground, approximately a dozen miles into German territory, Brinkhurst hid his parachute and started to walk towards Belgium. He managed to avoid capture for four days, despite the proximity of patrols with dogs, having to take shelter at one point near a German airfield, and suffering a debilitating bout of stomach cramp when he ate raw potatoes from a field. He walked 40 miles cross-country from the place he landed to the Belgian border, where he made himself known to 'a very fat lady at an isolated farmhouse who was putting out her washing'.[76]

He had chosen well; the woman took him in.

★   ★   ★

Cy's funeral was over, but the Bartons' suffering had only just begun. His distraught mother was tireless in her efforts to discover all she could about the last few moments of his life. She remained desperate to know whether he had experienced any pain, and to learn more about the nature of his injuries. His Commanding Officer at Burn replied to her letters, informing her that it was probably shock that killed him, and 'his cheery face with which we have become so familiar was still the same, even at the last'.

A more detailed picture of his last moments was provided by the Ryhope GP, Dr J. Bain Alderson, who had been with the rescue party. He described Cy's head injuries and traumatic blood loss. 'He was insensible when I saw him; he was not burnt in any way, as the plane only burnt a little and the crew were pulled out without any burns ... I very much regret that the hospital authorities and myself were unable to do any more for him ... Please also accept my personal sympathies in your great loss.'[77]

Her questions answered, it was time for the Bartons to start grieving the loss of their treasured son and to try and pick up the pieces of their lives. But the gap he left proved impossible to fill. Cynthia was particularly aware of the toll it took on her father. 'He almost became an old man overnight.'

Her mother appeared to cope better, at least superficially, but the girls could tell her heart was broken.

CHAPTER 18

A Charmed Life

Sam Harris and his crew flew on, nearing the end of their tour in May 1944. When they were five short of the golden target of 30 completed ops, their pilot Ken Murray told them that he wanted to volunteer for yet another five.

This announcement was met with a mixed response from the rest of them, to put it mildly. Chalky had only recently married, and Mac planned on doing so when his tour was over. There was no chance they were going to put their head back in the lion's mouth five more times if they made it all the way to 30.

Sam was the only one who said he might consider it, because he did not want to be sent to an Operational Training Unit, away from his crew-mates. But that wasn't enough for Ken. 'Right, that's it. You're a bunch of yellow-bellied bastards.' He turned and stormed out of the room.

The crew were quite perplexed by his attitude; if Ken was determined to do more ops, then the squadron would find him another crew. They wondered whether their Flight Commander had approached him with the idea. They were extremely short of experienced and battle-hardened crews; perhaps they were desperate to keep Ken and his crew together? Whatever the reason, it created tension and bewilderment where previously there had been comradeship.

'Well, that's it, chaps,' Chalky said after Ken walked out. 'We still have five trips to go and it looks as if they are going to be a right bundle of fun.'

Their last op as a crew came on 6 June 1944. They gathered around their aircraft that night, the warm summer air a stark contrast to the teeth-rattling cold of winter at the start of their tour. They were smoking their cigarettes, as they had on 29 previous occasions, when a voice came out of the darkness. 'One way or another, if we go to the target, this will be the last night we will ever stand here.' There was no more to be said.

The op was routine. At 2.39 a.m. they returned to base; they had flown together for the last time. As they sat on their bunks later that morning, unable to sleep, they smoked more cigarettes and reminisced. They talked of Nuremberg and its exceptionally high losses; and G2, their 'ropey old aircraft' which they had last flown on 13 April, before it was taken out of service. Luff summed it up: 'Well, lads, you have to admit it, we have been a very lucky crew.' They were all quick to agree.

Little more than a month later the brand-new Lancaster which they had been given to replace G2, and which they passed on to another crew as they left the base, collided with another aircraft and all but the gunners were killed. 'It could have been us,' Sam said.

Ken did return to a squadron, but not until 1945. Sam also returned to the front line, this time in a Mosquito.

★   ★   ★

The story of Cy Barton's heroism spread to the higher echelons of the RAF. One day in late June a dispatch rider arrived at the Bartons' house. He carried a letter from the Under-Secretary of State at the Air Ministry.

His father opened the letter. His mother asked what it said. He told her that Cy had been awarded the Victoria Cross for 'conspicuous bravery'.

Mrs Barton remained unimpressed. 'It won't bring him back,' she said.

'But it's the highest honour any serviceman can earn,' he explained.

'I don't care. It won't bring him back, will it?'

Newspaper reporters arrived at the house in packs to revel in the family's reaction. Mrs Barton stayed in her bedroom, still too distressed to speak publicly of her son's death.

The next day his citation appeared in the *London Gazette*, providing the world with the first official account of Cy's outstanding heroism. The honour bestowed on her brother was mentioned at Joyce's school assembly the next day. 'My teacher was so excited she put her arm round me and sort of lifted me up. I was excited, but I didn't really know why I was excited. I didn't understand what it all meant.'

The publicity brought a rush of letters through the Bartons' door, from hundreds of people wanting to congratulate Cy's family on the bravery of their son as well as offering their sympathy. Amongst them was a letter from Sir Arthur Harris, the Commander-in-Chief of Bomber Command.

My dear Mr Barton

I write to inform you that His Majesty The King has been graciously pleased to confer upon your son the Victoria Cross.

I ask you on behalf of Bomber Command, and for my own part especially, to accept our sympathy in your loss.

I hope, however, that this loss will be to some extent mitigated by the manner of your son's passing and by his high award, so well deserved, so hardly won.

Your boy set an example of high courage and, finally, of extreme devotion to duty towards his crew, which will go down in history in the annals of his Service and shine as an inspiration for all who come after him.

I hope indeed that a rightful pride in his achievements and his conduct will be of some consolation to you and yours at this time.[78]

These letters, sent by people she had never met from halfway across the world, did in time give Cy's mother succour. She kept every single one. Once the media frenzy had abated, she wrote to the lady who had looked after Cy when he was training in the USA. Her letter revealed both her stoicism and her profound sadness: '… I have been very brave, and try hard to carry on as he would wish me to. I feel so overcome when I sit down to write. Now he has been awarded the VC I have had to do a good deal of writing, we are very pleased this honour has been awarded him, but it has brought it all back again tenfold.'[79]

★   ★   ★

In June the Panton family was informed that, in his absence, Chris had been given a commission and made a Pilot Officer. But there was still no news of his whereabouts.

The weeks of waiting turned into months. Eventually, so much time had passed that Chris's status was now 'Missing, presumed killed'. But their father refused to give up hope. He wrote letter after letter trying to find out what had happened to his son. It was Fred's job to take them to the post office before school and check if there were any replies, a two-mile round trip, because his father couldn't wait until the postman's delivery later in the morning.

Fred and his little brother created a series of daily rituals to help sustain their hope that Chris would miraculously reappear. He would watch Harold run between two elm trees; if he made the distance before Fred counted to 10, then Chris was *definitely* still alive. Of course, he always made it, and just for a few moments both the boys felt better.

The waiting went on for half a year. Six months of agony, of clinging to the faintest hope; six months of wishing, in the face of mounting evidence to the contrary, that Chris was alive and well and being held by the Germans as a prisoner-of-war. Even more fancifully, they sometimes liked to imagine him making his way across Europe like Pimpernel Smith in the Leslie Howard film, evading the enemy pursuers, and finally arriving back in England, safe and sound.

Then, one autumn morning, there was a letter. The same sense of foreboding that told him Maurice Fenwick's envelope contained bad news told him this one did too. He ran back to the cottage and watched his father tear it open. The letter listed those on Chris's Halifax who had survived, and those who had been killed.

Chris was one of the two who had died.

Fred used to think that if anything happened to Chris, it would 'just about kill my mother', but she had come to terms with the possibility over the months that had passed since Nuremberg, and now, at last, she could begin to grieve.

For his father, it was different. 'It knocked the stuffing out of him.' He was never the same again. Christian Nielsen, Chris's pilot, travelled to Spilsby to see him when the war was over to explain what had happened that night, and told him how Chris had passed out the parachutes before the plane exploded and that those who had survived had been blown free. He also received a letter from another crew member, Canadian Jack McLauchlan, who was still grappling with the mystery of why everyone except Chris and one other airman had been spared on that dreadful night:

'What I cannot understand is if the Lord helped Chris [Nielsen] and Harry, why didn't I get killed and let your Chris escape unscathed. If anyone had a right to live it was this Panton! Gladly would I have laid down my life for Chris. He was the truest friend I have ever had. I believe Chris will be buried around a town called Bamburgh [*sic*] near Nurnberg. We were not allowed to attend the funeral and it broke my heart.

'At the time I went missing, no doubt Chris told you I owed him a pound note, so I have enclosed a postal order for the sum.'[80]

But that was it. Chris's death was never spoken of again in the Panton household, and neither was the war.

★   ★   ★

On a cold and damp day in December 1944, Cy Barton's parents received his Victoria Cross from the King at Buckingham Palace. They had been offered third-class rail vouchers to make the short trip to London, but their local MP, Sir Percy Royds, a former Admiral in the Royal Navy and himself a decorated veteran of the Battle of Jutland, asked to 'honour' their brave son by driving them.

Cyril's brother Ken took Joyce, Cynthia and Pamela to London by train, and they waited near the gates for their parents to emerge. There were no celebrations, just quiet pride at the honour bestowed on their son, and their lingering sadness at his loss. As they strolled around St James's Park, their mother told the girls that the King had praised Cyril's actions.

On another cold winter's day they made a sadder pilgrimage – to Ryhope, the place where Cyril crashed and died. But the distress of the visit had taken its toll on Mr Barton's failing health, and so they were unable to meet those who saw Cy make his last heroic landing. Among them was Mrs Richardson, whose house was half demolished by the wing of Cy's Halifax. She had exchanged letters with Mrs Barton. The two women shared the bond of motherhood, though one had suffered a great loss and the other had been spared. In May 1945 Mrs Barton wrote again: 'This has been a dreadful war and about time it was over. We all feel war weary, don't we?'[81]

Cyril was rarely mentioned at home. Mr Barton simply found it too upsetting. The silence heightened the sense of unreality for the girls. The Christmas after he died, Joyce believed he might come home, that it had all been a terrible mistake.

Cynthia says: 'This shadow that was cast over our family never went away. Mum never recovered. No one talked about him. Mum would have preferred people to talk about him and remember him. But it was a different time; people didn't talk about their feelings that way, did they?'

Mrs Barton carried the letter informing them Cy was to be awarded the VC in her handbag until the day she died, and gradually, over time, the sisters and their mother did speak more of him. 'All these years on, Cyril is clearly still a big part of our lives. There was something special about him, not because he's dead or because he won the VC, but just because he was a very special young man. He would have gone on to do good, I think.'

CHAPTER 19

A Wing and a Prayer

The decimation of their squadron at Nuremberg was so extensive that for a long time afterwards Rusty Waughman would scan the list of names on a battle order of those taking part and barely recognise more than a handful.

On 11 May, during a raid on the railway marshalling yards at Hasselt, Belgium, in the run-up to the Allied invasion of Europe, they collided with another Lancaster. The other aircraft's mid-upper turret and propeller blades tore into their fuselage and bomb bay before they had a chance to react.

A Wing and a Prayer shuddered and seemed to come to a halt in mid-air. At first Rusty was too stunned to do anything. Then the awful thought occurred to him that this was it – they had flown several raids over Berlin and its massed ranks of defences and survived the horrors of Nuremberg, only to have their lives ended by a collision with a plane from their own bloody side.

He tried to regain control but there was nothing he could do. They were riding piggy-back on their fellow bomber. It seemed as if the two lumbering beasts were 'intertwined ... in one final grotesque embrace of death'. Then the unknown Lancaster separated itself from Rusty's, and fell away at a 45-degree angle into the clouds.

Amazingly, the damage to *A Wing and a Prayer* – the name had never seemed so appropriate as it did right at that moment – was not as bad as they feared. It was a miracle that the thousands of pounds of high explosives in the bomb bay had survived the impact. The plane was responding, albeit sluggishly, but in an astonishing act of courage Rusty chose to go on and bomb the target rather than limp back to England.

On the return flight to Ludford Magna they discovered that one of the undercarriage wheels was badly damaged. Rusty considered his options. He decided to press on and land back at base, but he knew there were no guarantees they would make it safely. He felt he owed it to his crew to lay it on the line for them.

'This could be a bit dicey. If any of you want to bale out ...'

They decided to stick with their pilot and put their faith in his skill. As they came into land, he told them to assume their crash positions. Everyone braced themselves. Rusty held the heavy bomber on one wheel, before he reduced their speed and allowed the damaged starboard wheel to touch down. As it did, the aircraft began to career dangerously off course, but Rusty was up to the challenge. He managed to maintain control.

The plane started to veer towards the control tower. A WAAF on the Air Traffic Control staff fell over in fright as she saw the vast machine loom out of the darkness and hurtle towards them. With all the strength he could muster, Rusty managed to bring the bomber to a stop a matter of yards from the tower.

Slowly, breathing sighs of relief, the crew clambered from their battered aircraft. 'Best landing yet, Skipper,' Taffy said nonchalantly.

★   ★   ★

A little more than three weeks after Nuremberg, on a raid to Düsseldorf, Chick Chandler's Lancaster was shot up by flak and fighter fire. Two of his crew members had been fatally injured, two others wounded. Chick's parachute pack was shot off his back but he was otherwise unharmed. The aircraft was damaged by fire, the bomb bays door wouldn't close and the landing gear wouldn't open. He and others only survived because of the extreme skill and bravery of their pilot, Oliver

Brooks, who, with Chick at his side, managed to bring the stricken aircraft in to land at Woodbridge. 'A wizard effort,' Chick said, 'by the best pilot the RAF has seen.'

The Lancaster 'slid along on its belly. In a shower of sparks, dirt, dust, and debris and with the metal screeching on the concrete, the bomb doors buckled and collapsed under the weight of the aircraft and the propellers twisting as they struck the ground.'

Once his tour was over – and there were few more relieved crew members than Chick when he returned from his last flight in one piece – he was transferred to a training unit for what promised to be a six-month period away from the front line.

Unfortunately a 'personal dispute' with an officer led to him being given the worst jobs, including having to escort men detained by the RAF for misbehaviour to disciplinary centres. On his return from one such task, he was told that he had been 'volunteered' for another tour of operations.

Chick was understandably reluctant to return; he still had three months of the normal rest period left. He was posted to a Heavy Conversion Unit, where he met his new crew. But he told the Squadron Leader he would only carry out training flights, not ops, until his rest period had expired. He was dismissed immediately and replaced by a new engineer. While he waited for the bus in dispersal, the crew he was supposed to have joined took off. They crashed on landing. Everyone but the rear gunner was killed.

His refusal was to have severe consequences. Despite having survived some of the heaviest and costliest raids of the war, and completed a full tour, he was branded as having a Lack of Moral Fibre – the dreaded LMF. In a letter written many years later, Chick touched upon his experiences: 'I saw psychiatrists, medical officers, Group Captains, boards officers, Wing Commanders in charge of flying, etc, etc. At one time when being interviewed by a particularly aggressive Wing Commander I was threatened with facing a firing squad. I am not suggesting that this was the official policy and I really thought my man was bluffing, no doubt infuriated by my insistence that I [get] my full rest period. A threat that I did take seriously was the fact I could get demoted, transferred to the Army, and sent to a particularly unpleasant theatre of war.'

Chick endured 10 weeks of hell. 'It was worse than ops,' he said. Eventually he was allowed a hearing to state his case. He was given a job on the ground, but the hated LMF stamp still scarred his logbook: 'Withdrawn from aircrew duties.'

Remarkably, he remained in the RAF until 1978 as an air traffic controller, but still smarts from the way he was treated once his tour was over. 'I was shot up by flak, fighters, had my parachute harness shot off, crash landed, pinned by searchlights for 20 minutes and branded LMF. I had a hectic time in Bomber Command, but a charmed life. I was lucky and I can't have too much luck left to rely on. But the Air Force treated me very shabbily over the LMF issue.'

★   ★   ★

On 18 April 1944, on the way back from bombing a railway station at Tergnier, in northern France, Andy Wiseman's aircraft was ripped apart by cannon fire from a fighter they never saw. The pilot, sitting right next to Andy, was killed, as were the rear gunner and flight engineer. The navigator baled out. Andy quickly followed, carrying the lucky doll given to him by Jean. The navigator managed to make his way back to England, but Andy was captured and ended the war in the infamous Stalag Luft III prison camp in Sagan, Lower Silesia.

Another of its inmates was Dick Starkey. His broken, frost-bitten ankle had slowly healed, thanks to treatment in two different military hospitals. At the time of his arrival, security at the camp had never been more severe. A week before the Nuremberg raid, more than 200 Allied servicemen had tried to escape from it, and 76 had succeeded. Fifty of the 73 who were recaptured were executed.

All further escape plans had been abandoned. Not that Dick would have been chosen to go, given his disability. As 1945 dawned, there seemed to be another good reason not to risk going under the wire: word had spread that the Russian army was making significant advances towards them; Dick and his fellow PoWs would soon be liberated.

In January 1945, however, in a temperature of minus 20 degrees centigrade and a gusting blizzard, Dick, Andy Wiseman and thousands of fellow PoWs were marched from Stalag Luft III across the Silesian plain. They walked for 16 hours a day, dragging what few possessions they had behind them on sledges. At the rear of the column when they took shelter at a farm, Dick was one of the last inside the barns, which the prisoners shared with cows, sheep and horses.

They continued in this fashion for four days, and the effort began to take its toll on Dick's battered body. His neck was still so stiff that he couldn't raise his head above eye level, and though he was able to walk his ankle was not up to trudging for hours on end through heavy snow and ice. It became so swollen that he dared not take off his boots in case he wouldn't be able to get them back on.

Dick refused to give up. Rumours passed up and down the column that those suffering from frostbite, injury or exhaustion to the point of being unable to carry on were being shot. The periodic echo of rifle fire seemed to confirm it. Dick summoned up the last of his dwindling reserves of energy and determination, and soldiered on. Finally, after seven days of marching, they reached a train station and were transported to Luckenwald, where he became one of the 28,000 inmates praying for the war to end.

★   ★   ★

Thomas Maxwell, the 18-year-old rear gunner who had been shot down over Stuttgart and learned of the Nuremberg raid on an old wireless in a French farmhouse attic, continued to make his way back to safety with the help of the *Comète* line, a Resistance network which helped British airmen evade capture by offering shelter, clothes, false papers and transport, and guided them through occupied France into neutral Spain. They could then get home via a flight from British-owned Gibraltar.

His journey took two and a half months, but at the end of May 1944 Thomas arrived back in England to be debriefed by MI9. Before making his way back to Mildenhall to rejoin his squadron, he went to collect his possessions, which had been bagged up and shipped out to the Central Repository at RAF Uxbridge by the Committee of Adjustment, the branch of the RAF tasked with clearing away the personal possessions of missing aircrew, after his plane went down in March. One of his principal concerns was the eleven bars of chocolate he had been squirrelling away before he was shot down. But what he saw on his arrival immediately destroyed his appetite.

'The place smelled of death. All the personal effects of aircrew missing or killed in action were there, as well as huge piles of uniform, which were heaped on trestle tables. These were being sorted out with great care before being sent on to loved ones and next of kin. I imagined what it must have been like for the people who worked there, young WAAFs mainly, whose job it was to sort through these objects. I saw so many things: cigarettes, golf clubs, squash racquets, beer-soaked ten shilling notes, old theatre tickets, half-completed letters to girl-friends, chocolate and sweet ration coupons, a tin box containing pennies which a father had saved for his child. That was only a few of the items. Imagine the sort of trivia one might leave if you were all of a sudden taken out of existence and then multiply it by hundreds.

'The WAAF had the job of going through and sorting all the personal letters and, with the help of a squadron officer, would decide which would be sent on and which destroyed. This was only done when it was confirmed that someone was killed in action, or they had been missing in action for a certain amount of time. I can't imagine how they coped with reading all those words.

'I got the impression that it was a rare event for someone to turn up and collect their stuff like I had done. I was introduced to them and everyone stopped what they were doing and applauded! It seemed to bring a little bit of brightness to what must have been a terribly onerous task. I got my cardboard box. My chocolate ration had gone, "Returned to Catering Officer", but I was given a new ration book allowance in lieu.'

Thomas reached for his logbook. The last entry was written in red ink: 'LL828 March 15 Stuttgart: Failed to Return.' He was mortified. They had only been an hour and 20 minutes from landing in England when he had baled out. They had racked up six hours and 10 minutes of night-flying time before transmitting their first and last signal to base, none of which he had been credited with. There was no way he was going to be cheated out of that time; he entered the hours in the book himself.

'The next entry on a new page was three months later, by myself, and said simply in red ink: "Balls".' Thomas also added the details of his most recent flight, which had brought him back from Gibraltar to Whitchurch at 9.10 that morning.

Possessions in hand, Thomas returned to Mildenhall, the first of his squadron to have been shot down and return to operational duty. He went on to complete a further 26 operations.

★   ★   ★

Don Brinkhurst, the only airman from the Nuremberg raid to evade capture on the ground, was taken in by the Belgian Resistance near Liège. He was met at the safe house by a civilian carrying a revolver who led him into a back room where his mother-in-law was frying mushrooms.

'What is she frying?' he asked Don in English.

'Mushrooms.'

The man put away his revolver. 'If you had stopped or hesitated, I would have shot you as a German impostor.'

His credentials established, Don was even given a party to celebrate his 21st birthday three weeks later, though he had to flee when someone betrayed him to the Germans. He crossed into Switzerland, after being helped over a heavily guarded bridge by a *Résistante* who posed as his girlfriend, and then back into newly liberated France, where he encountered some Allied troops. From there, he made his way back to the UK and joined up with his old squadron.

On 2 January 1945 he took off in a Lancaster on the first of another 20 operations. The target was Nuremberg.

CHAPTER 20

Scars and Ghosts

For those whose loved ones were missing, the infamous radio broadcasts of William Joyce, more commonly known as Lord Haw-Haw, became required listening. In between snatches of jazz music and tedious passages of Nazi propaganda, Joyce read out the names of prisoners-of-war and often passed personal messages from them to their families over the airwaves. George Prince's family was listening to one such broadcast when his name was mentioned. He was alive! The joyous news was passed on to his friend, Jocelyn. She was ecstatic, but still surprised he had been captured. 'We thought that they were all invincible.'

Jocelyn started to write to George in Dulag Luft. Her letters were, she says, merely a mundane account of all the things she had been doing; friends she had seen, gatherings she had been to. Inconsequential, but she hoped they would be of some comfort to him. She also tried sending him cigarettes via the Red Cross. She only received one letter from him in return, but she kept on writing regardless.

Jocelyn had no idea that George treasured each letter she sent. It was a reminder of home, evidence that life was continuing as it had always done in New Malden and that, beyond the brutality and barbed wire of his prison camp, a normal world still existed.

A few days before VE Day in 1945, there was a knock at the door of her parents' place and, without any prior warning,

245

there he was on the threshold. They went straight to the cinema. It soon became clear that something had shifted in their relationship. Her correspondence had intensified their feelings for each other. They married in 1949. 'It's curious, I suppose,' Jocelyn says. 'I only started writing to him because he got shot down. I wonder what might have happened if he hadn't been? Things might have turned out very differently.'

Jocelyn was not the only object of George's affection waiting for him. His father travelled to Skellingthorpe, where George had been stationed, and drove his beloved MG down the A1 from Lincolnshire to Surrey. 'That car started the war with me and ended the war with me,' George says.

★   ★   ★

In the middle of April 1945, Dick Starkey's German captors evacuated Luckenwald, where he had been held since the New Year, and fought a running battle with the advancing Russian forces in a nearby forest. Eventually, to the joy of the inmates, the Russians rolled in: they were free.

Or so they believed.

The Russians refused to allow them to leave the camp until the Americans arrived and an exchange was agreed. There was an agonising wait as they were forced to stay inside the camp until the deal was done – whilst listening to the BBC announce that thousands of other PoWs had been released and were on their way back to England.

As time dragged on, their wariness about their new Russian overseers grew. One afternoon a group of elderly German conscripts, who had somehow survived the fighting in the forest, walked towards the camp with their hands held high. The Russian PoWs at the gate, now given the responsibility of guarding the place, shot them down in cold blood. 'We realised the Russians would show no mercy after the atrocities committed by the Germans in their country.'

Some became so impatient they decided to make a run for it, though that meant trying to force their way through Russian lines. Dick chose to stay, even if the frustration grew each day. The Russians started to ease the restrictions, allowing the PoWs to go for a walk within a one-mile perimeter of the camp. With an Australian pilot, Dick chose to walk into the forest, where the Germans had been hiding before the Russians had cleared them out.

They found a clearing and the remains of a field kitchen. German helmets were still scattered across the ground. Dick picked one up.

'Ah! What have we here?' a voice asked in English.

They turned. Two German soldiers and a young woman, possibly a nurse, were standing there. One of the men was holding a Luger. It was pointed at them.

'Do you know who we are?' he asked. He unbuttoned his tunic. He was wearing a black shirt emblazoned with a yellow skull and crossbones – the insignia of the SS.

The SS officer asked if they had anything to eat. Dick told them the Russians ran the camp very strictly and gave them little food. A thin smile played on the SS man's lips. 'Probably Britain and America will now fight the Bolsheviks,' he said.

Dick felt the kind of despair he had not experienced since his first few hours on German soil. There was no way that these men would let them return to camp and risk them telling the Russians that there were still German soldiers hiding in the forest. The safest option would be to shoot them.

Dick had survived being blown out of a burning plane, the impact of hitting the ground after falling 15,000 feet, more than a year as a PoW and an arduous week-long march through the Silesian winter. Now the war was all but over, he was about to be killed for taking a misguided stroll through the woods.

'Go back to your camp and get us food,' the SS man said.

Dick was stunned. Were they really letting them go? But he was not going to stay and argue. They turned and started to walk, expecting to be shot in the back at any moment. 'Those 25 steps back to the trees were the longest of my life. We dared not start running.'

As soon as they reached the trees they started to sprint, forgetting for a few panic-stricken seconds about his injured ankle.

At the end of May their agony came to an end. Dick was one of the last British PoWs to be repatriated; he landed at RAF Bicester a very relieved and happy man. He stayed in the RAF and was posted to RAF Dishforth in 1946 to familiarise himself with the new Avro York aircraft, used to bring troops back from the Far East.

But when he was asked to be Captain, Dick was forced to make a decision he had been putting off for several months. Ever since his arrival back in England he had been suffering from dreadful recurring nightmares, in which he was falling to earth without a parachute. These had become so disturbing that he began to dread going to sleep. He knew he would never be able to recover as long as he remained at the helm of the plane, so he asked to be discharged.

The scars of the Nuremberg raid ran deep.

★   ★   ★

Stella Wilton was deputy head of the American Red Cross in Naples. At the conclusion of hostilities she had plans to return to the USA to start a new life. But first she wanted to find her son, Andy Wiseman, who had been shot down a few weeks after the Nuremberg debacle. She had not seen him for seven long years. Their last meeting had taken place in such a different world it might as well have been on another planet.

Since then, she had divorced his father, who had later been gassed to death at Treblinka with much of his family. Stella had only survived because she had changed her name from

Wejcman, and been sent to an internment camp for US citizens. She had been liberated by the Russians at the end of the war, and made her way across central Europe by train to Naples.

She had exchanged letters with Andy's girlfriend, Jean, and learned that he was being held as a PoW, but during the past few weeks there had been no news of his release. Each day was torture. She vowed not to return to America until she discovered what had happened to him.

One morning, in the summer of 1945, she got into the lift at the hotel where she lived. The doors opened on the ground floor; she slid back the metal grilles and walked out into the lobby. Then she stopped in her tracks.

He was in RAF uniform, looking gaunter than before, and much older. But he was definitely her son.

She ran across the lobby and wrapped her arms around him. Tears flowed from them both. Neither spoke. Just mother and son enjoying a reunion each feared might never take place. Eventually Stella unclasped herself and fixed him with a stern look. 'What are you doing here?'

Jean had given him her address, he said, and he'd asked for a posting to Naples so he could see her. 'There's one more thing …' He paused. 'Jean and I are married.'

There were more hugs and tears. Andy told her that they had been on honeymoon in London, and were walking along Kingsway when they passed Adastral House, the Air Ministry headquarters. On the spur of the moment, Andy went in and asked the WAAF at reception if he could be sent to Naples to see his mother. A medical officer came down to see him, and it dawned on Andy that they thought he might be mentally unstable. Once they assured themselves that he was sane, and a former PoW, they noted his request. Within 48 hours his honeymoon was over and he was on a Dakota.

Stella dabbed at her eyes with a handkerchief. Then the stern look returned. 'If I'd been in England, I would have made you go to Oxford and stopped you joining the RAF!'

★　　★　　★

The years that followed were uneven and unpredictable for many veterans of Bomber Command. Some adapted to peacetime and civilian life with ease. Some desperately missed the comradeship and camaraderie they had shared with their crews. The contrast between their adrenalin-charged life on the edge and the humdrum world of day-to-day office and family life proved too great for others.

Jack Watson was one of the men who struggled to cope. 'A friend of mine, who was a flight engineer, said to me, "I was an absolute swine after the war. It must have been very difficult for my wife to put with me." Our mid-upper gunner married in 1946 and I was his best man. When we met up years later he said the same thing: "How she put with me, I do not know." It was just so difficult to settle back into a life that was so different. In those days, you went out one night and you were conscious of the fact that it might be the last night you were doing it. You lived life to the full. I think this is the real reason why it was so difficult for us to settle, because you have been living the life of a playboy and suddenly you have become a pauper.'

The boys who joined Bomber Command came back as men, and many yearned for the freedom they had experienced on base. 'It was really difficult to go back and live with a normal family,' Jack says. 'When I left the Air Force, family life in those days was obviously much stricter than it is now, and you went back and you were a man in your own right. You had grown up very, very quickly in Bomber Command, and seen things that most teenagers never hoped to see or wanted to see.

'I found it difficult. I went to work, and I was fine then, but in the evening you thought, I'll go down the pub. But then you realise you can't because you haven't got the money to do it. We weren't alcoholics, but we did like to go out and drink two or three pints a night, or more, as a crew. That sort of partying and drinking was a way of relieving the tension – there was no point in saving anything, because there was no use in having 50 quid saved up in your locker when you're on the other side of the Channel in a prisoner-of-war camp. Or dead in the ground somewhere. I got married in 1946 and it lasted for seven years but it was a very volatile situation. Eventually it failed, partly because of my experiences in the Air Force.'

★   ★   ★

Ron Butcher refers to the Nuremberg Raid as a major disaster. 'I call it The Night I Was Almost Robbed of my Twenty-third Birthday.'

He returned to Canada at the end of the war, but the sight of a full moon still caused him great distress. And that wasn't the only trigger. 'I think I was very affected by the raid. I still have images of those parachutes floating down ... For years afterwards, if I went to a firework display, I'd find myself back in that aircraft watching those men float down. Only a couple of months ago I heard my wife say to a friend, "Thank God he can at last watch fireworks with no problems." That's nearly 70 years on!'

Ron's flashbacks were a classic sign of post-traumatic stress disorder. After Nuremberg he continued to fly operations, though most of his remaining missions were in preparation for the Normandy invasion rather than deep penetrative raids on German cities. Life in Bomber Command would still be extremely dangerous, and many more crews would be lost, but the scale of losses would never again compare with those during the long winter of 1943–44.

The nightmare of the Battle of Berlin was over, but the memories remained. 'I still remember those days with clarity, especially that Nuremberg raid. It is imprinted on the film of my life. Of all of my experiences, all of my operations, Nuremberg occupies the biggest part of my memory. Yes, mistakes were made, but it was just one of those things that happen in war.'

There was one happy ending for Ron. Gord Schacter, his roommate and friend who had gone missing over Nuremberg, did survive. When he returned to the UK and was given his belongings, he found a note that Ron had slipped into his bags when he packed them for the Committee of Adjustment.

'In case you get back!' it read.

★   ★   ★

In 1949, when Fred Panton was 17, he expressed the wish to go to Germany to see where his brother was buried. His father would not hear of it. 'You've got no need to go there,' he told him sternly.

Even though Fred was no longer a boy, he knew better than to cross his father. 'Even when I was courting I was back in bed by ten o'clock, just like he said.'

A few months later Fred had learned of a Halifax bomber for sale, similar to the one Chris had flown. It had completed a full tour of operations and Fred reckoned he could pick it up cheaply, for about £100, because so many of them were being taken out of service. They had a smallholding where he could keep it. Once again his father put his foot down. 'No, you're not having one of those things here,' he said.

A couple of months later Fred was helping his dad pump some water for the ducklings to drink. As he worked, Fred told him again that he could pick up a bomber cheaply, and how much it was like the one that Chris used to fly.

The old man stopped pumping and fixed his son with a flinty glare. 'Fred, I'm going to tell you this once and for all. If you've asked me once, you've asked me a hundred times. You're not having one of those mucky things here.'

Fred gave up at that point. He knew his father would not be swayed and he dared not risk his wrath. He put to one side his project to commemorate Chris's wartime role.

* * *

Sam Harris was at home in Mablethorpe when the idea first came to him. His wife and children were on holiday in Scotland and he was at a loose end. In the 10 years since the war had ended – 11 since he and his crew had gone their separate ways – he had often wondered about what they were doing and what had become of their old base at Elsham Wolds. That August day he got into his car and drove up the coast, then took the A18 past Grimsby.

He was not sure what he would find, if anything, but as he got nearer he felt a quickening of his pulse. The two wooden posts that once marked the entrance to the base were still there. He drove between them. To one side, the guardroom had been reclaimed by nature, its timber frame entwined with weeds and bushes. He turned right, towards the airfield. The buildings were still there, but in ruins, their corrugated roofs rusted and dilapidated.

The road became so overgrown he was unable to drive any further, so he got out and looked for the narrow track that led to what was once their hut. Eventually he found it, wild and dense, but he could still walk down it. He and the lads had cycled along it countless times. On some mornings they would be rushing to get to the NAAFI and have their buns; on others they would be returning after an op, exhausted but happy to be alive.

He fought his way through the bushes and weeds. At the bottom he found it: the Nissen hut which had been their home for five months. The shell was still intact. He peered through one of the cracked windows. It took a few seconds for his eyes to adjust, but eventually he could see metal debris scattered across the floor. Then he saw what he was looking for and smiled: the stove that had given them much-needed warmth during that freezing winter, now rusted but still in place.

He looked at the spaces where their beds had been. He could almost see Mac and Luff, Ken and Chalky, Eric and Bert, lying on their beds, the smoke from their cigarettes curling into the air; the roaring stove, fuelled with pilfered coke, warming the soles of their feet. Sam walked away, in search of the ablutions hut. His memories of it were less warm, in every sense. It too had been claimed by an unruly tangle of weeds. The whole place had the feel of a Wild West ghost town in the movies.

Sam sauntered back up the track, trailed by a host of memories. He found the squadron headquarters. Grunting pigs snuffled and fed where he and his crew once sat doing the crossword. The navigation briefing building was another crumbling shell. As he squinted through a shattered window into the gloom, he heard footsteps.

It was the farmer who owned the land. Sam introduced himself and explained that he was on a pilgrimage to see the place where he had once served. As the farmer spoke to him about his plans for the site, Sam realised he was standing on the exact spot where the transport waited to take crews to their aircraft.

The farmer pointed to the Air Traffic Control Tower and said it was haunted – by the ghost of a pilot who had been reported missing, believed killed, over Germany. Several people said that they had seen him, clad in his flying kit, wandering about the control room, or staring out at the deserted, weed-strewn runway.

Sam cursed himself for not bringing a camera. He said goodbye and offered his thanks. The farmer went back to his work and Sam returned to his car. He climbed inside and started to head for the exit. But then he had another idea. He headed towards the runway. Soon he was driving along it, swerving around the potholes. He took the car to the far end and swung it around, then stopped.

'OK, everybody; here we go.'

Ken's soft whisper came back to him, the words he said on this exact spot so many times. He imagined the caravan beside the tarmac on the left, a small crowd gathered around it to wave them off, huddled together, all of them wrapped up in layers of clothes to stave off the chill. He closed his eyes and saw the darkness and the quivering flames of the paraffin lamps at the edge of the runway.

He could picture the crew around him and smell the glycol, hot oil and sweat, mingling with the stale, familiar smell of G-George, their old warhorse of a Lancaster; Ken, breathing heavily, almost gasping, as he went through his take-off checks; Mac replying in his strong Scottish brogue; Chalky, the bomb aimer, sitting silently beside Sam on take-off, lost in thought. Behind them, Luff sat in front of his wireless set, watching the crowd at the caravan from the porthole on his left side. Eric was in the mid-upper turret, saying little but keeping a beady eye on Bert, the rear gunner, to make sure he didn't nod off.

He opened his eyes and turned the key in the ignition, and drove down the runway, faster and faster. The car could only manage 60 mph with a following wind, but in his mind's eye they were approaching a ton and the roar of four Merlin engines filled his ears. Eventually he slowed down. They would be in the air by now, the old bird rattling and shaking as she lifted them and their world-shaking load.

He turned and headed for the road back to Mablethorpe, wondering what had become of the men with whom he'd shared so much.

It took until 1978 for Sam to find out. The reunion had taken much planning, but the day finally came when he met Bert in Saltaire, near Bradford, and they headed for London in Sam's Humber Super Snipe. It was late afternoon by the time they reached their hotel on Croydon's Aerodrome Way. He and Bert sat in the lobby as the others arrived: Mac first, then Luff and Eric. Chalky walked in with his wife and they recognised him immediately. They shook hands and smiled, and within a few minutes it was as if they had been away on a week's leave rather than spent 34 years apart. The only sadness was Ken's absence. He lived in Australia and had not been able to make it.

All six of them piled into the Super Snipe and headed for the local pub. As they stood supping their pints, Sam realised it was not that different from the first time they had all met, when they had lined the bar at the Golden Fleece in Loughborough. Mac had booked a photographer and they posed for a snap, standing in the same positions as they had when their photo had been taken in January 1944.

They left a space where Ken had been. Sadly, it was never to be filled. Ken Murray died of cancer in 1991, before they had a chance to enjoy a full reunion.

★   ★   ★

Cyril Barton's parents are buried beside him in Kingston cemetery. His brother Ken's ashes are also interred there. Cynthia and Joyce visit regularly, often finding that people – strangers usually, touched by the Barton VC story – have left flowers and messages. One, on the 50th anniversary of his death, read: 'Thank you for my future. From an "after the war" boy.'

Despite that attention, the VC, and a memorial that was unveiled in Ryhope in 1981 thanks to the ceaseless campaigning of Alan Mitcheson, who had been profoundly affected by Cy's bravery, his sisters have not lost sight of the fact that the story of the Nuremberg raid was about more than the death of one man.

'All those 55,000 men of Bomber Command who died,' says Cynthia, 'each one was an individual. We only know our boy, our brother, but all these thousands and thousands of other lads died too. It's disrupted so many families, hasn't it? Our brother died, but another 570 young men were killed that night. Those telegrams, like the one we received, went all over the country, didn't they?'

CHAPTER 21

Journey's End

In the early autumn of 1971, on the sort of sun-kissed September day that tempts people to forget that summer has passed, Fred Panton cycled to his poultry farm to make sure that his chickens were coping with the unseasonal heat. As he neared the hut, he could see his father and mother sitting outside the bungalow they had retired to, soaking up the warmth. His father waved across at him as Fred parked his bike.

'I'll be there in five minutes,' he shouted.

Once he had made sure the chickens were all right he walked across to the bungalow, the sweat breaking out on his brow. As he got nearer, his father hauled himself out of his chair. There was a serious look on his face. Fred thought, what's up here?

'Now, Fred,' his father said, 'I want you to get off to Germany and get me a photograph of our Chris's grave.'

Fred was speechless. 'He changed his mind, just like that. There was no clue or any indication before then that he wanted me to go. It was completely out of the blue.'

He was not going to waste this opportunity by grilling his father about what had caused his volte-face. He started planning his trip immediately. He had never been out of the country before, so it was more than a bit daunting, but each time he thought about it his heart would beat a little faster. He was desperate to go. He was finally getting the chance to see where his older brother had been laid to rest.

His travelling companion was Derek Pipkin, a friend he used to go running with in his bachelor days, and their transport was a Renault van. They spent night after night poring over maps, working out the best route to the small village near Bamberg, in Bavaria, where apparently the locals had buried Chris. It seemed an awfully long way to go, especially in a Renault van, but Fred was not going to be discouraged. A few weeks later he and Derek set off.

They reached Harwich at 10 in the morning, several hours before the ferry to Ostend was due to sail, but they had been petrified that they might miss it. It was nine at night by the time they docked in Holland, and pitch black. Fred gazed out from the stern of their ship into the vast, impenetrable darkness of mainland Europe, and grimaced. Have I got to drive through all of that? But then he thought of his brother – how, night after night, he had travelled over a much more hostile Europe, his life in mortal danger – and told himself to stop being so daft.

Though it took some time to adjust to driving on the other side of the road, they kept going through the night and into the following day, through Belgium, past Brussels and Liège and into Germany. Once over the border they skirted a succession of towns and cities that Chris would have flown over on his ops: Aachen, Cologne, Koblenz, Frankfurt, Wurzburg ...

They arrived at their destination near Bamberg in the early afternoon and found a campsite. Derek was all for putting up the tent and getting some rest after the punishing drive, and starting their enquiries the next morning, but Fred hadn't come this far to carry on waiting. He had been doing that for more than a quarter of a century. 'We're only six miles from where Chris came down,' he said. On the way to Bamberg he had spotted a range of hills; he knew they marked his brother's crash site. 'I reckon we'd better go and have a look this afternoon, before it gets dark.'

Derek was too tired to argue, and he could tell from the determined glint in Fred's eye that there would be no point in doing so. They climbed back into the van.

As they drew nearer, Fred could see that the hills were heavily wooded. He pointed to a large clearing at their centre. He had seen enough crash sites during the war to know the widespread devastation that took place when a Lancaster went down. 'That could be where Chris crashed.'

The road petered out well before the hills began.

'I reckon we should take a risk, Derek.' Fred started to drive across a vast field that still separated them from their goal. They parked at the foot of the hills and started to walk. The path, although steep, was easy to climb, but when they finally reached the clearing Fred felt his heart sink into his boots. 'This is natural, Derek,' he said. 'No aeroplane crashed here.'

As they walked wearily back down, Fred wondered what to do next. He knew they would probably have to wait until tomorrow, whatever they decided. But where to start? Neither he nor Derek spoke a word of German. They couldn't just criss-cross the countryside looking for Lancaster-shaped clearings in the hills. For a second he felt flat and disillusioned, but then he remembered the look on his father's face, and the reason he had come here. 'You mark my words, Derek,' he said, as they got back into the vehicle. 'We'll find someone who can speak English and help us find Chris before we go.'

They started to drive back across the field. It was a big one: 50 or 60 acres, by Fred's estimation. In the distance he spotted two figures, a man and a woman, and he wondered what they were doing in the middle of a field. Then he smiled to himself as he realised they might well be wondering much the same thing about the two wild-eyed occupants of a small van careering towards them across the turf. The couple were out mushrooming, and as they drew closer Fred wound down his window. 'Can you speak English?' he asked.

The man looked up. 'I can. A little –'

His wife interrupted him. Fred didn't like the look on her face. 'My father and mother were killed by a Lancaster that crashed on their house,' she said in English.

That's a great start, Fred thought.

'What do you want to know?' the woman asked.

Fred explained, glancing at her nervously out of the corner of his eye. He told them he had travelled to Germany to find the grave of his brother, who had been shot down during the Nuremberg raid and crashed somewhere in the hills that surrounded them.

There was a pause. Then the man spoke again. 'My brother-in-law is the *Bürgermeister* of the village nearby.' He started to scribble some directions and a note in German for them to pass on. Then he shook his head and scrunched up the scrap of paper in his hand. Fred's heart began to sink, but his fears proved unfounded. The man beckoned to him. 'We will take you there now. Follow us.'

They drove straight to the *Bürgermeister*'s home, where the brother-in-law acted as interpreter. It emerged that he too had fought in the war, had been captured by the English and held at a PoW camp near Ripon, only a few miles from where Chris had been stationed. He took Fred and Derek to meet a man who had been on fire-watch in Bamberg the night of the Nuremberg raid; he had seen Chris's aircraft go down, close enough to his family's home to fear for their safety.

'If you come here at nine o'clock tomorrow morning,' he told them, 'I will take you to the crash site.'

Fred barely slept a wink that night. The next morning he and Derek arrived early at the fire-watcher's house. They were ushered on to the back of his tractor and set off across the fields. The tractor wound its way slowly uphill. The slope became steeper and steeper and the trip seemed to take forever, but eventually they reached the place where Chris had crashed more than 27 years earlier.

As Fred had assumed, the site had been devastated by the flaming aircraft, and had not yet recovered. Debris from the Halifax was still strewn across the ground. He quartered the area, filling a plastic bag with fragments of the bomber as he went, trying to work out the flight path it had taken, and where his brother's body might have been found.

He took a series of photographs, then stood quietly for a moment, listening to the wind in the trees. As they made their way back down, Fred glanced back with a faint flicker of amusement. Chris had been based at Skipton-on-Swale; every time he had taken off, he flew over Sutton Bank. 'He left one big hill and crashed on another.'

Fred and Derek's next stop was the local cemetery, where they were guided to a peaceful, well-tended corner in the shadow of five fir trees. This was where Chris had been given a Christian burial. Fred was told that several local farmers had risked the anger of their Nazi overlords by taking time off their work to attend the ceremony. They felt it more important to observe common decency and give this young man the funeral he deserved, even though he had been sent to attack their country. The locals also found him a picture of the horse-drawn hearse that had brought Chris's coffin to the graveyard. He took snaps of the man who found the plane on the hill, of the village nearby, of every conceivable piece of the jigsaw that told the story of his brother's death and burial.

But the journey did not end there. Chris's body had been disinterred in 1948 and moved to the Durnbach War Cemetery near Munich, 200 miles away. The next morning he and Derek were on the road again. As they pulled up in the cemetery car park, Fred could see the rows and rows of white graves belonging to more than 3,000 British airmen.

After 10 minutes of methodical searching they located his grave. 'Pilot Officer C. W. Panton' it read. 'Flight Engineer. Royal Air Force. 31 March 1944'.

Fred put his hand on the cold stone before he knelt down. 'I knew then I was within six feet of my brother.' The memories flooded back, of the war years, of their rabbiting expeditions, of hearing the muffled voices of Chris and their dad in the front room, of watching the shadows of the departing and returning bombers on his bedroom wall. The tears started to flow.

When it was time to leave, Fred walked backwards to the car park so he could keep his eye on his brother's final resting place. 'I thought I might never see it again.'

Then, after 10 emotional days in Germany, it was time to return home and share what he had found.

His father was delighted. Fred had the photos enlarged and framed, and hung them on the wall. The one of Chris's grave took pride of place, above the mantelpiece, in front of the armchair where he so often sat. The old man stared at it for hours on end.

Three weeks later he died in his sleep.

'He knew,' Fred says. 'That's why he wanted me to go. I'm convinced of it. He wanted to see the place where his son was buried before his time ran out.'

Epilogue

The Sir Arthur Harris statue in London

Fred Panton's trip to Bamberg rekindled his determination to find out as much as he could about his brother's war years. He made contact with a friend, Canadian bomb aimer Wendell Burns, now a fellow farmer with 5,000 acres in Wynyard, east of Saskatchewan. The pair exchanged letters and Fred felt the itch in his feet once more. Chris's crew had included some Canadians, and he had been deeply touched by Jack McLauchlan's letter to his father. Perhaps he could track him down, and maybe the wireless operator, Harry Cooper, too?

In the spring of 1974 Fred flew to Canada; it was the first time he had been on an aeroplane. First he visited Wendell and spent some time helping him to till his land and sow it with barley and wheat. That job done, his attention turned to the real reason for his visit.

Harry Cooper lived in Vancouver, 1,300 miles from Wynyard on the Canadian Pacific Railway. But he had come this far; there was no way he was now going to be put off by a few days on a train. It rattled across the vast prairies of Saskatchewan, through the Rocky Mountains, past the glaciers and lakes of the Banff National Park and on to the Pacific coast.

Fred arrived exhausted in Canada's third biggest city. But there was no time to rest; he was on a mission. He needed to find Harry Cooper. There was only one problem: he had no idea where he lived – and in a city of almost two million people that might prove to be a challenge.

He turned to the phone book. To his delight, there were dozens of Coopers rather than hundreds, and not as many H. Coopers as he feared. He worked his way down the list and made a handful of unsuccessful calls. Then a woman answered. Fred made his apologies for the intrusion.

'Does Harry Cooper live there?' he asked.

'Yes,' she replied.

'Can I ask whether he served in Bomber Command?'

The woman paused. 'Yes, he did ...'

'Was he based at Skipton-on-Swale with 466 Squadron?'

'I think so.'

Fred couldn't believe his luck. 'Is he around?'

'Not at the moment.'

'Can you pass on a message for me, please?'

Mrs Cooper said she would.

'Could you tell him that Fred, Chris Panton's brother, was passing through town and would like to meet with him?' He gave the number of his hotel and expressed his thanks before hanging up.

Five minutes later the phone rang. It was Harry. He had been watering his lawn.

'Can I come and see you?' Fred asked.

There was a sigh. 'I can spare you five minutes,' he said.

Blimey, Fred thought. It's taken four years to find him, and I've travelled 6,000 miles to get here. All for five minutes ...

But it was better than nothing.

Later that afternoon, his mouth dry, he knocked on the door of a house in the outskirts of Vancouver. Harry answered, and Fred immediately sensed the tension in the air. They swapped uneasy small talk. Harry seemed edgy and Fred was unsure why.

'Why are you here?' Harry eventually asked.

Fred explained that he was trying to find out as much as he could about Chris. He told him how he had travelled to Germany to capture a photograph of Chris's grave for his father, and how it had reignited his passionate interest in his brother's wartime experiences. He told Harry that while he was at home on leave his brother had never discussed the war, and that after Chris's death his father had forbidden all talk of it. There was a gaping hole which Fred was desperate to fill.

As Fred spoke, he saw the Canadian's demeanour soften. His earlier guardedness seemed to fall away. 'I thought you were looking to blame someone,' Harry said slowly. 'What do you want to know?'

Fred got more than his five minutes. Harry asked him to stay the night, and told him story after story, until well into the small hours.

★   ★   ★

Fred's return flight to England was due to depart from Toronto, 2,700 miles and almost the width of the continent away from Harry Cooper's house. He looked at the map. Jack McLauchlan, the rear gunner on Chris's Halifax, lived in Winnipeg, 1,400 miles from Vancouver. That's about halfway, he thought.

Two days later, tired and dishevelled, he got off the train at Winnipeg and checked into the railway hotel. Again, there was no time to waste. He had a phone book to work through. There were even fewer McLauchlans than Coopers, and soon he was speaking to Jack's wife. She was picking her husband up later, she said. He was working at the local telephone exchange.

'I can come and pick you up too,' she suggested. 'Then we can go and get him.' She asked where he was staying. When he told her, she immediately insisted he stay with them instead. Only a few hours after he had checked in, he checked out.

He and Mrs McLauchlan sat in the car until Jack's shift finished at midnight. Fred asked whether she had told him he was there. No, she said, they hadn't spoken. She picked him up after every shift. He started to wonder if this had been a good idea. What would Jack's reaction be?

The door opened on the stroke of midnight. Out walked a dapper gentleman in his fifties. The two of them got out of the car. The man got nearer, a quizzical look on his face.

'Now then, Jack, do you know this fellow?' his wife said.

Jack's eyes narrowed. Crumbs, Fred thought, he probably thinks I'm an old boyfriend. He might thump me … Jack continued to stare at him. Fred glanced awkwardly between them, wondering if he should say something.

'You wouldn't be a Panton, would you?'

Fred smiled. 'I'm his younger brother.'

A broad grin lit up Jack's face. He clapped Fred on the back. 'I knew it. You have the same twinkle in your eye.'

★　　★　　★

Fred's Canadian adventures inspired an even greater interest in his brother's life in the RAF. In 1972 he had come across a Lancaster at a public auction, and although he did not buy it then, he had followed its movements closely ever since, and nursed a dream of starting a private collection of Second World War aircraft. Eleven years later he finally achieved his ambition, snapping it up – for far more than the £100 he could have paid for the Halifax in 1949 – in a private sale. NX611, more affectionately known as *Just Jane*, was built by Austin

Motors in 1945, and saw service in the Far East prior to Japan's surrender. She had then become the property of the French government, and travelled halfway across the world before winding up in Lincolnshire.

Around the same time, Fred and his brother Harold bought part of the airfield which had once been RAF East Kirby, where as young boys they had watched the Lancasters rumble into the sky. Rather than keeping *Just Jane* to themselves, they decided to renovate the airfield, restore the bomber to its former glory and open a museum to the public, honouring their brother and the thousands of young men who, night after night, put their lives at risk in the skies above Europe.

They opened the Lincolnshire Aviation Heritage Centre in 1988. *Just Jane* is still its centrepiece, now surrounded by a host of other Second World War aircraft and memorabilia, alongside the base's original control tower. She is regularly taxied along the runway, the roar of her Merlins filling the air. Now the brothers have launched a campaign to get her airborne once more.

The museum was built at a time when the men of Bomber Command had no memorial of their own – and indeed were relegated to the margins of history – but now the public, alongside surviving veterans and their relatives, flock there to pay tribute to their fallen heroes. Every year it hosts a reunion for Chris's squadron and the others that were based at the airfield. Every year the number of familiar faces dwindles, claimed by the passing of the years. But the memory of what they achieved, and the sacrifice they made, never fades.

'We're very proud of our brother and what he did, and what all those other young men did. It's terrible how for many years Bomber Command was forgotten; though we never forgot, and that's why we set up the museum – not just for us, but for everyone else. Those of us who didn't have to fight have had it easy. Sometimes it's good to stop and think, and be thankful.'

Postscript

The Nuremberg Raid haunts the memories and dreams of the dwindling group of men who survived it, and are still alive to speak of it. The horror of that hour of the long leg is seared into their souls. Never before had those airmen seen their brothers in arms die in such numbers. As Rusty Waughman says, 'We didn't usually see dead bodies; people just disappeared.' That fateful night they watched hundreds die, in graphic detail.

Ninety-five bombers were lost that night; approximately 545 airmen killed or missing.[82] The Air Staff Operational Summary of 1 April 1944, compiled from the logs of the squadrons across the country, stands as the official record of the events of 30–31 March. It states that 934 aircraft took part in the raid: 795 targeting Nuremberg and 139 sent on diversionary raids or other tasks. Under the subheading 'Results' it recounts the bare facts of the operation in the driest of bureaucratic language:

'608 aircraft, comprising 454 Lancasters, 146 Halifaxes and eight Mosquitos attacked, dropping about 2,148 tons of bombs (967 tons of H.E. and 1,181 tons of incendiaries). Among the H.E. bombs dropped were 6 × 8,000 lb and 322 × 4,000 lb, Flares were also dropped.

'The Pathfinders were over the target from 0059 hours to 0125 hours, with the Main Force attacking between 0103 and 0133 hours.

'The route to the target was comparatively free from cloud but over the target 6/10ths to 10/10ths cloud in layers up to about 16,000 feet was encountered. Some reports state that the attack opened slightly late and with only marker bombs occasionally visible through the thinner cloud, most crews bombed on the sky marker flares which are reported as being somewhat scattered with the concentration improving in the later stages of the attack.

'The weather conditions made assessment of the results difficult but the attack generally appears to have been widely scattered with no extensive area of fire, although a number of fires were seen in the target area and at least three large explosions are reported.

'Slight to moderate flak was experienced over the target, with a few ineffective searchlights. Opposition from enemy fighters was strong especially on the route in, and in the target area, and appeared to be particularly severe to the South of the RUHR and in the FRANKFURT area. One Me 110, one Me 109 and one Ju 88 are claimed as destroyed, one Me 110 as probably destroyed and three Ju 88 as damaged.'[83]

The causes of the massacre were clear. The Air Ministry's Night Raid Report states: 'An unexpectedly strong westerly wind scattered our aircraft, and cloud dispersed beyond Belgium, leaving them exposed in bright moonlight ... German fighters achieved considerable success on this night, helped greatly by the weather ... Nearly all the losses were caused by fighters. They destroyed at least 50 bombers between Aachen and the turning point near Fulda.'

Given the scale of the losses, some might find it surprising that there wasn't an official inquiry into what went wrong. It had been a costly operation, the worst yet, but there was nothing for it but to carry on. Bomber Command's Operational Research Section conducted a post-mortem a few days after the raid, as they did into every raid. Its conclusions were similar to those of the Night Raid Report, though they examined in greater detail the movements of the night fighter force.

Despite only four stations being employed, fighter opposition was described as 'unusually stiff'.

'Fighters were given instructions to enable them to find the stream at three separate points on the outward journey, and moonlight above the cloud and the presence of persistent contrails in conditions of excellent visibility made their task easy.'[84]

Intriguingly, the report goes on to address the vexed question of why so many of the bombers were caught by surprise, rather than having sight of their attackers, and what manoeuvre the enemy must have employed to avoid being seen. 'From the high proportion of damage caused by surprise attacks, by comparison with cases in which the fighter was sighted, it is to be presumed that most of the bombers destroyed in fighter attacks have been taken unawares.'

They were still unaware of the viciously upward-slanting *Schräge Musik*, the reason so many bombers exploded without their crews even knowing they were in the enemy's sights. It would be some months – and many more lost bombers and crews – before the secret of 'jazz music' was discovered.

What of the men responsible for orchestrating such a disastrous raid? Winston Churchill makes only a brief mention in his comprehensive *History of the Second World War*, even though smaller and less significant operations are given more detailed analysis. In Volume V he does say of Nuremberg: 'This was our heaviest loss in one raid, and caused Bomber Command to re-examine its tactics before launching further deep-penetration attacks by night into Germany.' But he declines to mention the pivotal part he played in developing those tactics.

Sir Arthur Harris does not mention Nuremberg in his account of his war years, even though it signalled the end of the Combined Bomber Offensive and his ambition to win the war by destroying German morale via a saturation bombing campaign.

The brutal winter was over, Germany remained fully engaged in the war, their night fighter force had proven itself more than equal to the tactics of Bomber Command, and Nuremberg remained largely untouched. The nights were getting shorter, spring was on its way and preparations for Operation Overlord – the Allied invasion of Europe – were taking precedence. Nuremberg would prove to be the end of the Battle of Berlin. Thousands had died in the skies and there had been no decisive victory. Harris's dream was over.

Harris never spoke publicly about Nuremberg. But according to Joan Dally, the WAAF Corporal in the Met Office of Bomber Command's High Wycombe underground HQ, he was deeply affected by the scale of the losses that night. 'I'm sure Harris was upset. He didn't say anything, but you could tell from his demeanour and the whole atmosphere that surrounded him.'

Later in life he would refer to it as the 'one real disaster' of his time in charge of Bomber Command. In a letter written to Geoff Taylor, the author of *The Nuremberg Massacre*, he admitted to his errors that night, but also issued a passionate defence of his tactics. It bears quoting at length, because the argument he constructs is forceful and compelling:

'It was a perpetual source of astonishment to me during my three and a half years as Commander-in-Chief, Bomber Command, that we did not suffer many more heavy reverses of the Nuremberg type and I cannot understand why the German defences did not improve much more rapidly and effectively as the bomber war developed over three long and terrible years.

'In Bomber Command we had to lay on and, more often than not, carry through, at least one and occasionally more than one major battle every twenty-four hours. That was a situation which no naval or military command has ever had to compete with. Navies fight two or three major battles per war. Armies, maybe a dozen. We had to lay on, during my three and a half years, well over a thousand. Naturally enough, we occasionally got a badly bloodied nose – but nothing like what we gave the Boche.

'There was a limit – and a small one – to the choice of tactical changes which we could introduce from time to time and occasionally such tactical changes had therefore to include doing something which the enemy would probably think so obvious that it would be the last thing we would ever choose to do.

'In the Nuremberg show we chose wrong and the Boche, aided by unexpectedly bad weather, guessed right.

'It is a wonder that coincidence did not occur more often during the thousand and more major battles which we fought ...'

As indicated in the letter he sent to Martin Middlebrook quoted earlier, Sir Robert Saundby, Harris's Deputy Commander-in-Chief, already held grave misgivings about the raid *before* it took place. He was later to describe Nuremberg as a 'thorough shambles'.[85] Had the weather not been against them, Saundby believed there would have been fewer casualties and the raid might have been more successful. He also confirmed the view of his chief: every time they sent a large force on a dangerous mission deep into German territory there was a chance there would be heavy losses. On this occasion – though thankfully on few others – the worst had happened.

Volume III of *The Official History of the Royal Air Force, 1939–1945* wastes few words on Nuremberg, but all of them are scathing. It describes the raid as 'a curious operation' ... blighted by 'unusually bad luck and uncharacteristically bad and unimaginative planning'. This verdict summed up the opinion of Pathfinder chief Donald Bennett. 'I opposed the long straight route because clearly the conditions were far too dangerous for such a tactic – particularly when we had been warned that there was a strong chance of there being bright moonlight. Nuremberg turned out to be an expensive raid.

I believe it would still have involved high losses, even without the proposed route; but certainly they would not have been so high as those which were incurred.'[86]

The terrible losses of that night did lead to speculation that there was a more sinister reason for the Nuremberg disaster than bad luck, bad weather and bad planning. Captured RAF crew under interrogation were told by the Germans that they knew they were coming, which led to rumours that Bomber Command had been infiltrated by a spy who had informed the enemy in advance of the location of that night's target.

The fact that many of the crews felt that the night fighters must have been waiting for them – because they flew almost straight into their path – gave this suspicion extra currency. And in 1963 the discredited revisionist historian David Irving alleged that a British wireless operator had been the one to disclose the target. But there is no evidence whatsoever that the Germans were tipped off, and they themselves have never subsequently claimed to have been. It was common for inter-rogators to tell captured servicemen their safety had been compromised by intelligence leaks, to destroy their morale and encourage them to believe there was little point in refusing to divulge their secrets.

The simple fact is that the designated route of the long leg took the bomber stream perilously close to two beacons where the night fighters had gathered, and that they were able to pick out the bombers clearly in the moonlight and radio their posi-tion to their comrades. The Germans *were* waiting for them, but only because of ill fortune and perfect night fighter weather.

Much has been made of the decision to send the stream so close to Ida and Otto, but others had done so; it was impossible to map a route across mainland Germany that avoided every beacon. A combination of the hunter's moon, the visibility of the contrails and the lack of cloud cover gave the Luftwaffe an advantage previously denied them, and they – and, arguably the entire German armed forces – did not enjoy a night like it for the remainder of the conflict.

As Sir Arthur Harris was the first to point out, the cost of a Nuremberg-scale raid was always likely to be high, given the relentless cycle of Bomber Command combat that winter. Their sustained offensive did help to stretch and weaken German defences over a crucial period, and though another hard lesson was learned that night – that the enemy could not be defeated solely from the air – they had been subdued, and a platform laid for the land campaign that followed.

30 March 1944 was a truly terrible night for Bomber Command. Yet those who ordered it were engaged in a relentless war, and seeking any means to hasten victory. And that meant sending brave young men, time after time, to risk sacrificing themselves for those they loved most.

Bibliography

Bennett, D.C.T., Air Vice Marshal *Pathfinder* (Panther, 1960)

Bishop, Patrick *Bomber Boys* (Harper Perennial, 2008)

Boiten, Theo *Night Airwar* (Crowood Press, 1999)

Boiten, Theo *Nachtjagd* (Crowood Press, 1997)

Bowman, Martin and Boiten, Theo *Raiders of the Reich* (Airlife, 1996)

Butcher, Ron *Been There, Done That* (Trafford Publishing, 2006)

Campbell, James *The Bombing of Nuremberg* (Futura, 1974)

Cawdron, Hugh *Based at Burn* (578 Burn Association, 1995)

Chorley, W.R. *RAF Bomber Command Losses of the Second World War 1944* (Midland Counties Publications, 1998)

Churchill, Winston *The Second World War, Vol V. Closing the Ring* (Cassell, 1952)

Connelly, Mark *Reaching for the Stars: A New History of Bomber Command in World War II* (Tauris, 2001)

Dally, Joan *A WAAF in Wartime* (self-published)

Delve, Ken and Jacobs, Peter *The Six-Year Offensive* (Arms and Armour Press, 1992)

Falconer, Jonathan *Bomber Command Handbook* (Sutton Publishing, 1998)

Feast, Sean *Carried on the Wind* (Woodfield Publishing, 2003)

Feast, Sean *Master Bombers* (Grub Street, 2008)

Ford-Jones, Martyn *Bomber Squadron: Men Who Flew with XV* (Kimber, 1987)

Harris, Sir Arthur *Bomber Offensive* (Greenhill, 1990)

Hastings, Max *Bomber Command* (Papermac, 1993)

Heaton, Colin D. and Lewis, Anne-Marie *Night Fighters* (Naval Institute Press, 2008)

Hinchliffe, Peter *The Other Battle* (Airlife, 1996)

Howell, Eric *The OR's Story* (B J & M Promotions, 1998)

Jacobs, Peter *Bomb Aimer over Berlin* (Pen & Sword, 2007)

Lowther, W.W. *Cyril Joe Barton VC* (Wear Books, 1994)

McKinstry, Leo *Lancaster* (John Murray, 2010)

Middlebrook, Martin *The Nuremberg Raid* (Cassell, 2000)

Middlebrook, Martin and Everitt, Chris *The Bomber Command War Diaries* (Midland Publishing, 1985)

Muirhead, Campbell *Diary of a Bomb Aimer* (Ditto Publishing, 2002)

Nichol, John and Rennell, Tony *Tail-End Charlies: The Last Battles of the Bomber War 1944–45* (Penguin, 2005)

Overy, Richard *Bomber Command 1939–45* (HarperCollins, 2000)

Probert, Henry *Bomber Harris* (Greenhill, 2001)

Revie, Alastair *The Lost Command* (Purnell Book Services, 1971)

Richards, Denis and Saunders, Hilary St George *Royal Air Force 1939–45, Vol III. The Fight Is Won* (London, 1953)

Saward, Dudley *Bomber Harris* (Buchan & Enright, 1984)

Starkey, Richard (Dick) *A Lancaster Pilot's Impression on Germany* (Compaid Graphics, 2004)

Thorburn, Gordon *Bombers First and Last* (Robson, 2006)

Verrier, Anthony *The Bomber Offensive* (Batsford, 1968)

OTHER PUBLICATIONS

The Means of Victory (Charterhouse Publications, 1992)

RAF News, special Bomber Command issue (2002)

Notes

Where an individual's reference for a source is given as an interview, book, document, etc. that source holds good for the remainder of the book.

1 The Barton family story. Barton family archive and interview with JN, February 2012.
2 Fred and Harold Panton. Interview with JN, July 2012.
3 Alan Payne. Interview with JN, February 2012.
4 Henry Probert, *Bomber Harris,* Greenhill, 2001.
5 Quoted from Sir Arthur Harris's personal papers in Leo McKinstry, *Lancaster: The Second World War's Greatest Bomber*, John Murray, 2010.
6 Dick Starkey. Interview with JN, March 2012, and his book, *A Lancaster Pilot's Impression on Germany*.
7 Rusty Waughman. Information from personal archive, interview with JN, March 2012, and the excellent book by Sean Feast, *Carried on the Wind,* Woodfield Publishing, 2003.
8 Chick Chandler. Personal archive and interview with JN, March 2012.
9 Jack Watson. Interview with JN, May 2003.
10 Sir Arthur Harris, *Bomber Offensive,* Greenhill, 1990.
11 John Nichol and Tony Rennell, *Tail-End Charlies,* Penguin, 2005.
12 Harry Evans. Private memoir and interview with JN, February 2012.

13 The National Archives. AIR 14/3513.

14 Thomas Maxwell. Personal archive and correspondence with JN.

15 W.R. Chorley, *RAF Bomber Command Losses of the Second World War, 1944,* Midland Counties Publication, 1998.

16 Ron and Sheila Auckland. Interview with JN, February 2012.

17 George and Jocelyn Prince. Interview with JN, February 2012.

18 Andy Wiseman. Interview with JN, February 2012.

19 'Sam' Harris was born Harry Harris, but was known to his crew-mates as Sam. To avoid confusion we have stuck with his wartime nickname.

20 Sam Harris. Personal memoir and interview with JN, February 2012.

21 Mark Connelly, *Reaching for the Stars: A New History of Bomber Command in World War II,* Tauris, 2001.

22 Roger Coverley. Personal archive and interview with JN, February 2012.

23 Reg Payne. Personal memoir, research by Kenneth Ballantyne and interview with JN, February 2012.

24 Ray Francis. Personal memoir, crew memoir by Don Harvey and interview with JN, March 2012.

25 Gordon Thorburn, *Bombers First and Last,* Robson, 2006.

26 Campbell Muirhead, *Diary of a Bomb Aimer,* Ditto Publishing, 2002.

27 The story of this escape would form the basis for the film *The Great Escape.*

28 The background to the planning of the raid is outlined in Martin Middlebrook's exhaustive book, *The Nuremberg Raid,* Cassell, 2000, which was of great help to the author.

29 Joan Dally. Interview with JN, 2012, and personal memoir.

30 Anthony Verrier, *The Bomber Offensive,* Batsford, 1968.

31 James Campbell, *The Bombing of Nuremberg,* Futura, 1974.

32 The National Archives. AIR 24/269.

33 Campbell, op. cit.

34 Len Lambert's written account is quoted in W.W. Lowther, *Cyril Joe Barton VC,* Wear Books, 1994, and Hugh Cawdron, *Based at Burn,* 578 Burn Association, 1995. Quotes from the account of Harry 'Timber' Wood also appear in both publications.

35 Quoted in Lowther, op. cit.

36 As above.

37 Ron Butcher. Personal memoir and interview with JN, April 2012.

38 Scouse Nugent's account appeared in *RAF News,* special Bomber Command issue, 10 May 2002.

39 The story of Jimmy Batten-Smith is taken from the 101 Squadron History and Martin Middlebrook, *The Nuremberg Raid,* Cassell, 2000.

40 Various authors, *The Means of Victory,* Charterhouse Publications Ltd, 1992.

41 Eric Howell, *The OR's Story,* B J & M Promotions, 1998.

42 Freddie Brice's account is taken from a letter sent to the Barton family. The Barton family archive.

43 Bruno Rupp. Interview with Christian Kuhrt, 2012.

44 Martin Middlebrook, *The Nuremberg Raid,* Cassell, 2000.

45 Theo Boiten, *Night Airwar,* Crowood Press, 1999.

46 Martin Bowman and Theo Boiten, *Raiders of the Reich,* Airlife, 1996.

47 Colin D. Heaton and Anne-Marie Lewis, *Night Fighters,* Naval Institute Press, 2008.

48 Friedrich Ziegler. Interview with Christian Kuhrt, 2012.

49 Fritz Fink. Interview with Christian Kuhrt, 2012.

50 Bowman and Boiten, op. cit.

51 Campbell, op. cit.

52 Middlebrook, op. cit.

53 Sidney Whitlock. Personal account courtesy of his daughter, Sylvia Oakley.

54 Peter Hinchliffe, *The Other Battle,* Airlife, 1996.

55 Campbell, op. cit.

56 As above.

57 Middlebrook, op. cit.

58 Peter Jacobs, *Bomb Aimer Over Berlin,* Pen & Sword, 2007.

59 Middlebrook, op. cit.

60 Tony Hiscock. Interview with JN, 2012.

61 Quote by John Chadderton, from Bowman and Boiten, op. cit.

62 Geoff Taylor, *The Nuremberg Massacre,* Sidgwick & Jackson, 1980.

63 BBC interview. 'Brothers retrace pilot's final flight over Germany': http://news.bbc.co.uk/local/york/hi/people_ and_places/history/newsid_8773000/8773448.stm

64 Alan Mitcheson. Personal archive, correspondence and interview with JN, April 2012

65 Taylor, op. cit.

66 Middlebrook, op. cit.

67 As above.

68 Campbell, op. cit.

69 As above.

70 Middlebrook, op. cit.

71 Howell, op. cit.

72 Martin Bowman and Theo Boiten, op. cit.

73 Campbell, op. cit.

74 The accounts of Les Lawther, Arthur Milburn and Tom and Ken Richardson appear in Lowther, op. cit.

75 Quoted in Middlebrook, op. cit.

76 The story of Don Brinkhurst's evasions features in the 101 Squadron History and Middlebrook, op. cit.

77 Barton family archive.

78 As above.

79 As above.

80 Panton archive.

81 Barton family archive.

82 Figure of bomber losses taken from Martin Middlebrook and Chris Everitt, *The Bomber Command War Diaries,* Midland Publishing, 1985. Figure of airmen lost or missing taken from Middlebrook, op. cit.

83 The National Archives, AIR 22/139.

84 The National Archives, AIR 14/4151.

85 Campbell, op. cit.

86 As above.

Index